A Path of Our Own

Culture of Enterprise series

Previously published:

Human Goods, Economic Evils:
A Moral Approach to the Dismal Science
Edward Hadas

Third Ways:
How Bulgarian Greens, Swedish Housewives, and Beer-Swilling
Englishmen Created Family-Centered Economies—and Why They Disappeared
Allan C. Carlson

A Path of Our Own

An Andean Village and
Tomorrow's Economy of Values

Adam K. Webb

Wilmington, Delaware

Webb, Adam Kempton, 1975–

  A path of our own : an Andean village and tomorrow's economy of values /
  Adam K. Webb. —1st ed. —Wilmington, Del. : ISI Books, c2008.

      p. ; cm.
      (Culture of enterprise)

      ISBN: 978-1-933859-77-4
      Includes bibliographical references and index.

  1. Economic development—Peru—Pomatambo. 2. Economic policy—Peru.
  3. Economic development—Political aspects. 4. Economic policy—Political
  aspects. I. Title.

HC228.P66 W43 2008   2008928225
339.5/085   0901

                        ISI Books
                Intercollegiate Studies Institute
                        P.O. Box 4431
                    Wilmington, DE 19807-0431
                        www.isibooks.org

            Manufactured in the United States of America

To the people of Pomatambo

Para el pueblo de Pomatambo

Pumatampu llaqtapaq, llapay sunquywan

Contents

I

Big Questions from a Backwater

"So we're in the middle of a war here," Quintín concluded matter-of-factly as he got up and shuffled through his papers. He had been sitting at a rickety wooden desk, pecking away at a typewriter that must have been thirty or forty years old. As one of the village schoolteachers, he had apparently had yet another official form inflicted on him to fill out. We had been talking on and off for the last few minutes, while other conversations went on within earshot and the occasional chicken fluttered around the yard. For this desk was outside, in front of a typical adobe peasant house belonging to one of his fellow teachers. With no electricity, it would have been hard to read anything inside.

Fig. 1: The central cluster of houses in the village of Pomatambo

Soon it would be hard to read anything outside, either. The sun was already sinking in the sky behind the house, and I could feel the first chill of an Andean evening. The nighttime cold goes through you quickly at this altitude. I was looking forward to the prospect of even a humble peasant soup, and perhaps a hot dish of rice and potatoes. It would be cooked over an open fire right there outside the house, in a corner where a low wall of mud bricks jutted out.

Despite the cold, I welcomed a respite from the searing sun of the daytime. I was feeling the discomfort of a sunburn and had been told a few times that my face had a reddish glow. At 11,500 feet above sea level, much more ultraviolet light gets through the atmosphere. And I had had plenty of time to get singed over the last couple of days, starting with the afternoon I had trekked four and a half hours out to this village, over grassland and hills from the nearest market town. It should have taken only two hours, but that estimate held only for locals. With lungs accustomed to sea level, I had gasped most of the way and made frequent stops, even though my twentieth birthday was still three weeks away.

It was July 1995, and this was my first visit to Pomatambo. I had come as a student that summer, in the waning days of the Sendero Luminoso (Shining Path) guerrilla movement, to learn more about the experiences and perspectives of the Andean peasantry. Maybe Quintín's remark about being in the middle of a war zone was no longer entirely true. But I had to admit to myself that I had at least stumbled into the *remnants* of a war zone. Guerrillas were no longer entering villages, for the most part, though there was still some activity in the area and Peru's state of emergency remained in effect. Later I was to learn that a column of Senderistas had recently been spotted about a two hours' walk away. Sitting there in the late afternoon with only the sound of Quechua conversations and chickens squawking in the air, it was hard to imagine what these people had gone through in recent years. The tranquility belied the carnage of a civil war in which some seventy thousand Peruvians had been killed or disappeared.

The trip to Pomatambo was not only a venture into the scene of years of turbulence. It was also a journey into deeper and deeper poverty. Over the last couple of decades, Peru's overall per-capita income has been roughly middling, considered on a global scale. Recent measurements, adjusted for real purchasing power, put it between $6,000 and $7,000.[1] But Peru is also a microcosm of the world, with an economic chasm between the coast and the highlands, and between the cities and the countryside. I had spent my first night in Lima in the upscale neighborhood of Miraflores, where the gloom of fifteen years of bombings and apprehension was slowly lifting. Today in Miraflores there are shiny new office buildings and renovated villas, signs of restored confidence among Peru's wealthy.

With each stage of the journey outward from Lima, I had stepped ever deeper into the poorer and forgotten part of the country. First to Ayacucho, the highland city where Sendero had planned its insurgency as far back as the 1960s. Then six hours by packed minibus on a jarring dirt road to the small market town of Vilcashuamán. And finally nine miles on foot to Pomatambo, this village in the heart of the remote area where the guerrillas had first taken up arms. Now I was amid the dire poverty of the Andean peasantry. They had no electricity, no running water, and a hard life of scratching a living from the soil, much as in centuries past.

Despite the lack of material comforts, the villagers had a fierce pride in their community. Pomatambo's residents saw it as a central village in that part of the district. Because of out-migration, its population had shrunk during the violence, from about three hundred to two hundred, but it was still slightly more likely than its neighbors to show up on maps. It occupied between three and six square miles of sparsely populated land, depending on where one drew the disputed boundaries with other villages.

It took little imagination to see why the insurgency, which had shaken the Peruvian state for fifteen years, had begun in this part of the country. Ayacucho lies in the "Indian belt" of the south-central highlands about halfway between Lima and Cuzco. It ranks as one of the poorest of Peru's twenty-five regions, with a living standard more familiar in countries like Mali, Nepal, and Bangladesh. In recent years about half the department's population has been rural.[2] And that proportion was much higher before the civil war drove so many peasants into the swelling urban shantytowns.

Ayacucho, the name of the region and its capital city of one hundred thousand people, means "corner of the dead" in Quechua, the indigenous language. Observers have long noted the aptness of the label for an area with a culture of suffering.[3] Even the folk music has a mournful air. A student at the university in Ayacucho once told me that the sound echoed the grief that centuries of battles had brought to the people of the area. While far from Peru's modern economic centers, the region has long been a strategic crossroads, where empires and movements have fought it out over the heads of the long-suffering peasantry.

Vilcashuamán, the capital of the province and district that include Pomatambo, is now a sleepy market town with a population of about six thousand. But six hundred years ago it had thirty to forty thousand inhabitants and served as one center of the Chanka confederation.[4] To the modern mind, Peru before the Spanish conquest was the timeless land of the Inka empire. Yet the Inka empire ruled over Vilcashuamán and the rest of what is now Ayacucho for only about sixty years before the conquistadores arrived. To peasants at the time, it must have seemed a short-lived occupying force.

The Inka empire's defeat of the Chankas was no easy task. Every July during the Vilcas Raymi festival, the conflict is reenacted in Vilcashuamán's square by secondary-school students in vivid battle dress—mainly blue for Inka warriors, and green, orange, and red for Chankas. By the end of the hour, the Chankas lie dead and their straw huts have gone up in flames. The real history did not see such a clean Inka victory. The fast-expanding empire met some of its stiffest resistance around this part of the highlands. Even after overcoming the Chankas in war, the Inkas ruled over a stubbornly independent local populace. The Chankas soon revolted again in a final lashing out against the overwhelming superiority of the empire. When the Inkas inevitably crushed the rebellion, the survivors took refuge atop Pilluchu, a nearly impregnable rocky hill that juts up from the horizon within sight of Vilcashuamán. There a few thousand Chankas held out for two years, relying on a hilltop spring, what they could grow, and dwindling food reserves. They surrendered only when starvation came. In one of history's ironic twists, however, the people of Vilcashuamán nowadays identify more with the Inka conquerors. Their

4

hearts are with them during the festival's battle reenactment, and in the square today stands an imposing statue of the Inka emperor Pachacutec, symbol of their pride in the greatest of Andean empires.

During the decades they ruled the area, the Inkas employed their usual techniques to suppress resistance. They depopulated much of the countryside, displacing the more difficult ethnic groups to far-flung corners of the empire, then resettling more loyal communities from elsewhere among what remained of the populace. These resettle-ments—*mitmaqs* in Quechua—wove around Vilcashuamán one of the most diverse ethnic tapestries of the Andes. The fragmentation and mutual distrust among communities, crucial to the Inka strategy of divide and conquer, lingered until well into the Spanish colonial era, when the various ethnicities gradually dissolved into a single Quechua-speaking peasantry.[5]

The town of Vilcashuamán did not decay once the Inkas overran it. In keeping with their general approach of integrating what they found, the new rulers kept it as one of their most important provincial centers. While their own capital at Cuzco was some 125 miles away, they con-sidered Vilcashuamán the geographic center of the empire. Even now you can climb the *ushnu*, a stepped pyramid near the square, and sit on the side-by-side stone thrones used during visits by the emperor and his consort. Perhaps the most visible legacy of the empire is the network of roads and fortifications that dot the landscape around Vilcashuamán. Several roads lead out of the town into the well-maintained system that extended up and down the highlands and out to the coast. Along these roads ran the *chaskis,* messengers who could relay communications in days from one end of the empire to the other.

Two of those ruined Inka roads forking out from Vilcashuamán meet again in Pomatambo and then descend as one to wind along the small stream that flows through the village, before the road again climbs over the hills eastward to Cuzco. The main road oddly curves out of its way to pass through Pomatambo, which suggests that there is more to the history of this village than meets the eye. What is now a tiny backwater must have been much more important five centuries ago. Stone outlines of fields on a nearby hillside, most no longer used, suggest that the land may have supported a thousand or more people long ago.[6] The name Pomatambo may hint at the road itself. Strictly *Puma-tampu* in Quechua, it means "puma resting place." That could mean simply that it was an area of pumas (a rare sight nowadays). But a *tampu* was also one of the way stations along the Inka road network, where messengers took over from one another every few miles. On the rock-strewn hillside near the road, you can see even now the possible remnants of a *tampu:* stones from an old dwelling, and a larger block with a hole that may have been used to hitch llamas.

Other traces of the pre-conquest period abound in Pomatambo. Fragments of Chanka and Inka pottery lie scattered on the ground, especially in an area near the village square that seems to have been a burial mound. Most impressively, when you approach the village along the present dirt road from Vilcashuamán you see on the right side a wall of massive and mysterious stones taller than a person. The wall seems to have been part of an Inka fortress, perhaps half-finished, that was to loom over the village and its burial mound. The locals call it Siqirumi, meaning "lined-up stones." One old woman told me that her grandparents had passed down a story about Siqirumi's origins. They said the Inkas had a magical iron rod that could move stones with no effort. They lined up the stones at Pomatambo, ready to build a huge bridge in midair over the Pampas River a couple of miles away. The arrival of the Spaniards rudely interrupted the builders' plans.

Nostalgia lingers among these folk for the Inka empire, for a golden age before the Spanish conquest, before the outsiders took their land and turned them into near-serfs. The conquistadores superimposed a new elite and a new religion on the Andes. Quite literally: at the edge of the square in Vilcashuamán, they built a Catholic church on top of the Inka-period temple. The white façade, red-tiled roof, and bell tower rise in Mediterranean triumph over the honeycomb-like walls of somber grey blocks. But through three centuries of colonial rule, the Andean peasantry clung to the dream of one day turning history upside down. At the end of a major revolt in 1781, an indigenous rebel leader reportedly declared before his drawing and quartering, "I will return, and I will be millions."[7]

The millenarian hope never quite died. Even after the 1824 defeat of the last Spanish royalist army in the Americas, at a battle near Ayacucho, the oppression of the Andean peasantry continued. The near-caste hierarchy remained intact in independent republican Peru, with those of Spanish blood at the top, until well into the twentieth century. Millenarian revolts broke out now and then in the highlands.[8] Small wonder that one of Pomatambo's villagers told me that, for her, to be Peruvian meant to be a rebel.

The rebel spirit and the mournful attachment to an impoverished land are reflected in a well-known verse from a quarter of a century ago:

> *Hierba silvestre, aroma puro,*
> *Te ruego acompañarme por mi camino.*
> *Serás mi bálsamo en mi tragedia.*[9]
> Wild grass, pure scent,
> I beg you to come with me on my way,
> You will be my raft in my tragedy.

The words were penned by Edith Lagos, an Ayacucho teenager who took up arms for Sendero in the early days of the insurgency. She won heroic status in the movement when she appeared in a press photograph, after her arrest in 1982, as a diminutive figure surrounded by police. After escaping from prison, she took to the hills again before being captured and tortured to death in Apurímac, some distance to the east of Pomatambo over the Pampas River. Aged only nineteen at the time, she became a martyr for the cause.[10] The wild grass referred to in the poem grows throughout the area, including around Pomatambo. Walking through the hills in the early evening, as the temperature drops and the wind picks up, you can hear the thin air whistling eerily through the tufts of grass.

A dry and sparsely peopled land, and centuries of turmoil and frustrated hopes for something better: these two themes run through so many outsiders' impressions of Ayacucho. The violence that wracked Ayacucho from 1980 to the mid-1990s had its origins in this history. Sendero appealed to the severe deprivation of the peasantry in places like Pomatambo.

It is hard to fill one's stomach in these villages. Vilcashuamán district contains some of the least productive land in the region, with a mix of sandy and clay-like red soil, dry grassland, and stony hillsides. Only about a sixth of it is now cultivated, mainly with maize, potatoes, barley, and broad beans. The rest is used as pasture, though even the llamas and alpacas raised in other parts of the Andes do not flourish here. With a harsh climate of frosts and irregular rainfall, and no mechanization of agriculture, peasants here can hardly subsist. A typical family struggles to eke out two harvests a year, one big and one small, on two to seven acres of land. Maize and potato worms threaten the crops. To make ends meet, most families scramble to secure sources of nonagricultural income, perhaps from migrant work.[11] Household cash income in Pomatambo averages around $40 a month.

These patterns hold across the region, in which, according to recent censuses, an overwhelming majority of inhabitants live in poverty, and over a third in "extreme poverty." Figures on that scale can seem abstract, but they translate into real deprivation. Outside market towns like Vilcashuamán, one finds no electricity and no household plumbing. People are chronically undernourished, and the infant mortality rate is high.[12] Add to this a frustration with governments that have done little if anything to improve matters—governments that have long signaled their disdain for the highlands and the indigenous people who live there.

Sendero promised the peasants it would relieve their plight through violent revolution. The guerrillas unleashed their armed struggle in May 1980 by burning ballot boxes in Chuschi, a small town in another part of Ayacucho. It was the eve of the first democratic elections after twelve years of military rule, but Sendero had been laying the groundwork for its insurgency since the late 1960s. This was no romantic and spontaneous movement of a Che Guevara flavor. Sendero, formally known as the Communist Party of Peru, was a Maoist faction that hoped to imitate the radical path taken by China during the Cultural Revolution. The movement's unquestioned leader, Abimael Guzmán, had been a charismatic philosophy professor at Ayacucho's Universidad Nacional San Cristóbal de Huamanga (UNSCH) in the 1960s. His fervent Marxist lectures inspired many students who would become cadres of the movement. Throughout the 1970s, Sendero used the university's agronomy and other programs as a recruiting ground and as a bridge to the countryside. By the time the Senderistas went over to violence in 1980, they were well prepared for years of civil war in which they hoped to surround the cities and topple the state.[13]

By the mid-1980s, the countryside had descended into bloodletting on a vast scale. Caught between the guerrillas and the army, thousands of peasants fled to the cities. Sendero broadened its struggle to Lima and elsewhere, undertaking a series of bombings and assassinations and taking de facto control of many shantytowns. By the early 1990s, some observers were wondering if Peru could avoid collapse. But the tide turned dramatically in September 1992, with the capture of Guzmán and soon thereafter most of the rest of Sendero's leadership. The movement slowly declined, and by the late 1990s it had shrunk to at most a few hundred insurgents operating in some remote enclaves. The violence from both sides had scarred a whole generation and torn the countryside apart. Some seventy thousand people had been killed or disappeared. The powerful and moneyed breathed a sigh of relief at their own survival, and the poverty of the highlands remained unchanged.

→ → →

My first visit to Pomatambo in 1995 was during Sendero's decline. I was an undergraduate at Harvard and was writing a thesis on how Ayacucho's peasants had experienced Sendero—above all, how they had regarded the alternative offered by the guerrillas. I previously had been elsewhere in the Andes, but this was my first time in Ayacucho. It took until the mid-1990s before a foreigner could go into what had been the heartland of the insurgency, and ask people probing questions about it, in relative safety.

Pomatambo became the focus of my research that summer by a fortunate chain of events. On arriving in Ayacucho, I knew that I wanted to look closely at one village. Through contacts at the same university in Ayacucho where Guzmán had once taught, I came to know an anthropology student who had been born in Pomatambo and still had relatives there. I went with him to the village, and returned for several more trips over a two-month period, sometimes with him and sometimes with other members of his family.

My friend's introduction was crucial in winning the confidence of people I wanted to interview. Andean peasants are hospitable people, with a genuine decency and warmth beneath the sober expression that one so often sees among mountain folk. But like many of these remote villages, Pomatambo had never dealt with such an obvious outsider before.

Children who had not been to the city had never seen a foreigner. I remember one late morning a few days into my first visit, when I was sitting outside the village school and jotting down some notes in the bright sunlight. A handful of youngsters, about seven or eight years old, gathered around and peered at me curiously. They chattered in Quechua. Amused, I waited to see what they would do. Suddenly one of them ran forward, touched the tip of my hiking boot, and then leaped back in delight at his heroism. There is, after all, the legend of the *pishtaku*: a phantom with white skin who roams the highlands at night abducting children. Old colonial legends die hard.

Among Pomatambo's adults, a different kind of apprehension was obvious in those first few days. The violence was still vivid in their memories and by no means clearly over. They had lived through reprisals from both soldiers and guerrillas against people who said the wrong thing or seemed to have the wrong associations. I could hardly blame them for not wanting to open up about their experiences to an outsider about whom they could not know anything for certain. Imaginations ran wild. My friend had to go to a village meeting without me at one point in order to convince the skeptics that I did not pose a threat. Apparently there had been some speculation, particularly among some of the older women, with their earthy apprehension, that I must be either a government investigator or some sort of international guerrilla.

On another occasion, when we called on one elderly villager to ask him for an interview, he was reluctant to come out of his house. My friend went in to explain in Quechua why I wanted to talk to him. I then heard a disembodied voice say through the door, in Spanish, that he could be interviewed later, but that he wanted to wait a few days to see what happened with the first few people who spoke to me. He proved true to his word and did talk to me on a later visit. With countless such small steps, none of them easy, we won the confidence of most of Pomatambo. I did thirty interviews that summer and had many informal conversations. I came away with a fairly good understanding of how the village had changed over the years, and how it had made sense of the insurgency.

It took some years before I got back to Pomatambo. I paid fleeting visits in 2003 and 2004 during trips to Peru, noting that it was much more peaceful and less apprehensive, though no more prosperous. Then in 2006, circumstances converged to let me spend six weeks there for another set of extended conversations with the villagers. This time I was coming back to Pomatambo with a somewhat different set of questions.

In the intervening years, my interests had turned to broader themes, and I had spent time in other parts of the developing world, including China and the Middle East. I have abiding sympathies for the best of traditional life and for social justice. I have written in *Beyond the Global Culture War* (2006) on those themes, and on misgivings about the direction of the modern world—including a concern for the deprivation in which much of humanity lives, and for the loss of worthy ways of life and types of character.[14] I am not alone in having such misgivings; they have cropped up in several rich traditions of political and economic thought over the last century and a half.

While my intellectual interests roamed far from Pomatambo in the years after my first visit, the place remained very much in my mind. My concern for the village stemmed not only from personal ties and the vivid memories of the time I had spent there that summer. It also came from a deeper preoccupation with the kinds of challenges that so many communities like it are facing. Pomatambo's story is the story of the world's peasantry. While its experience of a civil war has been unusually tragic, and while other details may vary, the broad experience and frustrations of this village parallel what has happened over the last half-century in countless other small villages across the developing world.

Ayacucho region alone has nearly six hundred recognized peasant communities like this one. Peru as a whole has close to six thousand.

India has over six hundred thousand. Between one third and one half of all humans on the planet are peasants living in small and quite traditional rural communities with a largely agricultural livelihood.[15] One would hardly know that by reading the *Economist,* or by watching Hollywood films or CNN news broadcasts, or even by attending to the media in countries like Peru. Rural people get a tiny fraction of the attention we should expect based on their numbers.

That such a huge chunk of the world's population fails to register in the public imagination is revealing in itself. These villages are neglected on many levels. Most obviously, they lack the infrastructure, comforts, and opportunities that more prosperous parts of the world enjoy. Anyone who walks around them can see as much. A snippet of a revolutionary folk song captures the common experience of so many who venture into the Andean highlands for the first time.

> *Cuántas veces detuve el paso, extasiado de tanta belleza.*
> *Cuántas veces detuve el paso, lacerado por tanta pobreza.*[16]

> So many times I halted, enthralled with such beauty.
> So many times I halted, lacerated by such poverty.

It takes no great sensitivity or idealism to believe that it does not have to be this way. Never before in human history has the world had such a chasm between wealth and poverty, along with so much capacity, given the political will, to do something about it.

One of the few consistencies in modern Peru has been the lack of that political will. Like many other countries in the developing world, Peru has cycled through a wide range of political alternatives. Since the 1960s, it has seen modernizing liberal governments, reform-minded military juntas, free-market neoliberal regimes, and ham-handed efforts at social democracy—as well as a Maoist insurgency that once spread over much of the south-central highlands. They have all made noises about improving the lot of the countryside but have delivered little. Usually their priorities in economic policy have lain elsewhere. Or, in the most generous view, their intentions have failed to connect with the experiences of people on the ground in places like Pomatambo.

This book is about neglect and misdirected policy as seen from the receiving end. It traces this village's difficult encounter with the modern world over the last few decades and tries to articulate the villagers' perspective on their own values and the threats to them. The failure of successive governments and movements to deliver real prosperity to places like Pomatambo runs deeper than mere neglect and ineptness. It reflects a fundamental disorder of values. It has to do with how policymakers—and most intellectuals, for that matter—imagine the place of these villages in a future world. In blunt terms, the future as now imagined has no place for such communities. Economic success means their disappearance, along with the way of life they represent. And this view holds across the global South.

In the middle of my stay in Peru in 2006, I took a side trip to another corner of the world. I had been invited to speak at a conference in Shanghai. Not only is Shanghai physically on the other side of the globe, but it also exemplifies what many people consider an achievement of globalization. The glittering new buildings of Shanghai's skyline stake coastal China's claim to the twenty-first century. On the outskirts of the city, proliferating billboards advertise luxury villa developments—McMansion tracts that, Epcot-like, offer a sterile plastic imitation of one or another style of European architecture. These suburbs for China's new moneyed status-seekers spread over what used to be farmland and absorb what once were small villages.

This newly wealthy Shanghai and the Andean highlands, with their unpaved roads and adobe huts, represent the two sides of globalization and modernity. Observers comfortable with the world's present trajectory will say that suburban Shanghai and rural Ayacucho simply represent success and failure, the creations of go-getters and laggards, respectively. But they are also linked by a common vision of a future without peasants.

Walking around Pomatambo in the quiet of an afternoon, with nary a soul in sight and the locals out in the fields, I have tried many a time to imagine what this village will be like half a century hence. In a future Pomatambo afternoon, the sun will still be blindingly bright. One will still be able to breathe the same thin but crisp air of the countryside and gaze out on the rocky hillsides and expanses of yellow-green wild grass.

The village will probably be wealthier than it is now. There will be tractors in the valley, and a few farmers will have made a go of selling cash crops, perhaps out-of-season vegetables for the tables of Shanghai's villa owners.

But what of Pomatambo as a community? What of the fellowship that now binds the poor together? Its loss has long been the price of modernization. The usual story is one of agriculture declining, peasants packing up and moving out, and traditional communities withering. Just as Edith Lagos's poem had wild grass growing over her grave, so might the wild grass of an abandoned countryside grow one day over the grave of the traditional Andean way of life. If so, only the open space of the highlands and a few scary bedtime stories about ghosts in the hills will endure.

In this book, I tell the story of Pomatambo over a couple of generations from the bottom up. In many ways, it is the usual story of villages as they face modernity's promises and threats. I try to let the values of the peasants themselves come through, to give voice to an outlook that neither the state nor the guerrillas have ever really respected. But beyond bringing to life the experience of humanity's forgotten half, I also want to suggest a more hopeful path for the future, both for Pomatambo and for similar communities across the global South. They deserve a path of their own.

Development strategy is ultimately a question of vision, of a commitment to strengthen some ways of life rather than others. I firmly believe that people in villages like Pomatambo should have electricity, running water, health care, education, and a prosperity that will allow them to live in dignity and broaden their horizons. But there is more than one way to deliver such goods of the world. The way that nearly all policymakers today take for granted disdains the values of the people who are supposed to benefit. The prevailing vision of development neglects these villages or misdirects its efforts precisely because it denies them a real place in what development offers. Free-market enthusiasts, liberal and social democratic reformers, and the radical left alike have shared this disdain for the peasantry. They have assumed that economic development must erode these traditional communities. They have assumed that progress means setting people free from centuries-old habits of mind. And they have assumed that the best way to help peasants is to turn them into something other than peasants—to draw them into the cities, to consumer culture, to markets or state-owned factories. In short, they all want to eradicate poverty by eradicating the peasantry.

Here is the crux of the issue. Either we can drag the peasantry to prosperity and destroy it in the process; or we can bring prosperity to the peasantry, raising its living standards while building on its time-tested values. The path I shall propose in the second half of this book is one of bringing prosperity to the peasantry, *as a peasantry*. It does not assume that agriculture need remain the mainstay of these communities forever, nor does it assume that institutions and habits must remain exactly as they are. But it does take peasant values as a starting point, and it seeks to avoid the many ways in which antitraditionalist efforts from left and right have assaulted them. Places like Pomatambo need an economic base for the long term, built on traditional foundations, so that fifty years from now they can be prosperous but also recognizable as communities. They want, and perhaps can have, the best of both worlds.

Outlining such an alternative is no easy task. I hope only to take a first step here. I lay out what I think is at stake, based on the experience of this village and the threats that face it. And I propose several levels on which like-minded people could begin working together to craft a truly pro-peasant development strategy. The most modest level would presuppose no broader political change; it would rely wholly on the resources that communities like this one could marshal alone and in civil society. More ambitious would be a political strategy at the national level in countries like Peru. It would aim for a policy environment hospitable to the efforts of the peasantry to build its own kind of rural prosperity. It could also form alliances to reach out to the urban sector, in the name of more placeless values grounded in tradition and community. And on the most far-reaching level, I want to suggest how such a tradition-centered alternative could link up across borders and gain real momentum across the developing world. In short, I do not just want to protect traditional villages where they still survive. I want to show how their deepest ethical commitments can inspire a global cultural resurgence. We have to redefine what it means to be modern.

In putting forth this argument, I am speaking to several types of readers at once. Andean peasants are not going to read this book—at least, not anytime soon. But those who work closely with them in development and education often come from peasant backgrounds and share many of their values. I know enough of them well enough to see their discontent with the world as it is, and their desire to bring community and prosperity together. Beyond the countryside, people who reflect on public policy and its failure in the highlands are looking for new approaches to rural development. I hope to challenge their assumptions and provoke the open-minded, even if they may differ with some of my conclusions.

Still farther afield, the challenges and potential of villages like this one are truly global. They recur beyond Peru, up and down the spine of the Andes, and throughout much of the global South. Even many nonpeasants share the values, aspirations, and frustrations of peasants like these. With the surge of rural–urban migration around the world, well over a billion people are still only a generation removed from the countryside. The memory of a way of life built on the small decencies, on a sense of belonging, of fellowship amid adversity, is woven in subtle ways into the texture of their lives. They welcome some of the advances of modernity, but more of them than one might think want to recover what they have lost. That such a recovery now seems an idle fancy does not invalidate their yearning. Sometimes the sentiments we dismiss most hastily are the truest of all. The alternative is for these uprooted folk, too.

This book thus aims to draw on and foster several conversations at once. It amplifies the voices of some of the most voiceless and marginalized people of our time. It brings to bear on their challenges a rich tradition of economic and political thought, focused on community, human dignity, and the challenges of modernity. It puts the neglect of the Andean countryside in global perspective, with lessons for other parts of the world. And, not least, it suggests that modernity's ills can be overcome, in history's strangest twist, by listening to precisely the people whom modernity has put on the defensive. The Pomatambo that we now see is humanity's past—but it can also inspire humanity's future.

II

Small Worlds, Small Fortunes

The modern world came to Pomatambo, as it often comes, at the point of a gun. It was 1923, and Amadeo was not yet born. His mother was several months pregnant when the people of Pomatambo heard gunshots echoing through the valley. The noise had come from the next village over, he told me, waving in the general direction of the Pampas River.

It was a general wave because his house stood between us and the valley, blocking the view. He had a fairly comfortable dwelling by local standards—adobe like nearly all the others, but a bit bigger, right-angled, and covered with a cheerful layer of orange plaster. Amadeo had grown

Fig. 2: A peasant woman preparing to feed her chickens

up in Pomatambo, but as an adult he had settled up the hill here in Colpa-pampa, some twenty minutes' walk away. In good years, he had prospered raising horses. I had come looking for him because of his reputation as the area's amateur historian. He was now in his eighties, with grey hair visible under his wide-brimmed blue hat and grey stubble on his chin. But he still had his wits about him, and sparkling eyes that must once have had plenty of youthful mischief in them.

Amadeo went on with his story. The mystery of the gunshots was cleared up swiftly, because about twenty well-armed Spanish-looking men suddenly arrived in Pomatambo. They may have been Spaniards, or more likely Peruvians from the coast, but fine distinctions like that mattered little to Andean peasants at the time. Outsiders were outsiders. And these were an odd breed of outsider: fortune hunters brandishing guns and swigging the alcohol they carried with them. Seeing Amadeo's pregnant mother, they gave her wine and chocolates and told her not to be frightened. They were only looking for Inka treasures, they announced. For eight days they lodged in one of the bigger houses in Pomatambo, gorging themselves on milk, tuna, melons, and other delicacies they had brought. They poked around the local ruins for remnants of Inka gold and silver but found little. Apparently all their efforts so far had netted only a few gold crucifixes from post-Inka days. Then they moved on to other villages beyond Pomatambo in search of treasure and women. The latter were easier to find than the former. "Miserable son of a Spaniard" became a favorite insult hurled around among the next generation of Pomatambans.

Centuries before those modern gunshots shattered the peace of the village, another set of Spanish fortune hunters had made their way through the Andes. The conquistadores had disembarked on the Inka empire's northern coast and ridden up into its heartland. Numbering in the mere dozens, but on horseback and armed with steel swords and primitive guns, they managed to take advantage of a succession crisis in the Inka royal family and overcome an empire of millions. God, gold, and glory, the saying went. The sort of men who came to the Americas were adventurers, invoking Christianity for a veneer of legitimacy but more often than not simply lusting for quick riches. One drawing in a chronicle of the conquest depicted a curious Andean asking a Spaniard if the latter had to eat gold.[1]

The conquistadores and their descendants, along with later settlers from Spain, installed themselves in the Andes as semifeudal lords. The image of society they brought with them was, as one historian has noted, "feudal, oligarchic, authoritarian, and élitist."[2] Compared to the rest of late-medieval Europe, the members of Spain's ruling class and its American offshoot paid more attention to the advantages they could extract from their position than to any webs of obligation that might bind them to their subjects. Such a view of the world combined in unhappy ways with the racial fault line between conquerors and conquered. Andean peasants were turned into serfs, granted in blocks of hundreds or thousands to serve the new landowners as an agricultural workforce.

Spain's hunger for gold, silver, and mercury also drove a mining economy that relied heavily on levies of forced labor. The colonial state took over the *mita,* the tributary labor system that the Inkas had used for building roads and storehouses. As the underground metals trickled away in shipments to Europe, so did the lifeblood of the peasantry. Thousands of men were worked to death in the mines. And the new European diseases to which the indigenous people of the Americas had no immunity, such as smallpox, kept killing off victims for two centuries. By the time the Andean population reached its nadir in the 1700s, it had shrunk to around a tenth of what it had been at the height of the Inka empire.[3]

Seen from the bottom, the shock that the highland world experienced in those generations after the conquest was disastrous. Historians have written of a kind of collective psychological crisis in the sixteenth and seventeenth centuries. Local communities and practices were no longer anchored in a larger Andean empire and cosmos. The new rulers seemed alien, and the economic burdens they imposed bred resentment.[4] They violated one of the first principles of Andean culture: a decent reciprocity, in which you give back something for what you get.

But once the worst exploitation abated, the mountain folk gradually settled into a routine in which the Spaniards and their descendants mattered less than one might think. The colonial viceroyalty and the independent republic that replaced it in the 1820s affected daily life for these people only now and then. Even by the late nineteenth and early twentieth centuries, the state still cared less about the hinterland than about foreign interests. The most lucrative niches of Peru's economy were mining and agro-exports from coastal plantations. Trade and finance were dominated first by British and then by American investors.[5] The Quechua-speaking peasantry of the highlands generally had little to do with these economic sectors. It lived in its own cultural universe, for the most part. The villages remained the true repository of Andean values, and under varying names the preconquest *ayllu,* the Andean hamlet, persisted as the basic unit of rural life.

Such was the condition of villages like Pomatambo. The sturdy independence of these small worlds gave them much in common with peasant communities all over the planet. Today we tend to think of peasants as those who farm the land and live at the edge of subsistence. That is true, but they also live differently from other kinds of rural people. They are not like hunter-gatherers or others who live in isolated settlements and have no ties to a larger civilization. Nor are they modern farmers of the sort we now see in Europe and North America, who raise crops for sale and broadly share the culture of the rest of their country. Peasants live locally but fit into a larger social structure. Usually they fit at the bottom of it and try their best to keep at bay the demands that press down from the wealthy and powerful. They live and work in traditional ways and devote more energy to subsisting among kin and neighbors than to earning money from an outside market. The community plays a vital role in shaping the economic life of its inhabitants. Customs restrict how land can be used, and often the villagers either own the land in common or at least have strict rules against selling it to outsiders.[6]

Until well into the twentieth century, peasant life in Pomatambo went on this way. It had an air of the timeless present about it. When I asked members of the older generation who they felt were their ancestors, they did not talk about ancient legends or ethnic groups. Instead they talked about their grandparents and great-grandparents. History on a large scale does not much impress people with more immediately human interests. The real texture of rural living comes from the family and a life cycle shaped by custom. The most important inequality among peasants is a hierarchy of age. Indeed, commentators on the peasantry have remarked that you can know the character of a village quite well by looking at the typical biography of its inhabitants.[7] Young children in Pomatambo join in the tasks of subsistence from an early age, for example. They first learn to look after their younger siblings, then move on to managing the livestock, and finally take up full agricultural work in their teens.[8]

One old woman fondly remembered her childhood as a peaceful time. Above all else she enjoyed taking her family's sheep and cows up the hills to pasture. She told me that they had good meat and milk in those days, though the animals in the area started suffering many more illnesses after she was an adult. Her nostalgia was nearly universal among villagers of her generation. One venerable fellow insisted that things were better when he was a child, partly because in those days parents knew how to bring up children. Another of his cohort remembered the austere moral teachings handed down to him by his parents, as their parents had done before: "Don't be envious. Don't steal. Don't lie. And you have to work."

Generations of peasants in Pomatambo and nearby villages managed their own affairs well enough. Their poverty was something of a blessing in disguise, for no outsiders or authority figures had much reason to interfere. No really large estates emerged around Vilcashuamán, because the sparsely inhabited grazing lands could not support them.[9] If Pomatambo had anything resembling an enemy in the first part of the twentieth century, it was probably neighboring villages (and vice versa). The elders today remember conflicts over pasture land between Pomatambo and other communities, conflicts that now and then erupted into violence. When they were children, their parents would sometimes use slingshots and stones in skirmishes with their counterparts. Apparently one dispute got so hot that a police officer came out from town to intervene. He must have made matters worse, because he ended up getting beaten to death.

Occasional lawlessness was one side of the coin, a sturdy self-reliance the other. Pomatambans used to meet most of their needs by farming their small plots in the village. Even several decades into the twentieth century, over half of what rural Andeans consumed came from subsistence agriculture.[10] The rest came from bartering directly or indirectly with peasants much like themselves. Llama-drivers and other petty trad-ers used to circulate among villages in different ecological zones. This age-old "vertical complementarity" took advantage of microclimates that could change with as little as a few hundred feet in altitude. Some traders brought coca leaves, others clothing, and so on. In exchange, Pomatambans would offer cows they had raised. The average household might have a couple of cows, five to ten pigs, and anywhere from five to thirty sheep, though the pigs and sheep were usually of poor quality and had to be kept for domestic use.[11] Between what they could scratch from the land and the animals that grazed it, Pomatambo's peasants managed to feed themselves over the generations.

The land itself defined much of community life, in a way that modern people without a sense of place have largely forgotten. The history of this village centers on the land. Pomatambo first appears in official records in 1648, with a recorded land sale to the Rudas family. Apparently they were minor estate owners who used some of the area as a cow pasture. The village is mentioned again in 1887, when a justice of the peace certified that it covered three square miles.[12] Most of the intervening details are hazy, as we might expect among a people who could not read or write until a century ago.

Handed-down stories make up for what the official history lacks. Some settlement clearly goes back to the pre-Inka period, and the village site has probably been inhabited continuously for centuries. But accord-ing to the elders, it was very sparsely populated two hundred years ago. The present core group of families goes back in semilegendary fashion to a woman named Elena Carrasco. Apparently she moved into the area around the early nineteenth century and bought a large chunk of the land in Pomatambo and neighboring villages. Then this formidable woman scandalously took up with three different men in succession, including a priest with the surname of Remón. Her eldest son, by this same priest, was Agustín Remón, the progenitor of Pomatambo's most influential family for a few generations. Younger sons by Elena Carrasco's other lovers founded families with other surnames that persist in the area.

As the story goes, punctuated by moments of intrigue, these families divided up the land among them. Divided inheritances and population growth combined over three or four generations to spread land ownership more widely. A few plots were bought by outsiders, some of whom married into the village, others of whom were small traders who wanted to settle down. All these trends turned Pomatambo by the mid-twentieth century into the collection of smallholding peasants we see now. If more or less true, this story fits broader patterns in the Andes.[13] These villages are still bound together as tightly as the pre-conquest *ayllus,* but a significant portion of the land is owned in individual plots, much as in peasant communities all over the world.

In the early years of the twentieth century, landownership was by some measures more unequal than it is now. The Remón family had more land than other villagers and enjoyed some advantages from sitting at the center of the village's kinship networks. They gave out land in small parcels to be farmed by other peasants, who paid them a kind of rent-in-kind by working on the Remón family's own plots from time to time. While the Remón landowners are remembered now as having ill-treated their tenants, it bears noting that they were not much better off materially. They were certainly not rich estate owners, and they had to do some manual labor themselves to subsist. Apart from the rent-in-kind, they were little more than somewhat richer peasants among poorer peasants. And with the ongoing sales of land to newcomers and the pressure of dividing up plots in each generation, Pomatambo's leading family lost ground fast. In fact, by the time I got to looking over lists of surnames and wealth in the 1990s, there was no longer any real difference between the Remón and other formerly richer families on the one hand, and the rest of the community on the other.[14] Small advantages dissolve quickly amid the equalizing pressures of the countryside.

Pomatambo's peasants are keenly conscious of a rough equality among them. They repeatedly told me that no one has much land but everyone has at least some. So while the fragmenting of inheritances reduces wealth at the top, the wide dispersion of landownership also gives the poor a vital security. In other parts of the highlands there were large estates owned by descendants of the Spaniards, but among the Andean peasantry equality has been the norm. Efforts to find peasant "classes" have usually ended up identifying a narrow spectrum of wealth and poverty. Middling peasants manage to subsist independently on their plots. Richer peasants have enough extra crops and livestock that they can sell or barter the surplus and live a bit more comfortably. And poorer peasants, short on land, have to make up the shortfall in income by doing work on the side for others.[15] These are gradations within the same way of life, not sharp differences.

Andean communities like Pomatambo hang together well because they have built-in buffers against insecurity. One such buffer is the web of customs that regulates land use. Only some of Pomatambo's land is in private hands. This land includes the plots under and next to houses in the village, as well as parcels for growing maize down in the valley. The maize-growing land is farmed intensively every year and yields the most important part of every family's food. It is the most valuable land in the village, because it enjoys some natural irrigation and an ideal microclimate at the slightly lower altitude. The average family has a few acres of maize land in total, scattered over as many as six plots in Pomatambo, and sometimes even some plots in nearby villages.[16]

The scattering of plots is an age-old and cross-cultural peasant strategy for hedging one's bets. It limits risk from frosts and crop diseases, and it lets each household take advantage of several different soils. But it also comes from patterns of inheritance. Maize and house plots in Pomatambo are passed down between generations and get mixed and matched over time with intermarriage and transfers.[17] In one sign of the tenacity of custom and the observance of small decencies, title to these parcels rests entirely on informal recognition. The parcels are marked off by rows of plants or small stones. Villagers say that they have wills, and that ownership comes down "from the ancestors," but you will not find these plots on any official land registry. Custom has sufficed so far. Everyone knows who owns what, and the fact of being properly given or buying a piece of land, and then working it with one's own hands, is enough in these people's eyes to sustain a moral claim. Only a long-abandoned plot can be taken away, perhaps to give to a newly married couple short on land.[18]

Important though it is, this kind of informal private land makes up but a small part of the territory that Pomatambo covers. About five-sixths of the land in the area, mostly in the hills, is communal land of two sorts.[19] One part is communally owned but used privately, in plots that the village authorities distribute each year to households based on the number of members they have. This custom of allotting land according to family size goes back at least to the Inka period.[20] Since this land is higher and drier than the irrigated land in the valley, it has to be rotated in use. The poor soil, exhausted easily, can withstand only about three years of cultivation before it has to lie fallow for up to fifteen years. The other type of communal land is not divided up at all. It consists of the sweeping expanses of *puna,* or grazing land, on which Pomatambans let their cows and sheep roam free. They also pasture animals on the agricultural fields nearer the village once the harvest is over. The animals themselves, of course, belong to each household separately, even though they are fattened on communal land.[21]

As with much of peasant life, this system works well even though it exists only in the minds of the villagers themselves. No laws or documents support it. Peruvian law today only says that each community formally owns all of the land within its borders, and that it has to settle for itself how much land to use collectively and how much to give out to individual households.[22] All the intricacies of land use in Pomatambo come from customs that long predate the Peruvian state. These are tried and tested ways of making a living in harsh conditions while maintaining some level of goodwill among neighbors.

The village is not a utopia by any means. Apart from the severe poverty that affects everyone, it has real albeit narrow inequalities. But the system does work on several levels: ecological, economic, and cultural. Irrigated plots in the valley are ideal for maize, the higher and drier land above for potatoes. Rotation adjusts land use to sustainability and the number of mouths each family has to feed.[23] And, perhaps most importantly, no one starves, and the community is woven into the texture of daily economic life.

Alongside customs of land use, the village is bound together in economic life by labor exchange. This, too, reflects the pressures of agriculture. The need for manpower surges during the time of sowing, and even more during the big harvest each year. Two quite simple practices, *ayni* and *minka,* allow families to pool labor for such occasions. *Ayni* is a one-to-one exchange of labor that even the poorest villagers can afford: help me for one day on my plot, and I will do the same for you tomorrow. *Minka* is a larger undertaking that requires more resources. A family facing a large harvest or a house-raising, for example, will invite friends and neighbors to work for the day in exchange for food, drink, and music. Traditionally, no money would change hands for either *ayni* or *minka.*

Both these practices go back centuries. They rely on powerful norms of reciprocity, of a balance between help one gets from others and help that one gives in return. Many of the older villagers remember quite fondly the years before the violence, when *ayni* and *minka* were natural cycles of daily life just as sowing and harvesting were natural seasons of the year. Studies of communities throughout the highlands have shown how vital these labor practices are in sustaining a whole system of subsistence.[24] Production has a collective, even festive, atmosphere, but the harvest that emerges from it is still owned by each individual household. "The harvest is private," declared one elderly rich peasant in another village when I asked him how far cooperation went. The exchange of labor as neighbors work on each other's plots also amounts to an ongoing ritual that recognizes ownership and boundaries.

Most of the time, this mix of cooperation and self-reliance works well. But it has its tensions, which come into sharper relief in villages with a wider gap between rich and poor. The poor can always do *ayni,* since it costs nothing except a few hours of hard work. And it builds solidarity by creating a debt of help that has to be repaid another day. But for *minka,* a family needs to be at least comfortable enough to afford the quite extensive hospitality for neighbors who come to work. *Minka* has an equalizing effect, simply because generosity is expensive and Andean culture expects a rustic camaraderie between hosts and guests. But looked at in a certain light, it can also highlight wealth disparities. When richer and middling peasants host a *minka,* they become employers in all but name. They pay workers, in kind, to bring in the harvest or build a house that then ends up as private property.[25]

In more unequal villages, or villages where the cash economy made inroads early on, *minka* can open the way to wage labor. First a token payment of cash becomes part of the hospitality offered. Then the hospitality gets rolled back, and eventually wages become the main motive for doing work. Complex ties of custom and goodwill between households give way to a wage contract between rich farmers and day laborers.

In the highlands, at least until recently, this unraveling of communities was never complete. It had built-in limits not because of any softhearted idealism—though norms against greed are powerful—but because even rich peasants found it in their interest to stay within these customs. Their slight advantages in resources and productivity never went far enough that they could afford to go it alone. Sometimes they might hire labor so that they could devote their own energies to working outside their villages. But even the most hard-nosed and profit-minded rich peasants still found unpaid labor, attracted only by hospitality, cheaper now and then. Keeping their neighbors on reasonably good terms meant playing the game by contributing to festivals and the like. They had to keep one foot in the wage market and one foot in tradition.[26] Peasant communities like this hang together not only because long-standing values demand it, but also because most of the time cooperation is in everyone's interest.

All these pressures for and against solidarity were at work in Pomatambo in the first decades of the twentieth century, as elsewhere in the highlands. But Pomatambo had no great inequalities to weaken the fabric of the community. The Remón family was not rich by highland standards, and it was declining anyway. All households practiced *ayni* and *minka*. Any disruption to the relatively comfortable equilibrium in the village could only come from outside. Not that these villages were ever completely closed off from one another or from the towns—some rural folk did move about for seasonal work and the like. Still, it took a special kind and intensity of contact to change age-old habits.

✣ ✣ ✣

That new contact came around the middle of the twentieth century from an upsurge in migration to the cities. Many forces drove this shift, but one of the most basic was that moving around became slightly less arduous and expensive. Starting in the 1930s, the state began building

27

A Path of Our Own

roads to connect major cities as part of an effort to bind the national territory together more securely. New economic activity on the coast also offered employment for migrants who wanted it.[27]

Perhaps fittingly, one of this wave of new migrants was none other than Amadeo, the lively fellow who was born in 1924 after the fortune-hunters shot their way into the area. His mother was from Pomatambo, and his father was *personero* of Colpapampa, a kind of mediator with other villages. Amadeo grew up in Pomatambo and lived there until his teens. Then he went to work as a general hired hand for his godfather, a prosperous man who lived in Vischongo, the next town northward from Vilcashuamán. He learned some rudimentary Spanish by moving around a lot with his godfather on business.

When Amadeo was about eighteen, his uncle, who worked in Ica on the coast, offered to take him there. Eager to see city life for himself, young Amadeo went with his uncle on horseback. He was disappointed, for Ica at the time was little more than a cluster of mud buildings on a plain. He worked for a while as a servant, but he quickly concluded that he would rather go on to Lima, in the hope of becoming an apprentice in a city workshop.

Amadeo got to Lima soon enough, and he liked it better than Ica even though he still had to struggle with Spanish. He got a job as a uniformed steward in one of the city's mansions. Lima in the early 1940s was a far more peaceful and human-scale city than the sprawling and chaotic metropolis it has become since. It included little more than what are now the central neighborhoods, with their wood and adobe houses and old colonial buildings. But it was also a city of opportunity, of plentiful work and new horizons. After a few months, Amadeo's uncle urged him to go to night school and then to a proper state school. At the ripe age of nineteen, he earned a certificate for having completed the second-year level of primary education.

With this accomplishment under his belt, Amadeo went back to Pomatambo. A primary school had opened in the village in his absence, led by a female teacher from town who was about his age. She put him into the fifth-year class. Within a few months the two struck up a romance that lasted until he returned to Lima with one of his friends. He went

28

back to his previous employer for a while, then moved around doing odd jobs over the next thirteen years in an ironmonger's, a launderette, and a granary.

Afterwards he came back to the countryside, married a woman from Colpapampa, and settled there, just up the hill from his home village. He liked the two villages well enough but felt a bit out of place after having moved around so much. As a returned migrant, he poured his ample energy into farming and horse-raising, improving the piece of land he owned, and building three houses. He also drew on his newly honed political skills. While in Lima, he had served as president of an association of migrants from these villages. At first Colpapampa's inhabitants were unwilling to elect this semi-outsider to office, but after only a year they made him the local constable, the first of several posts he would hold.

Amadeo was not the only Pomatamban in that important wave of migrants. Another, about the same age and now half-blind and walking with a cane, was Alejandro. He went to Lima in 1947 and remembers waiting on the street every morning for odd day jobs. He liked the city, especially the novelty of having such a variety of fruit in the markets. But migrant life had its lonely side, too. Lima had few highland folk in those years, and the city people who did not know Quechua could not talk to him. Ignacio, another migrant a few years younger, felt similarly out of place and hated getting lost in the city streets. He remembers the ethnic tapestry of the city, with blacks as well as immigrants from Japan, China, and Europe. The blacks used to look down on Quechua-speaking highlanders, and Japanese employers would shout at him; whites and Chinese were a bit nicer on average, he thought. Perhaps the most striking image of city life Ignacio recalled was the daily scene in a cafeteria where he worked. Unlike the hearty conversation and warmth of an Andean village, lunchtime customers would come in hurriedly, eat alone, then pay and leave as soon as they finished. By working there and in an electric plant, he managed to make enough money to help his parents in their twilight years.

Along with Amadeo, Alejandro and Ignacio also came back to their home village after a few years. The familiarity that returned migrants like them had with the outside world later made them key figures in their villages. But many who left to seek their fortunes from the 1940s onward stayed permanently in the cities. Over the second half of the twentieth century, Peru, like much of the developing world, saw a vast movement of people from rural to urban areas. When you drive around Lima today, with its huge and jumbled shantytowns that hold a third of the country's population, you can see that the highlands have disgorged their swelling millions onto the coast. Between 1940 and 1961, nearly a hundred thousand more people moved out of Ayacucho region than in. In the 1970s, the province that included Pomatambo even had its total population decline, despite a very high birthrate. Young men who could not earn a living in a depressed countryside left in droves in the years leading up to the civil war.[28]

This steady outflow of youths was one reason the landscape in Pomatambo changed in the mid-twentieth century. But while migration often affects villages, it does so in different ways and to different degrees. Short-term seasonal migration, for example, usually involves men adding to their annual incomes by going to other parts of the countryside to work in agriculture. Longer-term migration tends to involve younger villagers, both male and female, going to the cities for menial work in industry or services. Their earnings are put toward education, or housing, or small businesses, but are not usually enough to alter significantly the distribution of wealth in their home villages.[29]

In Pomatambo, as in other fairly isolated and equal communities, this wave of migration did not create a new class of rich villagers: the money was too meager and the local economy too stagnant. What mattered most was the exposure to a new way of life and new values. This exposure can come through other channels as well, of course. It can come from periodically visiting a market town, if that market town is itself changing. Or it can come through listening to battery-powered radios.[30] But in Pomatambo, as in many other villages, migration to the coastal cities exposed a critical mass of peasants to new ways of thinking and new habits, which they in turn brought back to the countryside.

Some changes are superficial, such as the wearing of more modern clothes. Others run deeper and involve a shift in what kinds of status symbols attract people's attention. Data from different countries has shown that migrants who circulate between villages and cities tend to acquire a new frame of reference. Traditional villagers gain social standing from joining in festivals and performing community duties. The new men, while they might keep a foot in village life, put more stock in symbols of modernity and in taking advantage of outside economic opportunities. Over time, as one anthropologist has put it, a clash of personal image emerges "between the poor stay-at-home yokels and the sophisticated dark-glasses-wearing urban dwellers."[31]

I do not want to exaggerate this fault line in Pomatambo. Back in the 1960s and 1970s, you would not have seen much visible difference between returned migrants and the peasants who had stayed put. And by most indications, men like Amadeo who came back from the cities fitted quite smoothly back into village life and continued to participate in the usual customs. But no one could deny that by learning basic Spanish and how to navigate the cities, they had gained new knowledge and new horizons. Alejandra, Amadeo's younger sister who is now in her sixties, remembered of that era that "there were some who understood, and some who didn't."

The modern world made its first inroads into Pomatambo after the 1940s, but it did so in a distinctive way. Usually modernity comes through commerce and industry, through the new power of money and the fevered preoccupations of those who are making it. Here in the impoverished Andean highlands, however, modernity came first through ideas and experiences. It did not buy up the countryside; it offered a new lens through which some people *looked* at the countryside. The shifting values at stake come into sharp relief here precisely because daily material life did not change much.

Migration was only one point of entry for new values between 1940 and 1980. The other was education. Before the twentieth century, education could not have lain further outside the universe of the Andean peasantry. In Europe and Asia, peasants had been broadly part of the same cultures as the ruling strata. Whatever the obstacles of class and caste, high culture was in some imaginable sense their culture, too. An intelligent and aspiring young peasant could find transmission belts to lift him into the ranks of the educated, perhaps as a teacher or cleric. In the Andes, the racial hierarchy, with descendants of Spaniards at the top, was much less permeable. The Andean peasantry kept to itself, or at most circulated into small provincial towns, because it had nowhere to go.

This changed dramatically for the generation that included Amadeo, Alejandro, and Ignacio. In the 1930s, the first significant group of Pomatamban children began getting a rudimentary education. It began as an entirely informal arrangement. Ignacio remembers that when he was a child, he and a few other children used to collect firewood every week and take it to a neighbor who had learned to read and write. He would then teach them a little. The first proper school started in the early 1940s. At first, the parents themselves had to pay the salary of the teacher, who only showed up when he felt like it. Eventually the village got fed up with this arrangement and sent one of its leaders to the city on horseback to bring back another teacher, whom the state began to pay. These and other early teachers came from the city of Ayacucho and from small provincial towns. This group included the young woman who became involved with Amadeo.

In those early years the school stood on the village square, next to a small church that had been built twenty years earlier. It would stay there until the current school building was erected down by the stream in the late 1970s. The first school was made of stone and adobe, much like the houses in Pomatambo. The children helped build it. Ignacio recalled a fearsome teacher who gave him and his classmates an especially difficult first exam that they all failed. As punishment, they had to pick up rocks and carry them to the school site. But despite that teacher's sternness, he took his responsibility for his pupils to heart. He taught them all subjects, including a smattering of religion. Sometimes he would stride through the village streets at night with his walking stick, and if he found children playing outside too late he would walk each of them home.

Pomatambans in those early years had a thirst for education and thought quite highly of the school. They took pride in the fact that Pomatambo had been chosen as the site, that other villages contributed to building it, and that students came from around the area to attend it. This enthusiasm for education was evident across rural Ayacucho. One observer has compared the village schools to a "capsule of modernity," a first outpost of the modern state, a device that vaguely promised upward mobility—even if peasants who had never seen anything like it before could not quite grasp how it worked.[32]

Such expectations were strangely prescient, even though, on the surface, the early reality of the schools was not very promising. Few observers exposed to a fully modern education system elsewhere would have picked this very modest school as a crucial element in changing Pomatambo. The first few students who attended it barely benefited from doing so. Only a couple kept studying beyond a year or so; most were lucky if they left knowing how to read at all. The oldest men in the village today either remained functionally illiterate or later studied somewhere else. Girls did not gain even that limited benefit, because the school at first was only for boys. Alejandra, Amadeo's much younger sister, only started learning to read and write a couple of years ago. Their father was a village leader who wanted his sons to be educated, but he believed that his daughters at most needed only to know how to write love letters. Comparatively broad-minded for the time, he eventually sent Alejandra and her sister to Lima to learn Spanish.

Despite the humble beginnings of the village school, it became a formidable agent of change in the 1950s and 1960s. The average age of entering students plummeted. Whereas at first the classroom consisted of mostly older teenagers, a decade later the entering pupils were of normal primary-school age. Education for girls in Pomatambo started around 1966. By the time the insurgency erupted in 1980, primary-school attendance was nearly universal in rural Ayacucho. In the region as a whole, illiteracy fell rapidly, including a drop from 60 percent to 45 percent in the 1970s.[33]

Unlike in some other parts of the highlands, the school did not make enemies in Pomatambo. Elsewhere in those years, teachers whose own sympathies lay very much with national Spanish-speaking culture sometimes took a disparaging view of the peasantry.[34] In Pomatambo, no one remembers such tensions. They may have struck good fortune with the types of teachers posted there. One teacher who taught in Pomatambo for a few months in 1975, now an innkeeper in Vilcashuamán, spoke fondly of the village he remembered. He said that the teachers made a point of staying on good terms with the community. They used to work side-by-side with the locals making tiles for the church and school roofs.

In the long run, what mattered most was not the villagers' perception of the school, but what access to education, both in the village and in the towns where some Pomatambans circulated, was doing to the inner workings of the community and the types of people who had influence within it. The upsurge of migration had been an equal-opportunity agent of change. It provided real familiarity with the outside world and the crucial Spanish-language skills necessary to navigate it. But which young Pomatambans became exposed to urban life, and which did not, followed no particular pattern. Furthermore, more or less anyone could learn Spanish well enough, given the opportunity.

Education was a trickier area, one in which more lasting differences emerged among villagers, at least during the transitional twenty years or so between when virtually no one went to school and when virtually everyone did. The social positions and aspirations of families, even within the narrow range of differences in the area, mattered somewhat. Even after the state started paying teacher salaries, primary education still had accompanying costs, and it took children and teenagers away from household work. More prosperous families were more likely to be able to afford education.

Take as an example a Pomatamban family that I know well, one that has experienced remarkable upward mobility over the last generation. Their ancestral village is nearer the Pampas River, where they had a fairly comfortable middle-sized farm in the early twentieth century. They could fairly be called rich peasants, though still within the typical range of wealth in rural Vilcashuamán. According to one story, a great-great-grandfather was a cattle trader from northern Peru who put down roots in the area in the nineteenth century. They had the money in the 1940s to send three sons to a prestigious secondary school in Ayacucho. One of those boys, the father of my close friend, would become a rural schoolteacher as an adult. Some social advantages, however modest, made it easier for them to take advantage of the new educational opportunities that arose at midcentury.

Undoubtedly a good chunk of the newly educated from rural back-grounds came from among the richer peasants. At the same time, even a few years of education gave credentials, status, and access to outside resources that dwarfed the modest advantage a couple of extra acres of highland soil might have provided in earlier days. Becoming a schoolteacher gave a person a cash salary in a cash-poor village. Even the more modest accomplishment of basic literacy and fluency in Spanish allowed a young peasant to find his or her way around the urban bureaucracy without being paralyzed by fear of the unfamiliar.

Any population has a range of talents and temperaments. They are released in different directions and esteemed to different degrees, depending on the nature of the society. In a world of small-scale subsistence farmers, abstract intelligence and the ability to manipulate impersonal rules carry little weight. Today's lawyerly types disdain villages in part because they would never flourish in them. What matters more in a village is a knack for building networks of goodwill among kin and neighbors. By the 1960s, the old bases of influence were weakening in places like Pomatambo, while the personal abilities that allow one successfully to enter a modernizing national society began counting for more. Education shifted the terrain like an earthquake, particularly since the village had no real concentrations of wealth that might have been converted into significant advantages in a modern economy.

For villages like Pomatambo to feel the full impact of migration and education, still more had to change. After all, a traditional peasant, still oriented to the small world of the village, should have had no reason to care much about the new experiences of a few youths. Exposure to Lima, a basic grasp of Spanish, and a smattering of book learning might have opened up more options for those who had them. But all else being equal, such alien accomplishments should have had no purchase on life within the community. The customs and values of Pomatambo should have gone on as usual for the more traditionally minded. And influence in the village should have stayed where it had always been: with the Quechua-speaking elders, those enforcers of austere highland mores.

But change did come, and it came because Pomatambo could continue as its own small world no longer. So far I have traced mainly what was happening in Pomatambo, and in the lives of Pomatambans who ventured outside. After all, this was how these people themselves experienced the world. Larger political forces would matter to them only later on, when they began to feel new changes pressing down on them from powerful external actors.

The turning point was an ambitious national agrarian reform program launched after 1968. Without this political initiative, migration and education would have affected individuals, but not so much the workings of the community itself. Simply put, the agrarian reform and events surrounding it made the Peruvian state vastly more important for highland communities than it had ever been before. To understand why, we must step back and look at national politics. Then we can see how a changing political environment broke down the walls around these little communities and shifted power within them in subtle ways.

The agrarian reform did not come out of the blue. By the early 1960s, the state had already begun making inroads into rural life. The liberal government of Fernando Belaúnde, inspired in part by a wave of moderate reforms in Latin America, started trying to bring the Andean countryside into the national mainstream and open the agricultural sector to market forces. One concrete step in doing so was to give peasant communities official, full standing under the law. The pace of community recognitions picked up in the early and mid-1960s, including in Vilcashuamán and other remote parts of Ayacucho.[35]

Pomatambo, perhaps because of its slightly greater size compared to neighboring villages, was ahead of the curve. As early as 1951, it had taken the first steps from being a mere name on a map to being a full-fledged legal entity. Some families saw recognition as a way to finish off what remained of the local power of the Remón family. But bureaucracy's wheels turned slowly, as they usually do in Peru. Eventually an association of migrants in Lima, seeing that the process needed greasing, managed to cobble together money to bribe an official at the ministry of agriculture. Full recognition came in 1964.

This part of the highlands had no large estates and no wealthy landowners directly oppressing the peasantry. The only estate anywhere near Pomatambo, visible in the distance down towards the Pampas River, was small and unproductive. So this village did not have any struggle with a Spanish-speaking, landed oligarchy during the years leading up to the agrarian reform. Elsewhere in Peru, however, pressures were building by the 1960s. More and more large landowners were moving to the comfort of the cities, and absentee ownership meant a slackening of semifeudal controls on the poor.[36] The success of the 1959 Cuban Revolution inspired a guerrilla movement that took to the hills in 1965 preaching redistribution of land. Within a few months, the army crushed that handful of romantics with guns, but fear of revolution still hung in the air. And in national politics, the moderate left could not make headway against the oligarchy. It became clear that civilian reformers would never be given the leeway needed to implement real change, and that a backward-looking landowning class would never let go of its stagnant fiefdoms.

Something had to give. And give it did. On October 3, 1968, the army lost patience with the political impasse, seized Belaúnde, and swiftly put the ousted president on a plane into exile. Then the military leadership set about changing Peru in ways that the civilians had never managed to do. The officers who would rule Peru for the next twelve years were an odd bunch. Most coups in Latin America in that era came from the right, from officers tied to the wealthier classes and bent on suppressing any threat to capitalism. Peru's new junta had much humbler roots and a leftist agenda. Its leader, General Juan Velasco, came from a working-class family, and the broader officer corps had become ethnically diverse. Moreover, the officers who supported the coup had little patience for the oligarchy that was clinging to power and letting too much pressure build up from below. These new, professional soldiers saw internal security, development, and the alleviation of social conflict as intertwined priorities. They wanted to head off a Cuban-style revolution and keep order, but they saw that doing so would mean imaginative reforms. To modernize Peru, the old landowning oligarchy had to go. Almost uniquely in Latin America, this military regime would attempt a "populism from the top."[37]

The Revolutionary Government of the Armed Forces, as it styled itself, at first won the applause of many leftists in Peru and abroad. Its ideology was complex. The junta claimed to represent the true national interest, in contrast to the shortsighted partisanship of the rich and the radicals. It proposed a "society of solidarity" that was "neither capitalist nor communist." This third way had some Catholic undertones. In 1973, the minister of energy and mines declared, "[t]his is in reality the first revolution in the world that is trying to be, simultaneously and inseparably, humanist, Christian, socialist, and libertarian."[38]

Most such pronouncements were just the army's incoherent flattery of Peru's various political blocs. The common thread was usually little more than order and development, intended to defuse social tensions and thereby prevent worse chaos. But whatever the high-flown rhetoric, the most striking slogan for Peru's peasants was "Land for the one who works it." The urgency of agrarian reform had become clear among the new officer corps in the years leading up to the coup, and it was the strongest point of consensus for the military leadership once it found itself in power.

In a series of decrees between 1968 and the early 1970s, the junta launched a series of measures intended to "dynamize and modernize the traditional ways of using land." Large estates, including sugar plantations on the coast, were expropriated with some compensation to the owners. One aim was to get the landowning oligarchy to transfer its capital and any energy it still had into the expanding industrial sector. The military regime claimed to side with the more up-to-date and productive business classes against the decayed remnants of the Spanish gentry. Another aim was to turn expropriated land over to peasants and workers, so that they might farm it more efficiently in cooperatives. The junta resisted simply handing out parcels to individual farmers; they feared that this fragmentation would hinder modern economies of scale and the use of machinery.[39]

In practice, this effort had mixed results. On the one hand, where there were big estates to expropriate, the agrarian reform was carried through swiftly. New provincial authorities, appointed from Lima and beholden to no local interests, swept away resistance as they implemented edicts from above.[40] Peasants all over Peru had no doubt that the regime was on their side against the large landowners. But the result was anticlimactic. For one thing, only some areas in the highlands had much land to redistribute. The small estate in the valley below Pomatambo, for example, remained mostly intact because of its modest size. When Pomatambo's claim against it was adjudicated in 1969, the village gained a mere forty-four acres of land on top of the 1,900 acres it already had.[41] Few farmers elsewhere in Ayacucho benefited, either.

Economically, the agrarian reform was a disappointment. Its proponents had expected it to jump-start economic development in Peru's countryside by organizing land more efficiently and promoting cash crops. Stagnant subsistence farming was supposed to give way to commercial dynamism, in which even the poorest farmers would have a stake in a flourishing national economy. But there was no economic boom. The benefits were few and tended to go only to middle-class commercial farmers and government employees on the coast. The most lasting effect involved an expansion of the state's role in the economy. Between 1965 and 1975, the state's share of new investment in Peru swelled from 16 percent to 50 percent of the total.[42]

The agrarian reform failed for three reasons. First, even where substantial land was expropriated, the regime's plans for it were usually out of touch with highland life. Farming practices had developed over the centuries in each community based on its soils, climate, and ecological niche. On this tapestry the reformers tried to stamp preconceived models of modern agricultural cooperatives, models based on large coastal sugar mills and the like.[43] Second, the junta underestimated the importance of culture and ethnicity. They insisted that the chasm between the Quechua-speaking peasantry and the Spanish-speaking cities involved nothing more than class conflict and economic backwardness.[44] Third, top-down reform may have swept aside some of the roadblocks in Peruvian politics, but it never overcame the disconnect between the regime and civil society. The officers rammed through the changes they wanted, at first taking some satisfaction from not having to listen to businessmen, unions, or landowners. But a few years into the experiment, it became clear not only that a national consensus was lacking, but also that powerful economic interests were beginning to regroup and frustrate the junta's agenda. Military populism had failed to grow roots.[45]

By the mid-1970s, most observers concluded that the "Peruvian experiment" was doomed. For all the talk of participation, of worker- and peasant-managed cooperatives, the agrarian reform remained a top-down exercise. Even the employees of those agricultural cooperatives on the coast that made a go of it economically had no real input in decision-making. The officers could not break the mental habit of trying to run a country like a barracks. Indeed, the regime aligned more than it wanted to think with the hierarchical political culture of the nineteenth and early twentieth centuries. On top of that legacy, it made matters worse by creating a new layer of bureaucracy. The same administrators who carried out the agrarian reform became the kernel of a new top-heavy state apparatus. As masters of the new Peru, a modern officialdom arose on the wreckage of the defeated rural oligarchy.[46] Even a generation later, a teacher in Pomatambo still complained about the corruption and highhandedness among the administrators of that era who thought they knew better than peasants how to work the land. "Who's in charge?" he asked. "Farmers or 'experts'?"

In short, the agrarian reform was a blunt instrument. It ignored local conditions and tried to improve the countryside with scant regard for practices that had worked over centuries. In addition, redistributing land could work only where there was land to redistribute. As the saying goes, if all you have is a hammer, then everything begins to look like a nail. The Andean peasantry did not fit the mold of technocratic modernization that the junta took for granted as Peru's future. On the surface, a third way that was neither capitalist nor communist, neither liberal nor socialist, might share common ground with rural Andean customs, which blend cooperation and self-reliance. But for all the junta's talk, it ignored what was right under its nose. Villages like Pomatambo were not consulted because they supposedly had nothing to contribute to the discussion.

As the years went by, the failures of the military regime mounted, and the experiment lost momentum. General Velasco, in declining health since 1973, was ousted by his fellow officers in August 1975. The idealism of the incoming leadership had worn thin. They had closer ties to Peruvian business interests, and they knew that radical reforms had run their course. Disillusioned with power and declining in popularity, they had little choice but to put the country back on a path toward civilian rule. Presidential elections were held in 1980. Parties linked to the military regime got a negligible percentage of the vote. And the new civilian president was none other than Belaúnde, the same moderate liberal whom Velasco had thrown out of office twelve years earlier.

Peasants are down-to-earth people. They tend to be skeptical of grand political visions until they bear fruit. Perhaps for that reason, the agrarian reform's failure to deliver did not cause any great disappointment in Pomatambo. It would be easy, therefore, to conclude that the "Peruvian experiment" meant little to the people in this village.

But the agrarian reform did transform Pomatambo in unintended ways. It made migration and education matter as they would not have mattered otherwise. The national government's increased involvement in the countryside meant that the community had to deal with outside forces more than ever before and could no longer keep to itself. The junta set up Agrarian Tribunals to carry out the expropriation of large estates and to settle disputes in favor of peasants where possible. But even where little was ultimately at stake, as in the area around Pomatambo, the burdens of dealing with these new legal bodies were unprecedented. Every new decree or statute affecting peasant communities gave them new tasks, including recordkeeping, carrying out official correspondence, and so on.[47] The average citizen in a developed society would find these responsibilities challenging. Imagine how they must have seemed to peasants, most of whom could neither read nor speak Spanish.

A new kind of villager stepped into the task. Perhaps the best example is Fortunato, born in 1933 into a typical village family. He attended school for about seven years, first in Pomatambo and then in Vilcashuamán. After that, like many of the migrants we have already met, he went to Lima to seek his fortune. Several years of work in a factory and in construction did not bring him wealth, and he remembers being disdained by city dwellers. But he did learn fluent Spanish, and he acquired a sharp sense of how to navigate the world outside his home village.

When Fortunato came back to Pomatambo, he held a series of local elected offices. In fact, when I first visited Pomatambo in 1995, he was president of the community. During the years of the agrarian reform, he had come into his own as a local leader. He traveled to Lima several times to represent the village in boundary disputes with neighboring communities and with the estate owner down in the valley. When poking through the archives of the ministry of agriculture in Ayacucho, I came across a file of legal documents and correspondence from this era. One of the letters from Pomatambo to a tribunal complained in vivid detail of the misdeeds of the nearby landowner, who was allegedly married to two different women.

Fortunato was not the only returned migrant to take up the responsibility of dealing with the new bureaucracy. Most of the other migrants mentioned so far also started holding community offices in those years, as justice of the peace, constable, registrar, treasurer, and the like. In anthropological parlance, these types of local representatives are often called "brokers," because they have the cultural skills to bridge traditional villages and the modern state.[48] Starting on a modest scale with the community recognitions of the early 1960s, and then much more after the agrarian reform was launched, they became indispensable to villages like Pomatambo. In the nineteenth century, no one really needed to know the law or how to deal with city life; custom and the goodwill of a basically self-governing village were quite enough. Those days were drawing to a close.

To appreciate how the balance of power in Pomatambo shifted, we have to look at who lost out. Prestige and influence are more or less a zero-sum game. The new brokers rivaled and largely displaced the traditional authorities of the village. The most important figure in a community like Pomatambo had long been the *varayoq*—literally the carrier of the *vara* or staff of office. Even when the post did not exist under that name, something functionally very like it was always a fixture of Andean life.[49]

The sort of man who served as *varayoq* is as crucial to understanding the office as are the responsibilities attached to it. I spoke at some length with one such elderly fellow, Teodosio, on my visits to Pomatambo in both 1995 and 2006. He was born in 1923, making him chronologically the same age as Amadeo. In a more profound sense, though, he is much older. He has never lived outside the village of his birth. On my last visit, he stood in front of his humble house, wearing a hat and slightly threadbare grey jacket, munching matter-of-factly on coca leaves with his few remaining teeth. He held forth at length in Quechua about his experiences serving as *varayoq* three times over the years. The first time he was in his twenties—quite unusual, since typically the *varayoq* was a much older man. To be a *varayoq,* he said, you had to get along well with the community, and people had to be sure of your basic decency. The main duties of a *varayoq* included settling disputes between villagers, presiding over festivals, and organizing collective labor for tasks like repairing a meeting hall or cleaning the irrigation canals.

A *varayoq* was chosen by informal consensus based on experience and qualities of character. He served a one-year term. While in office, he and his wife had to exhaust a significant chunk of their savings to cover festival expenses and other duties of hospitality. Anthropologists writing about the *varayoq* system have noted that expenditure in traditional villages is oriented to the community. Money is spent to earn prestige and goodwill—unlike the individualistic conspicuous consumption that lets people in modern societies show off their wealth to others. To the traditionally minded, the honor of serving in this kind of post was a powerful motive. At the same time, the demands of such offices had an equalizing effect. A peasant elected as *varayoq* would spend money more or less ungrudgingly and would enjoy the honor, but he would spend money nonetheless. This is yet another method Andeans devised over the centuries to split political from economic power.[50]

This traditional authority system lost ground fast in the 1960s and 1970s. It existed all the way up to the start of the insurgency, but its prestige diminished once the landscape of power shifted with the agrarian reform. This trend was not unique to Pomatambo, of course. It held across Ayacucho and the rest of the south-central highlands. As some of the younger generation embraced schooling and the cities, the Quechua-speaking *varayoqs* began to seem backward.[51] This perception had to do partly with the nature of the role itself. Overseeing village festivals and enforcing an austere highland morality hardly seemed *au courant* to outward-oriented youngsters. The backwardness also had to do with the kind of people who still wanted to serve as *varayoq*. In 1995, I went through my list of interviewees by age, wealth, and whether they had held the *varayoq* post. The villagers most likely to have served as *varayoq* during the twenty years before the civil war were older and poorer.

In another sign of this power shift, the literate and Spanish-speaking brokers took over the modern offices more completely than ever before. The state-mandated positions of president, constable, treasurer, and so on had existed on paper since the 1920s, but they had not carried much weight. Now they had much more to do and needed new men to fill them. I found signs of this generational shift while poring over yellowed copies of Pomatambo's old village election documents in the ministry of agriculture. In 1972, the older slate of candidates won. In 1974, they were defeated by a younger and more educated slate better suited to handling the bureaucracy outside Pomatambo. This pattern held until 1981, the last election before the civil war disrupted everything.

The same divisions emerged elsewhere.[52] In short, communities like Pomatambo had a fault line opening between two different types of leaders. On one side were traditionally minded elders, oriented to the small and self-contained world they had always known. On the other side were the brokers, with broader horizons, more individual aspirations, and the skills to deal with the vast forces pressing down on Pomatambo from above. It is a truism among those who study the world's peasant communities that local leaders carry a great deal of weight in shaping opinion and getting things accomplished.[53] But here there were two very different *kinds* of local leaders, side-by-side in a snapshot of two worlds colliding.

In some ways this is the usual story of how peasant communities have cracked under the pressures of the modern world. Changes come from outside, and the balance of power shifts. In other ways, Pomatambo's story has some peculiar twists. For one thing, conflict between the old and new worlds did not come out in the open here. In most places, the broker types, with their experience of the outside and their valuable new skills, come to dominate their backward fellows. Prosperity comes to depend more on external connections than on controlling resources within the community that are bound up with age-old customs. Trade flourishes while the rough equality of traditional life unravels. The brokers and wealthier peasants profit by bringing in new seeds, fertilizer, and machinery, and by selling to an urban market. They lose patience with the value-laden give-and-take of the past, mark off private property more clearly than before, and reject most obligations to other locals. Meanwhile, traditionally minded poor peasants go under one by one, losing their land and turning into a dependent workforce. They resent the new rich with their hard-edged competitive instinct, and they cling to the *varayoq* system and other customs as long as they can. But their way of life gradually fades away.[54]

The story in Pomatambo unfolded along very different lines. The brokers did gain in influence in all the ways we have seen, but they did not become the avowed enemies of tradition and community. To appreciate why, remember *how* the modern world found its way into Pomatambo in the first place. It came through migration, education, and an expanding state bureaucracy—not through trade. This was a modernization centered on education and cultural capital. Local economic life changed very little in the mid-twentieth century. Pomatambo's peasants kept scratching a living from the soil, bartering for what they could not make themselves, and perhaps spending some extra cash brought or sent back by migrants. Even in the region as a whole, the economy stagnated in those decades. Ayacucho had only fifteen tractors in 1951 and forty-seven in 1957; as late as 1967, it had a mere forty-five people working in industry.[55]

Because Pomatambo in those years had no real profit-making opportunities, it did not give rise to a new business-minded class of rich farmers and entrepreneurs. Those young villagers with the drive and ability to go beyond the older way of life had to find other outlets for their aspirations—at least if they were to stay in Pomatambo rather than head to Lima. People who in a booming economy might have been the first to go out and make a buck instead turned to politics. They won prestige by holding community office and dealing with the outside world. This choice was not too different, on one level, from how respected peasant elders a generation earlier had put their energy into serving as *varayoqs,* except that now the most desired offices were oriented to the outside rather than to inside the village.

There *was* a real tension between old and new, however. Many of the brokers still felt at home with Pomatambo's traditions, and many thought their facility with Spanish and the written word was little more than a way to help the community press its claims. But some in this new group had a harder edge and a real difference of mentality. Take one fellow of that generation, used to living by his wits and, by some accounts, his fists. He had never served as a *varayoq*. He once told me disdainfully that the *varayoqs* had been "ignorant people." Unlike most in the community, who remembered those stern elders fondly, he had nothing good to say about them. That attitude carried over to how he saw the rest of the village. Once he approached me in the square, after I had interviewed many other Pomatambans, and said I should feel free to talk to him whenever I wanted to clear up the "mistakes" in what such ill-informed folk must have told me. Furthermore, some of the old Andean reserve about begging for a personal handout seemed to have worn thin in his case.

So among the brokers there was a spectrum of attitudes. At one extreme there were people who were much like the old traditional leaders but with more skills and broader horizons. At another extreme, there were those whose hearts seemed to lie with the modern world. In villages like Pomatambo, the encounter with modernity opens up a fault line between those who want to get along and those who want to get ahead. Modern society is arranged to benefit the shrewd and competitive, those who can figure out how to manipulate the new rules of a larger society to their own advantage.

Where the bearers of that new mentality can do so, they break ties to their communities even if physically they keep living there. They wall off their private economic interests from the duties that tradition would impose on them. If they can afford to offend, they usually will.[56] Here in Pomatambo, they could afford neither economically nor politically to do so. Private land title in these villages is shaky. Ownership of private plots, and the right to rotated and common land, rest entirely on custom. According to the Peruvian legal code, a community like this owns all land collectively, and private land-use rights within it can be extinguished merely by a vote of two-thirds of villagers.[57] So even if trading opportunities had existed, an enterprising peasant with a bit more land would still have relied on the goodwill of neighbors to protect his or her property. Even more obviously, brokers who sought the prestige of local office had to stay on good terms with the voters, even if they thought the voters were ignorant rustics.

Because the modern world came to Pomatambo through education and migration, not through economic growth, the village hung together better and longer than it might have done otherwise. From the standpoint of community cohesion, we might even see the economic stagnation of the 1940s to 1970s as a blessing in disguise. In a country that changed so much over those years, this region experienced surprisingly little economic development. Rural Ayacucho had barely a 1 percent economic growth rate in the 1970s. By the end of the military regime, most non-subsistence economic activity in the region was under the auspices of the state: government-employee salaries and the like.[58]

Pomatambo had no prospect of an economic takeoff under those conditions. The first dirt road into the village was built between 1968 and 1975, largely through the backbreaking labor of villagers with picks and shovels. Traders came from time to time, offering the usual purchases of rural folk: sugar, salt, oil, matches, and perhaps rice and noodles to supplement the potato crop.[59] Such traders had little impact on the village, partly because of the limited activity and partly because most of them came from the countryside and small towns themselves. Pomatambans sometimes resented having so little bargaining power in these exchanges. Cash prices were unfamiliar to many of them. Traders would collude with one another to fix prices through the area. Sometimes they would try to buy peasant products like livestock en route to the Vilcashuamán market rather than letting villagers get the town price for them.

Still, these tensions did not erupt into open conflict. Elsewhere in the highlands, particularly in small towns and villages with better road access, trade posed a more visible challenge to traditional life. Economic life shifted more decisively away from subsistence to exchange. In some areas, half or more of what a family consumed came through the cash economy, even if they still grew most of their own food. Peasants started thinking more about ways to earn money. And ever more intense contact with merchants brought festering resentment of swindling and shoddy goods. When a bout of inflation hit Peru in the late 1970s, peasants linked to the market felt the effects.[60]

For Pomatambans, neither the benefits nor the ills of economic development had been felt much in the years before the insurgency. But most of the older generation who spoke to me of the 1970s remembered that they felt neglected anyway. Alejandro, the old man who now walks with a cane, said they did not even have proper shovels to dig. I once read a letter he wrote in 1971, asking the government to put windows in the school and send a bulldozer to flatten the square properly. It took years before they got even that much.

What struck me most about the letters from those years and the reminiscences of Pomatambans was how little these people were really asking. They only wanted basic equipment for the school, or the loan of digging equipment for a couple of days to improve the way into the village or make the construction of an irrigation ditch less arduous. These modest aspirations came out of the small deprivations of daily life in the countryside, not from any grand imagination about consumer culture. At most, some younger villagers' exposure to the cities had made them aware that resources existed outside Pomatambo to help take the edge off poverty.

It is telling, however, that despite the modesty of their aspirations, Pomatambans were quite cynical about the government's willingness to meet them. Many said that state officials were corrupt and inefficient, and that Pomatambans had always had to rely on themselves to get anything done. This attitude toward aid from the state is pervasive among the Andean peasantry. They want help jump-starting local economies when they can get it, but they fear the hidden agendas that the government might have, especially agendas that involve taking control of land and resources. If they think there is a real threat of losing control of their own lives, they will opt for less aid.[61]

Not that such aid was forthcoming in the 1970s anyway, as we have seen. As elsewhere in the highlands, the military regime did virtually nothing to improve Pomatambans' lot. The government promised a burst of economic development that it did not deliver. The meager benefits that flowed from land reform went to already comfortable farmers on the coast, not to Peru's poorest. Ayacucho ranked near the bottom among regions in its share of state spending, despite its dire poverty. But all the talk of state-led development had one unintended effect. It drew attention to the state as part of the economic problem and a potential tool for its solution. By 1980, peasants throughout the highlands were much more conscious of the state than ever before. Their aspirations had multiplied, even though Peru's mainstream political parties had exhausted any confidence they once enjoyed.[62]

As military rule wound down in the late 1970s, such was the condition of rural Ayacucho. The Vilcashuamán innkeeper who taught in Pomatambo for a few months back then remembered a deceptive quiet during his stay. The peasants kept sowing and harvesting, raising livestock, and celebrating their festivals as they always had. He saw no sign of any tensions among them, and nary a whiff of impending violence in the air.

But all the changes of that generation had remade in subtle ways the landscape of this village and countless others like it. Pomatambo had been exposed, unevenly, to the modern world. New aspirations had arisen and had been frustrated by the neglect and ham-handed efforts of two reformist governments. Pomatambans were now ready to give a fair hearing to anyone outside the system who promised to improve their lot. Little did they know how soon their lives were going to change—for the worse.

III

Socialism and Scorched Earth

When Quintín the teacher first saw a member of Sendero Luminoso, he was only eleven years old. It was the mid-1970s, and he had only just left his home village of Pujas, near Pomatambo, to start secondary school in Vilcashuamán. That year a young engineer came to Vilcashuamán and gave a talk about simple technologies that could improve rural life. He mentioned the prospect of building cisterns to collect biomass, which as it decayed would produce a burnable gas. A few years later, that same young engineer, Óscar Ramírez Durand, was to become "Comrade Feliciano," one of the top leaders of the insurgency.

Fig. 3: Memorial to a villager killed during the civil war

Senderistas in the making popped up often around Vilcashuamán in the late 1970s. When Quintín was about fourteen, an assortment of teachers, nurses, and other professionals used to wander in and out of that small town speaking of Maoist ideology. A breakthrough was in the air. These activists held forth to anyone who would listen about an uprising that would start shortly. They promised a struggle for social justice, a revolution that would destroy the corrupt regime in Lima and bring development to the long-neglected poor of Ayacucho. Like other young people in the area, Quintín found much of what the Maoists were saying persuasive and hoped they would deliver.

And the insurgency did come. Years into it, Quintín returned to the area after teaching in the jungle and was posted to Pomatambo's primary school. The war for Peru's future was raging through the highlands. One afternoon, Quintín found an ominous note addressed to him from Sendero guerrillas. It demanded that he appear on the outskirts of the village at 7 P.M. that evening to talk with them. When the hour came, he climbed the twilit hill trembling in fear. The guerrillas who met him matter-of-factly announced that they had heard of cattle thieves in the area and wanted to know who they were. The guilty parties were to be killed. Quintín did his best to defuse the situation. He told the guerrillas that the rustlers were only poor peasants desperate for food, and he begged for their lives. Eventually the guerrillas relented and gave a temporary reprieve. He hastened back to the village and called together twenty or so peasants he thought were involved. When he warned them of the danger and told them he had got them one final chance, they broke down in relief and gratitude.

Over a few short years, a movement that had held out the promise of social justice had become a source of terror. The biogas tanks that Comrade Feliciano had described never appeared in Pomatambo. And Quintín, who as a teenager had listened with genuine interest to Sendero's activists, ended up quaking with fear as he begged for the lives of his fellow villagers. Hope turned into carnage and tragedy across the highlands. Clearly this movement had gone very wrong.

Sendero's first armed action had been the burning of ballot boxes in Chuschi on May 17, 1980. On Christmas Eve the same year, violence came to the Vilcashuamán area. Senderistas attacked a small estate on the

Vilcashuamán side of the Pampas River, torturing and killing the owner. In March 1981, the guerrillas dynamited the rum-processing mills and other buildings at one of the larger estates.[1] It was not long before the war moved to small towns. The municipal building, bank, and police station on the square in Vilcashuamán were blown up in a five-hour pitched battle in 1982.

For all the talk about fighting for the poorest of the poor, these were hardly the poor taking up arms on their own behalf. The initiative for this insurgency came from outside, not from places like Pomatambo. The energy and ideology started with a circle around Abimael Guzmán, the philosophy professor whose lectures on Marxism stirred up a generation of students at UNSCH, Ayacucho's university, in the late 1960s. Guzmán became "the heart and soul of the movement."[2] His *nom de guerre,* Presidente Gonzalo, was duly added to the pantheon of what Senderistas called "Marxism-Leninism-Maoism-Gonzalo Thought." Guzmán himself was a Spanish speaker from the prosperous southern city of Arequipa and only came to know the Andean peasantry as an adult. Fired by radicalism and a short trip to China during the turbulence of the Cultural Revolution, he saw his task in Peru as but one prong of a global communist revolution that might take a century to accomplish. Sendero Luminoso, in the eyes of Guzmán and his followers, was merely applying universal Marxist principles to Peruvian conditions.[3]

This enthusiasm for revolution was hardly unique to Guzmán's circle at UNSCH. Campus radicalism was a staple on the left in Latin America in the 1960s and 1970s. A smorgasbord of ideological sects was on offer, from the Stalinists to the Trotskyists to the Castroites. But Sendero took its Maoist vision more seriously, in the sense that it always planned for much more than the usual idle cafe banter and occasional student protests. It regarded as a waste of time the romantic Che Guevara-style adventure of taking to the hills and hoping peasants would join. For Sendero, Peru's revolution was a deadly earnest program that required the groundwork and perseverance of a generation.

Guzmán's circle cleverly used UNSCH as a launching pad. Many of the university's students, then as now, hailed from the villages of rural Ayacucho and were the first educated members of their families. Wanting to move up in the world but feeling out of place in the city, they had a natural receptivity to the Marxist doctrines of this charismatic professor. He claimed to make sense of their frustrations and to offer a way out. The crucial importance of UNSCH in this poor highland region in those years has been noted by many observers; without an economic transformation, the university was the most visible sign of modernity. To be modern meant above all else to embrace a modern way of thinking. And the modern ideology lived and breathed by Ayacucho's intelligentsia was Marxism, in one form or another.[4]

Sendero recruited youths who were seeking the excitement of a cause. The movement took over campus organizations and some of the agronomy programs that did projects in the countryside. Along with those programs, Sendero could also count on the students themselves to link the movement to the peasantry. The students had personal ties in both city and countryside and circulated between the two.[5] Over several years, cadres painstakingly laid the foundations for armed revolution.

All this preparation was as yet unknown to the villagers in Pomatambo, of course. But like the more educated youths who came and went, they were willing to listen to what any radical movement might say. Pomatambans had a broadly satisfying way of life given the strength of their community, but they held no illusions about their poverty. They felt the state could do much more for them, and they were disappointed that the little they did request for rarely if ever materialized. They rightly suspected that the government did not think of them as a priority: in those years, state spending on the southern highlands was far below its share of Peru's population.[6]

Moreover, an endemic bad situation was getting worse when Sendero burst on to the scene. Inflation in the late 1970s and especially in the early 1980s shifted the terms of trade against the peasantry. Rising prices for items like rice, oil, sugar, and fuel hit peasants hard, because they had so little cash income in the first place. Since rural folk in Ayacucho kept growing most of their own food during those years, the impact on poorer communities, such as Pomatambo, that bought less from outside was more limited.[7] But even in Pomatambo, villagers remember paying more for items like coca leaves and alcohol.

To say the countryside around Vilcashuamán was ripe for revolution, though, would be an overstatement. In some ways it was, in others less so. The usual pattern leading to peasant revolution is clear. Villages become more dependent on an outside market, which benefits rich peasants much more than poorer ones. Tensions build up between those who gain from such changes and those who lose out. The poor and more traditionally minded resent a style of development that cuts them out. They also have enough of the old community spirit left to be able to organize politically. When a crisis comes—a threat to subsistence, or perhaps a reversal of economic growth—things reach a breaking point. The poor join in whatever revolutionary struggle is unfolding because it offers the most obvious way to solve their local grievances.[8]

In the decades before Sendero, as we have seen, Pomatambo became more connected to the outside world. Some villagers gained broader horizons and new experiences. The community felt neglected by the state and wanted more aid. And the inflation crisis did touch it enough for frustrations to rise at the crucial moment. But all this discontent remained too shapeless for revolution to follow as a matter of course. These people simply did not have enough experience of development to have much of an opinion about its good and bad versions. Tensions over values and interests within the village stayed beneath the surface, with no real polarization between rich and poor. When inflation came, Pomatambans did not blame it on traders, richer peasants, or other local exploiters. Instead, they blamed it on mismanagement by the distant political classes in Lima. The restored president, Belaúnde, was "a murderer of the poor," as one villager remembered bitterly.

In short, social tensions of the sort that feed revolutions were not part of life in this village or in other traditional villages like it. The changes of a generation had not created the energy for revolution so much as they had complicated the landscape on which revolution would be waged. The revolutionaries would come to Pomatambo from outside. Pomatambans would listen to what they had to say, but as an audience rather than as eager participants at the outset.

The Senderistas' first appearances in Pomatambo around 1980 were low-key. They attempted to size up the community and get people used to their presence and to the idea of an uprising. Guerrillas came in ones and twos, at first. They walked house to house, focusing on villagers likely to warm to the cause. They talked casually before steering the conversation to politics. The corrupt authorities were going to disappear soon, they promised. As the insurgency got going, some of the guerrillas benefited from Andean hospitality and slept in the houses of sympathetic villagers. The movement also took advantage of its ties to teachers. A couple of older men said that they first heard of Sendero when the children in the village school suddenly started chanting revolutionary slogans.

These first signs of Senderista activity stayed below the surface. Someone who seemed an unlikely supporter or did not pay attention might have missed them altogether. That was to change soon enough. Once the insurgency was in full swing, the guerrillas began calling occasional meetings of the whole village. They said that the meetings were mandatory, though a few uninterested and daring souls chose not to go and either hid at home or left the village when the guerrillas were there. These big meetings happened at night, away from the square. Preferred sites included a secluded grassy area down the hill behind some trees, where the valley dropped away in three directions. The army would have difficulty finding them there, and if they were found, the guerrillas could scatter quickly.

The guerrillas wore typical peasant clothes and carried guns. They started the meetings by ritually invoking "Marxism-Leninism-Maoism-Gonzalo Thought." Then they would hold forth on Peruvian politics and the changes that revolution would bring to the countryside. They claimed that the large landowners and other exploiters were going to disappear. This was a war for unity and equality for all. One of the Senderistas, nicknamed "Comrade Pablo," won support from some younger villagers with his fervent talk about fighting for social justice. One man who was then a child remembers the community being urged to join in and "accompany" these armed men in their struggle. The Senderistas also painted a rosy picture of how the revolution would bring to the poor a living standard previously enjoyed only by the rich. Alejandro, the elderly former migrant, recalled reacting with some skepticism to the promise that in the Peru of the future, peasants would all ride around in cars.

For some other villagers, those talks made little impression because of the language barrier. Guerrillas speaking at the big meetings used a mix of Spanish and Quechua, so peasants with no grasp of Spanish found them hard to follow. Many cadres came from the coast and barely knew Quechua. Apart from language, some of the vocabulary and references to world-historical struggle made little sense to people who had been digging potatoes their whole lives. Senderistas loved to talk about China's accomplishments during the Cultural Revolution, about Mao Zedong and the like. According to one story from rural Ayacucho, some guerrillas even spouted Chinese phrases at blank-faced Andean farmers. The tale is probably apocryphal, but the impression is telling nonetheless.

Despite these obstacles, Sendero won some sympathy in the early years of the insurgency. As one young woman from a small town elsewhere in Ayacucho told me, for many peasants the movement "was like a light that illuminated them." Pomatambans at first were somewhat open to Sendero, at least when they compared it to the Peruvian state that had given them almost nothing. They were divided on how likely it was that the guerrillas could prevail in the long struggle to come. The dominant view was described to me as "an unlikely hope" that they would.

Senderistas came into communities like Pomatambo prepared. They knew what needs were unsatisfied in each area and would highlight the lack of infrastructure, health care, agricultural aid, and so on. They prepared a diagnosis of each area so that they could emphasize specific sources of discontent. When their focus shifted to Lima's shantytowns a few years later, they rallied support around squatter grievances about land title and services.[9]

The topics raised at meetings in Pomatambo fit this pattern. The poverty and the state's neglect were easy to point out. Interestingly, however, they also talked about wiping out the large landowners as "principal exploiters." At first glance this seems odd, since the Vilcashuamán area had no really big estates and conflict with the smaller ones was marginal. But the effort to play on that theme reveals something about Sendero's natural audience. Pomatambans who were more educated and more familiar with the outside world already knew—and surprisingly well—the Marxist vocabulary employed by Sendero.

Fortunato, the broker *par excellence* who represented Pomatambo's interests during the agrarian reform, is a case in point. Estates were not a pressing concern for most villagers, because they affected local economic life much less than in some parts of Peru. But for Fortunato and others who had spent years attempting to wrest away part of the neighboring estate's land, this was an issue close to their hearts. When I asked him about Sendero's promises, Fortunato seized on their antilandowner rhetoric. They offered "land for the one who works it," and "took over the conflict with the landowners." Words swiftly turned into very tough, even if not constructive, action. Shortly after the first meetings, Senderistas set fire to the estate in the valley. The owner was lucky to escape alive. Today you can see the ruined, roofless outline of the buildings if you look down from Pomatambo on a clear afternoon.

Support for Sendero at the outset was soft but widespread, and it cut across village divisions. Men and women, old and young, literate and illiterate—most vaguely hoped that the insurgency would bring what the government had not brought. But brokers, the young, and the more educated supported the insurgency more consistently. They knew city life well enough to have more vivid expectations of the material benefits that might come. They could also understand Sendero's message better. The level of education needed to make sense of these armed outsiders was quite modest. In 1995, I ran a simple statistical test examining the relationship between early levels of support and years of education. I found that the threshold lay between two and three years of primary education—roughly the level that would let you read a newspaper and understand radio broadcasts in Spanish.

Sendero thus encountered a split between people who could understand their political language and those who could not. That split reflected the differences that had arisen in Pomatambo over a generation. Literate and Spanish-speaking villagers had very different horizons from their more traditional and insular neighbors. Indeed, their very experience of being socialized into political values was new. Some anthropologists have suggested that in Peru's countryside, two kinds of socialization happen side-by-side. One, which goes back through the ages, happens face to face. It looks inward and gives people a sense of belonging in the community.

In the twentieth century, a new socialization has arrived through schools and radio broadcasts. It is more individualistic and orients rural youth toward making it in an emerging national culture.[10] By the early 1980s, these processes had produced two subcultures in Pomatambo.

More locally minded and traditional people were not Sendero's natural audience. Peru's peasantry lacked—still lacks, for that matter—a real ideological compass in national politics. Highland folk wanted hope and would give a fair hearing to a movement that offered it. Sendero's novelty even gave it an edge over the moderate leftists in Lima, whose opposition had grown stale over the decades. But Maoist ideology alone could not connect with the life of the Andean peasantry. Peasants are moved more by sentiment, symbols, and charisma than by abstract political theories.[11]

For this reason, enthusiasm for Sendero got shallower the farther out into the countryside its cadres ventured. Villages less attuned to the market economy and Spanish-speaking culture regarded Sendero's rhetoric as less relevant to their lives.[12] Indeed, more traditional peasants responded warmly only when the Senderistas addressing them twisted the message into recognizable language. Militants who had themselves grown up in the countryside sometimes dropped the Maoist slogans and instead invoked old Andean touchstones instead, like restoring the Inka golden age. Yet that adaptation was more the exception than the rule. It was frowned upon by the strictly Maoist higher echelons of the movement.[13] Officially, this movement spoke to class, not culture.

In any case, peasants care most about what they see. A movement that acts according to peasant values will fare well. Of Sendero's actions in those early years, what most struck a chord with Peru's poor was the enforcement of a strict morality. Some Pomatambans told me that the best thing Sendero did was clamp down on womanizers, wife-beaters, and thieves. One Sunday, for example, Senderistas dragged into Pomatambo a man from another village. He had beaten his wife one too many times, and justice was due. The guerrillas called everyone together in the Pomatambo square and asked the assembly to decide whether he should be executed. Many, mostly women, called for death. But in the end the community found it best to shave his head—an old Andean humiliation—and give him fifty lashes instead.[14] On another occasion, while most former cattle rustlers had taken to heart Quintín's warning that they were risking their lives, one habitual rustler could not control himself. When the Senderistas discovered that he had stolen some cattle, they took him to the outskirts of the village and killed him as a lesson to others.

Stern measures against crime and disorder won support for Sendero throughout Peru for a time. The further social breakdown had gone, the more receptive an area was to a no-nonsense crackdown. In Lima's shantytowns, with their vicious crimes and degeneracy, cadres won support as "harsh but fair imparters of justice and social order." Local political leaders were a target, too. Where corrupt officials had worn out the patience of peasants, they met their end in so-called "popular justice" executions.[15] One Pomatamban who closely follows national politics remarked on the appalling corruption of Peru's political class and told me that at least Sendero would have stopped it.

This punishing of transgression ran into problems, however. Senderistas soon overstepped the bounds of what Andean peasants could accept. One day in Pomatambo, Senderistas brought into the square a woman from outside, a petty trader, who had been accused of swindling the locals. They announced that they were going to slit her throat in front of everyone who had gathered. Murmurs of protest ran through the crowd. A few courageous souls, including the father of my close friends from the village, spoke up and urged the Senderistas to "punish, but not kill." Others agreed. After some persuasion, the guerrillas relented and let the woman off with a shaved head.

Pomatambans had recoiled not because of sympathy for the trader. They often felt cheated in local markets, as Sendero knew when it invoked the idea of a "just price." They also lost little sleep over the guerrillas' confiscatory demands for "donations" from traders who still ventured into the area. But slitting the woman's throat in the square would have crossed the line. When Andean peasants moralize about economic behavior, it is to preserve the community. They want excessive gains to be shared, and they teach lessons to people who flout norms. But greedy people are deviants, not enemies. Andean peasant thinking does not carry over to the slaughter of abstract "class enemies."

Sendero's talk of wiping out "rich peasants" in Pomatambo did not go over well. By local standards, a rich peasant had little more than a bigger flock of sheep or a bit more land and was usually related to poorer villagers.[16] Andean economic morality builds on relationships among people and buffers them from the excesses of greed. Sendero's war against greed and inequality slid all too easily into inhuman excess, tearing apart the community rather than restoring equilibrium within it.

In any case, Sendero's authority was only exercised on vivid occasions like these. It was intermittent because the insurgents never controlled enough territory on an ongoing basis to set up their own government. They could move freely in some areas, including much of Vilcashuamán for the first few years. A congress of Senderista leaders from all over Peru met near Pomatambo around 1983, for example. But so-called "liberated zones" were mainly areas of potential Senderista control, where the guerrillas could coerce most of the people most of the time. They could not redistribute land because there was none to redistribute. At most they could informally authorize poor peasants who took over plots abandoned by others who had left. They could also disrupt trade between the countryside and the cities. By threatening traders and patrolling roads, they tried to force the peasantry back into a rough self-sufficiency. This strategy was supposed to aid in their long-term encirclement of the Peruvian state.[17]

The effort to cut market ties to the towns alienated many Pomatambans. Indeed, several of them related to me the risks they took to get to the weekly market in Vilcashuamán. They would even hide cash in their shoes in case they ran into any Senderistas on the two-hour walk. The same happened in other villages in those years. Most of what these people consumed they grew themselves, but they did want their salt, matches, oil, and so on.[18]

It is important to understand what was at stake and how Sendero misread it. Andean peasants—peasants anywhere, really—are not hostile to commerce on principle. They take advantage of exchange with near and distant others when they can. The vertical flow of goods between different altitudes in the Andes over the centuries is a case in point. These are practical people, after all.

Their reservations about commerce come instead from two concerns. First, they appreciate that profit-seeking often needs walls around it to prevent it from poisoning the human relationships that make up their communities. Traders who offend those norms run into trouble. Second, peasants worry about self-reliance. The modern world being as it is, they think twice about changes that will subject their communities to the undue influence of outside powerholders. In short, they are not anti-commerce; they just care a great deal about power and values. Sendero's version of self-sufficiency was alien to their thinking.

Tension between Sendero's plans and peasant sensibilities went well beyond trade. Guzmán's movement had a particular vision of rural development under socialism. On the surface, what some Senderistas said seemed to align with what peasants wanted. As far back as 1969, Antonio Díaz Martínez, a UNSCH agronomist who would join the movement, outlined an alternative development model for Ayacucho's countryside. He complained that existing agricultural aid programs had failed to deliver and had remained disconnected from peasant life. Proper development would build on peasant know-how and give agronomists a more advisory role. For rural Vilcash-uamán specifically, he called for technical training in water conservation, fertilizers, and composting. That would be followed by the introduction of modern agricultural technology, more scientific land rotation, communal barns, hybrid clovers to regenerate exhausted pastures, and reforestation.

In an appendix to a 1985 reissue of his book, Díaz Martínez praised Sendero's "molding of the new republic." He highlighted the practice of redistributing land to those who worked it. Supposedly the guerrilla-controlled countryside was bringing new socialist practices into the villages, amid other kinds of cooperatives.[19] In practice, much of this praise was mere talk. What Sendero did to act on Díaz Martínez's writings involved symbolism more than constructive solutions. Senderistas regularly blew up electricity pylons as symbols of modern technology that brought no benefit to the rural poor. And in 1982 they destroyed UNSCH's experimental farm, Allpachaka, because its products were market- rather than peasant-oriented.[20]

Symbolic acts like those wear thin after a while. Rural folk like to see results. One axiom in the history of revolutions is that insurgent movements only gain full backing from peasants when the latter start to see genuine benefits.[21] Concrete material gains from Sendero were few and far between. In villages with more trade and more visible local exploiters, guerrillas won popularity by canceling debts and handing out goods taken from dishonest merchants.[22] But such gains were, by their very nature, small and one-time events.

Ultimately, the guerrillas implemented none of their abstract promises. "It was all talk," as one elderly Pomataman put it. In Chuschi, site of the first armed action, villagers similarly lost patience because everything they were offered was prefaced with the phrase "When we govern. . . ." Man does not live by bread alone, but he does not live by ideology alone either, especially when he cannot understand it.

The strategic situation in the countryside remained fluid throughout the 1980s and early 1990s. Sendero did not control territory reliably enough to implement a whole new style of development. But surely the guerrillas could have done more than they did. Many of them had training in agronomy and other useful skills. They could have shared their knowledge, helped build simple technologies, and the like. A few afternoon workshops would have made a real difference and shown genuine commitment. But they chose only to talk and fight without proving themselves where it mattered.

✤ ✤ ✤

The tension ran even deeper than this failure to deliver, though. Even if Sendero had controlled enough of the countryside to act on its promises, its vision had fundamental problems. Based on my conversations in Pomatambo, I detected two different versions of Sendero's alternative, depending on which guerrillas had been speaking and when. One was a moderate reformist agenda, broadly appealing to those hearing it, but hard to implement unless some far-fetched assumptions became valid. The other was a much more radical alternative that ran counter to peasant values.

The moderate agenda, if we might call it that, hinged on three themes: a safety net, redistribution, and aid. A revolutionary regime would support the most vulnerable people. Sometimes widows, orphans, and others without kinship ties and labor power do fall through the cracks of the traditional safety net.[23] Senderistas also repeated the slogan of land to the tiller and promised to take more land from nearby estates. They said that they would change Peru's strategy of development, which was sucking the lifeblood out of the poor. Instead of exporting food from a malnourished country, a Maoist regime would give Peruvians priority. It would cancel the crushing foreign debt. All these measures would free up resources to help the poor. More locally, the guerrillas identified other sources of funds for Pomatambo. The village would be allowed to exploit mines in the valley and sell the ore. And revolution would bring an influx of aid from abroad: supposedly, Chinese experts would flock to Peru to speed up development.

The idea of a more consistent safety net made sense, but safety nets cost money that has to come from somewhere. In much the same way, talk of redistributing land assumed that there was land to redistribute. Somehow a postrevolutionary regime would generate vast new resources from outside the peasant communities; it would have to do so, if everyone within them was to win. The moderate vision had no hope of working under any other set of assumptions. It had to rely on one or another *deus ex machina*: ore deposits nearby (which would have become state property anyway), a rolling back of international exploitation, or an influx of foreign aid. The last idea was particularly misguided, because a victorious Sendero would have had no allies abroad. The promise of Chinese advisors came from lower-level militants who failed to understand recent Chinese history. Guzmán did praise the Cultural Revolution, but he also thought that Mao's successors after 1976 had betrayed true socialism. To drive the point home, Senderistas in Lima even bombed the Chinese embassy and hung placards denouncing Deng Xiaoping as a "son of a whore."

The moderate agenda probably appealed to even some people who saw its contradictions and unworkability. The radical version of Sendero's vision is more interesting, however. It would have remade villages like Pomatambo in far-reaching ways. And the opposition it provoked, even without being implemented, sheds light on much more than just Sendero's heavy-handedness. For the radical vision offers a more extreme version of many tendencies in the antitraditionalist left around the world. It exemplifies one prong of the modern assault on the peasantry everywhere.

What was the radical vision? As Quintín phrased it, it was communism, a cooperation "like *ayni* and *minka,* but more so." In the new society, work would rotate in a spirit of equality with one for all and all for one. Other villagers remembered the guerrillas talking about everyone being "well organized" to "work together." Sendero promised to set up cooperatives and transfer all private plots into communal ownership. Such speeches aligned with the movement's written commitments. The 1985 appendix to Díaz Martínez's book, for example, included plans to pool livestock and employ peasants as wage laborers on collective farms.[24]

Such ideas met stiff resistance. One anthropologist noted in the 1980s that Ayacucho's peasants, accustomed to working together in kinship networks, looked askance at Sendero's one-size-fits-all collectivism.[25] But the radical vision provoked opposition for a host of deeper reasons. Indeed, the radical left elsewhere in the world has encountered many of the same problems when dealing with smallholding peasants.

For example, the plan to work land collectively was like waving a red flag to a bull. Every family in Pomatambo owned some land, and none cared to lose it. Those who had a bit more than average, while far from wealthy, took exception all the more. Ignacio, the former migrant, remembered that he and others who moved to the cities to escape the violence had their land taken away. A Senderista leader decreed that absentee owners had forfeited their private maize plots in the valley. He distributed them to peasants from Pomatambo and neighboring villages who were short on land and seemed to support the insurgency more. Those people apparently then shrugged their shoulders, took over the plots, and began cultivating them for the rest of the war.

Economically, the harm to the owners was negligible, since they were not there anyway. And the community had always maintained the right to extinguish dormant title and give it to needy households. Despite the legal vagueness of private property, however, the principle ran deep in the consciousness of Pomatambo's smallholders. Ignacio and others thought it deeply offensive that the guerrillas—outsiders—would barge into the village and reassign what clearly belonged to some people rather than others. If this sporadic and ad hoc expropriation of land caused such resentment, it is easy to see how unpopular full collectivization would have been.

Resistance to Sendero's vision of rural socialism might seem overdone. Peasants might have grumbled about collectivization, but would they not have quickly forgiven it if living standards improved? After all, were the traditional peasant practices of mutual aid not communal in spirit? This misconception underlay previous failures of collectivization around the world. Norms of mutual aid, sharing good and ill fortune, and the other small decencies of traditional life are certainly very different from a harshly competitive capitalist economy. But they are not socialist in the sense that many movements of the far left have convinced themselves.

The military agrarian reform of the early 1970s had run into the same problem. As one anthropologist pointed out at the time, collective planners all too often think that peasant practices will be easy to translate into modern cooperatives. Peasant practices have never been about exploiting land in common. They have been a way to prop up the subsistence of individual households.[26] By pooling labor for major tasks and letting everyone use common pasture land, villages like Pomatambo made it easier to keep one's head above water. The poor did benefit, in the sense that some might otherwise have starved. But this primitive safety net ultimately benefited individual households. A patchwork of collective production, if we stretch enough to call it that, supported what was still basically a system of private consumption.

That private consumption had its unevenness, its cracks, its inequalities. Peasants in Pomatambo, as around the world, have had advantages and disadvantages in their ranks. They treat one another more or less decently, and cut down to a rough equality anyone who puts on airs or tries to profit at the expense of others. But some do have a bit more than others, and traditional practices like *minka* underline those facts.

Some of Sendero's plans to replace traditional forms of cooperation with socialist collectives undoubtedly reflected an awareness of these subtle ways in which tradition impeded the building of communism. Karl Marx himself once called peasants "potatoes in a sack," because their stubborn independence got in the way of his desired revolution.[27]

For Senderistas walking into highland villages, *ayni* and *minka* must have seemed backward. Those habits, along with the fragmentation of plots, got in the way of rational planning and the use of modern machinery. And since peasants seemed to share often enough, they would presumably not howl for too long if dragged into the shining future.

Another problem with Sendero's radical vision hinged on how the rural poor weigh the risks of change. A guerrilla who took the time could probably have made a reasonable case that collectivizing land would raise living standards through economies of scale. One cannot use tractors on tiny maize fields, for example. But such a drastic restructuring of the village required a high level of trust in the people doing the restructuring. When it comes to putting food on the table from year to year, peasants are notoriously risk averse. As one political scientist has observed, peasants judge innovation first and foremost against security of subsistence. Countless studies of peasant economic decision-making have borne this out. Peasants will normally choose a low but secure living standard over a higher but more uncertain one. They will adopt at first only new techniques that reduce fluctuations in the harvest from year to year. Only when subsistence is secure will they make the leap to selling cash crops to earn more money, and then only in stages.[28]

If small innovations like these are weighed against the risk of starvation, it is easy to see why collectivizing land and working in cooperatives would seem too drastic. Sendero's type of collective agriculture would mean trusting the state to get things right year after year. One misstep and your children gnaw on grass. Given the government's failure to bring real benefits in the 1960s and 1970s, Pomatambans could be forgiven for not wanting to entrust their lives to these new outsiders with guns. No state they had ever known had been able to feed them as reliably as they had themselves. Even the Inka empire, with its vast grain storehouses and occasional labor levies for road building, knew that it could not reliably employ and feed a dependent workforce all the time.[29]

We have seen some of the reasons Sendero's radical vision clashed with peasant sensibilities: peasants' attachment to private property, the limited purposes of traditional cooperation, and their worries about subsistence. Digging still deeper, we find that the revolution also would have changed the relationship between the household and the public sphere in troubling ways. Since women run so much of the Andean household economy, these changes threatened long-established male and female roles.

Traditional Andean practice fits the more or less universal model of peasant gender roles. Men and women have equal yet distinct responsibilities. Men take charge of the political affairs of a village, including representing their families outside the village. They handle the heavier tasks of ploughing and planting, slaughtering animals, and the like. But economic life as a whole—taking in the harvest and stretching it over a year's meals, juggling domestic priorities, keeping a tight rein on expenditures, even engaging in small-scale trade—is much more a female concern. In other words, there is a gendered split between the external and political sphere on the one hand, and the household and economic sphere on the other.[30]

Even the texture of subsistence and reciprocity demonstrates this traditional balance between gender roles. Subsistence breaks down into two parts: producing the food, and then managing how the household will consume it. These parts tend to be male and female responsibilities, respectively. *Minka* is a particularly good example of how they are balanced. Men do most of the agricultural or building work involved in a *minka*. Walking around a *minka* site, you would think that women are not involved. But then the mealtime arrives, and this centerpiece of the day relies on hours of food preparation undertaken by the women. Moreover, the household hosting the *minka* enjoys prestige because of the hospitality that the women provide. Feeding displays power.[31]

Andean peasant families are not made up of domineering breadwinners and timid housewives. Males are not as dominant as it might first appear. I have heard many stories of outsiders meeting with male elders in these communities and putting one or another proposal to them. They will ask questions, mumble among themselves noncommittally, and then conclude that they all want to go home and think it over for a day or two. Most of the time this means going home to consult their wives, who are often tougher skeptics. In the 1970s, I was told, women took charge of small-scale trade because men were inept at judging prices—and if they received any cash they would soon drink it away.

While the traditional model endures in much of the highlands, it has come under pressure as the modern world has penetrated these villages. The effect on women's influence has been mixed. On the one hand, a new political universe has opened up for them. Women have become more familiar with the outside, Spanish-speaking world. They have begun to participate in the national political system by voting. With each successive village election in the 1970s, for example, more Pomataman women appeared on the local register with a voter identification card. And all offices and occupations are now at least formally open to women.

On the other hand, modern life can sometimes diminish the real economic power that peasant women hold. The Spanish-derived culture of Peru's cities probably has a larger dose of *machismo* than is found among the Quechua-speaking peasantry. Migrants, mostly men, often come back to villages disdaining women's authority. They buy into outside images of progress and master the new skills of city life: literacy and Spanish. Women who stay in the home village hold to traditional ways longer and become defenders of the community.[32] Women's empowerment, at least of the traditional sort, becomes a sign of backwardness.

At the same time, the bases of women's power in a traditional village economy start to crumble. Economic activity moves from subsistence into the market. Families need cash, which comes mainly from men's wages. Trade expands, so peasants barter less with local peddlers and instead buy and sell with merchants in a national market. Men have an edge in the skills necessary to deal with outsiders. The more the household loses its age-old functions, the more power men wield over women.[33] If *minka* hospitality gives way to wage labor, for instance, then women have little to contribute. Partners in subsistence turn into dependent housewives, except for the few women who can transition quickly into the modern economy and earn wages of their own.

This has been the prevailing story across the highlands—indeed, around the world, as modernity makes inroads. Villages like Pomatambo were quite isolated when the insurgency broke out, so they had experienced few of these changes. Migrants had brought new ideas back to the village, but its economic ties to the outside world remained weak. The household was still the core of the village economy, and women had lost very little of their influence. Nevertheless, the trend was clear. In its early and middle stages, at least, modernization reduces women's economic clout. Anything Sendero offered, therefore, was weighed both against women's influence in Pomatambo's traditional economy and against how women in Peru's cities seemed to live.

Sendero did take up the feminist banner. Women made up nearly a third of its membership and played a highly visible part in the armed struggle. Sendero's posters and murals commemorating battles showed women as making up half or more of the combatants. Women sometimes dominated the "people's committees" in Sendero-controlled shanty-towns. The guerrillas said that their agenda in the countryside included "reclaim[ing] male–female unity in community development."[34] Among their moralistic appeals was one urging men to respect women rather than treating them as objects.

Pomatambo's women responded unevenly to Sendero, however. A simple statistical comparison of my interviewees in 1995 showed no difference in the *overall* level of support between men and women. I found only two possible patterns. Perhaps because women were less familiar with Sendero's language, many of them had no strong opinion one way or the other when they first met the guerrillas. This reaction probably had little to do with gender; most women were illiterate and did not speak Spanish, and men with similar horizons thought the same way. The other pattern was that, at least according to informed people who spoke to me in confidence, most of the villagers who actively helped Senderistas with food and lodging in the early years were women. Again, this probably had to do more with personal goodwill and the hospitality of Andean culture than with any deep political sympathies.

More interesting than these general reactions, however, were Pomatambans' feelings about specific ways Sendero proposed to transform the household economy. Several women mentioned unfavorably the idea of a *wawa wasi* or "baby house." To free women for work in collective agriculture, children were to spend much of the day in a communal nursery being educated for the new order. Women also said that the Senderistas told them that the village would have communal storehouses, from which food would be served in a communal dining room. Both proposals would have destroyed much of women's traditional influence in managing each hearth independently.

Of course, the Senderistas thought such apprehensions were misguided. Like other Marxists, they insisted that women's empowerment would not come from clinging to traditional life any more than it would come from the bourgeois ideal of breadwinners and housewives. Rather, women's full participation in a modern socialist economy would be truly liberating. Even if it had been explained to them in such terms, however, Pomatamban women would hardly have been convinced. Much of Sendero's rhetoric about women's equality and how to bring it about must have been bewildering and implausible. In the end, it promised the same disempowerment that their migrant sisters had found in Peru's cities.

Not only women resisted this version of rural socialism. The prospects of a communal nursery and dining room may have threatened women's roles in a crucial way, but were they really only women's issues? No, they were *peasant* issues. Collectivizing local economic life would have disempowered households, not only women. It would have ruined the social fabric of the village. It would be like replacing a fine hand-woven Andean shawl with a monochrome polyester straitjacket.

The analogy fits in more ways than one. Senderistas said that everyone in the village would one day wear uniforms as a symbol of equality and comradeship. Whether they planned to clone the Mao suits of China or do something else was left vague. In any case, both kinds of clothing one now sees in Pomatambo would have vanished: the Andean shawls and brightly colored skirts, and the Western-style jackets and brimmed hats that migrants bring back from the cities. Each allows for some self-expression, despite poverty. To an enthusiast for collective equality, resistance to uniforms indicates either a blind attachment to habit or petty concerns about status symbols. But to a flesh-and-blood peasant, uniforms offend human dignity.

Sendero's vision of the countryside unnerved people as a *style of life*. Perhaps it would have improved material living standards, perhaps not. But regardless of its performance on the usual economic indicators, and even if no one had been killed, it would still have cast a shadow over the village. Pomatambans at first glance seem reserved, even glum, like most

71

farmers in cold highland regions around the world. But when you get to know them you discover a genuine joy and sociability in their daily life. Those qualities run deeply and have to do with the nuances of how individuals and families relate to one another. They rely on one another a good deal, but by choice rather than compulsion. The tapestry of the village has both the warp of cooperation and the woof of household self-reliance. Pick away at one strand, and the whole fabric unravels.

A postrevolutionary Pomatambo would have had plenty of sharing and cooperation, but of a peculiarly joyless sort. It would have headed off the excesses of capitalist individualism and offered a different image of what it meant to be modern. Yet control would have shifted away from peasants and toward party administrators. Work would have become disenchanted. Poverty in villages like this is bearable in large part because strenuous work is often surrounded by camaraderie, even festivity. Peasants talk, joke, and drink formidable amounts of corn beer while working. But the Senderistas gave a taste of what was to come when, in about 1984, they tried to prohibit all alcohol because it led to "foolishness." Socialist cooperatives would have replaced the humble pleasures of the *minka* with efficient but supervised team production, punctuated by breaks for meals and perhaps a bit of indoctrination at the village canteen.

Peasants are more perceptive than arrogant outsiders assume. Pomatambans' apprehensions concerning Sendero's plans suggested that they foresaw these likely outcomes, even though the guerrillas had no opportunity to carry out the radical vision. Despite the movement's rhetoric about rescuing the rural poor, it was no respecter of peasant custom. At first, I was puzzled when Quintín told me that Peru's national governments, unlike Sendero, had always respected the customs of the community. I knew that Lima politicians had no great sympathy for what they saw as backward highlanders. Then I realized that he meant respect in the limited sense of salutary neglect—the national authorities did not try to suppress peasant customs because they could not care less about them. Sendero, however, would stop at nothing. When I asked Quintín which village traditions he thought a Senderista government would have left intact, he listed only easily disembodied customs like festival dances. The avowedly atheist movement would have stamped out religion, along with any mutual aid or community authorities that it did not supervise itself.

A Sendero victory might have raised rural living standards in the narrow material sense: more clinics, better roads, a safety net for the destitute. In power, Guzmán's circle probably would have made the same policy choices as Mao and other radical leftist leaders. Such regimes do tend to deliver some modest but real benefits to the poorest of the poor, even if their economies lack dynamism and are prone to planning disasters like the Great Leap Forward. But whatever the overall economic performance, a Maoist regime would have accelerated Pomatambo's unraveling as a traditional community. This version of rural socialism would have meant the disappearance of the peasantry's long-standing habits of self-reliance.

What other changes would have taken place in the first decade or so of a Maoist regime in Peru? In villages like Pomatambo, who would have benefited most? Surely the fate of the brokers hung most in the balance. At the outset, villagers with a few years of education and fluency in Spanish took Sendero seriously. The old, the poor, and monolingual Quechua speakers did not quite grasp the guerrillas' rhetoric. Their responses ranged from apathy to personal hospitality that was not politically motivated. The brokers, however, understood what the Senderistas were saying and often liked it.

How would a postrevolutionary government have changed the brokers' lot? Among Sendero's promises, Quintín picked out equal access to education and an end to racial discrimination against highlanders. While he went through university to become a schoolteacher and displays an intense curiosity in conversation, Quintín has also met one obstacle after another in trying to pursue further studies. (He even once signed up for a correspondence course in neurophysiology.) For people like him, how Sendero would change conditions *within* the community was beside the point. More investment in rural development would have benefited everyone, since all Pomatambans were poor by national standards. Brokers cared far more about whether Sendero could remove blockages in Peruvian society more generally. Whatever edge Spanish and literacy gave them locally, they still saw their country's social structure from the bottom. Unlike more traditional Pomatambans, they also saw more of it, every time they went to the city or came up against petty bureaucrats.

Brokers in these villages probably would have bettered their lot in a postrevolutionary society. They would have had easier access to education and new avenues of upward mobility. They would have been natural candidates to staff an expanding state. But people with such abilities and acumen do well whenever the world outside their villages opens up. A larger-scale society with fewer blockages and less discrimination releases their talents. It may not satisfy them in a deeper sense, but it offers them a way up in the world. This pattern holds across social and economic systems. In a booming capitalist economy, they go into business. In a learned culture without racial divisions, they find a place in the clergy or mandarinate. And in a Maoist state, they fill the ranks of cadres.

But as with most things, what Sendero would have given the brokers with one hand, it would have taken away with the other. An expanding socialist state would have had a place for literate Spanish-speakers as the tools of rural transformation. But they would have been foolish to think they could be installed as local administrators, unanswerable to more backward villagers, without themselves answering to higher echelons of the ruling party. Sendero triumphant would have slotted these villages into a much bigger political structure.

With enough credentials, managerial skills, and proven loyalty to the party, a broker might rise higher in a revolutionary state than he ever imagined. Yet a broker whose local importance stemmed only from being the villager best equipped to represent an isolated community in the outside world would have come up against new limits. He would have experienced the expanding state as the source of a thousand new nonnegotiable demands. And the new state's activism would have thrust coastal contempt for Andean culture even more into the face of the peasantry. Fortunato, the broker who handled many of Pomatambo's external affairs in the 1960s and 1970s, saw something along these lines when he complained that so many Senderistas were urban coastal types.

In short, a victorious movement would have changed some of Peru's social hierarchies more than others. Lima's wealthy—at least those who got out alive—would have lost everything and settled in Miami, no doubt. Economic life would have been transformed within a few years. But the political arrangements pressing down on villages like Pomatambo would have been no more egalitarian in spirit. Every study of Sendero's behavior in the countryside has revealed a profoundly undemocratic mindset.[35] It hinted darkly at what would have come with victory. Local administration would have relied on decrees, not consultations.

Even without thinking through all these likely political outcomes, Pomatambans had growing misgivings about the insurgency. By the 1990s, the guerrillas' conduct on a day-to-day basis had left a sour taste in everyone's mouth, even among villagers who could appreciate some of their slogans. Quintín, for example, remarked on the Senderistas' utter lack of respect for human life. Andean communities aim to bring people who make mistakes back into the fold. The guerrillas would not even try to change those they disliked, whether criminals or those with opposing political views. Everyone even *potentially* on the wrong side of the revolution had to die. Quintín said that if Sendero were in power today, it would rule by fear through a system of austere and needlessly harsh laws.

✧   ✧   ✧

Luckily, Pomatambans never had to find out what a Senderista government would mean for their village. When I asked them what they thought it would have been like, few could describe it. None thought it would have been good on balance. Indeed, the starkest commentary on Sendero's failure was that the peasants kept coming back to one overriding theme: the carnage of the insurgency. Abstract plans for a postrevolutionary order mattered less to them than the blood that Senderistas had shed. The early hopes turned into fear once the radicals with guns began acting on their slogans. Sendero was remembered not as a cause, but as a band of thugs and murderers. Nélida, one of Quintín's fellow teachers, said that the guerrillas' actions spoke volumes about their real values. They killed people, and no one should have the right to do that.

My many conversations with ordinary peasants in Pomatambo brought out similar memories of those years. One such conversation took place when five or six villagers, both men and women, sat down with me next to a low mud wall for an hour's break. They had just finished castrating four young black pigs, which had staggered off whimpering in various directions. We chewed coca leaves and swigged some formidably strong clear alcohol while we talked.

The first three years or so of the insurgency had affected them little, because the government had not yet realized the scope of the threat. The real violence came when the army started pushing back. The two sides never had a pitched battle in the village; neither side valued Pomatambo enough to risk their own lives in defending it from the enemy. Instead, both the soldiers and the guerrillas wandered in and out, shooting peasants who had supposedly collaborated with the other side the last time it was there.

The violence was the worst period Pomatambo had ever experienced. Of the men and women sitting with me that day, some had stayed in the village throughout it all. Everyone admired their bravery. Others escaped to the city when things got unbearable, sometimes coming back for a time. Several had close relatives killed by either the guerrillas or the army. With the usual sober Andean understatement, they tossed around numbers of how many Pomatambans had died: a couple here, three there, seven on one bloody occasion, and so on.

Other villagers had the same stories. Amadeo, the prosperous horse-raiser and local amateur historian, lost his first wife because Senderistas targeted him as a rich peasant. One of the community leaders, now in his forties, promptly answered my question about what Sendero offered them by saying simply that they killed so many people. When pressed, he said that all their slogans had turned out to be about "deceiving people," and "when people didn't go along they wanted to kill them." This brutality recurred through southern Peru, in the countryside and in the cities. Nélida the teacher grew up in a family of mule-drivers who used to peddle their goods up and down the mountains. Many times, she said, her parents narrowly escaped death as they passed through a village just before or just after Senderistas arrived to slaughter supposed enemies. She lived in the city of Ayacucho when the violence started. The first outbreak had been when Senderistas shot a vendor at the market near her house. Within a couple of years, bullets were flying daily in the neighborhood, which was next to an army base. You could not go out safely after 6 P.M., and 8 P.M. marked the start of a shoot-on-sight curfew. The carnage left countless widows and orphans.

By the mid-1980s, the downward spiral of violence had worsened. Officially, some 1,300 people—about one in twenty—were killed in the Vilcashuamán area, though there were many unreported deaths.[36] Both sides shot first and asked questions later, while the fate of Peru hung in the balance. As the peasants got caught in the middle, their sympathy for both sides vanished. That the early enthusiasm for the cause did not last should not surprise us. A civil war is a long, hard slog, and innocents always get killed. But this was an unusually bloody and conscienceless civil war on both sides, with no quarter and no decency. One day, in the hills above Pomatambo, a female Senderista was injured in the leg during a skirmish and captured. A fat army captain saw an opportunity to amuse himself and exact revenge on his prisoner. He tortured her with thorns for some time before shooting her point-blank in the head.

On Sendero's side, the shift to brutality was partly an expression of authoritarian impulses that had been present at the movement's founding. It also reflected the growing number of guerrillas. Success breeds opportunism. The insurgency attracted all manner of people who wanted to be on the winning side. Many of these new lower-level militants joined less out of belief in the cause than because they had grudges to settle. Some had pathologically aggressive tempers or were otherwise mentally unbalanced. Peasants saw more and more of these guerrillas as experienced cadres moved into the shantytowns and other new fronts of the civil war. Intoxicated with power, the new guerrillas saw no reason to exercise restraint. They targeted people who failed to attend mandatory meetings, as well as rich peasants and others whom they disliked. Public executions proliferated, without the reprieves that pleading from other villagers had sometimes won. Frightening stories circulated about "la Gringa," a fair-skinned woman who slit people's throats in front of their neighbors.

A number of writers agree that the Senderistas' brutality lost them the support of the peasantry.[37] Selective vigilantism against unpopular targets gave way to violence against peasants who had done little if any-thing wrong. So-called rich peasants, for example, were usually related to poorer neighbors, whose support for Sendero evaporated when they saw their kin killed. Whatever tensions existed in these villages before the violence, the small decencies of traditional life had buffered. Most people wanted to keep the peace and rely on norms and social pressure to correct greed and bad behavior. For Sendero, the chief guides to action were ideology and the relentless display of authority.

Sometimes, ironically for a movement that claimed to fight for social justice, that display of authority turned into a scorched-earth dispossession of the poor. As their power grew, guerrillas made confiscatory demands for material support. At one point Pomatambo had saved enough money to buy bricks and tiles for a second story on the village meeting hall. This hard-gained cash did not last long. A Senderista leader appeared one day and demanded that the community leaders hand it over to him to support the guerrillas. Something as unimportant as the meeting hall had to wait. Refusal would have meant death. And while most Send-eristas were not thieves, a few were. The aged Alejandro remembered times when people's most valuable belongings were snatched from them. Sometimes a wanton show of force, perhaps because of a momentary irritation, threatened the very livelihood of villagers who struggled to feed themselves. "They might shoot a hen," one peasant told me. "And that hen might be all you have."

Reports on the countryside from those years tell of agricultural shortages due to the violence.[38] The greatest disruption, though, came from people fleeing. Between the mid-1980s and the early 1990s, over a third of the region's rural population headed for the shantytowns, sometimes in the city of Ayacucho and sometimes in Lima. A famous song from that era, with the mournful tone of highland music, is called *Adiós pueblo de Ayacucho*—"Goodbye, Ayacucho." Pomatambo numbered over three hundred inhabitants in 1980; by the time of my first visit in 1995, it had shrunk to below two hundred, made up of the determined as well as those who lacked the money and connections to find a new life in the city. By 1993, over a third of the houses in the district were abandoned.[39]

For those who stayed, Sendero's intermittent presence added up to a reign of terror. The guerrillas made every effort to wipe out rival sources of authority. They threatened to cut off Quintín's nose and ears—even his head—if he taught children the existing Peruvian national anthem or national symbols or anything to do with religion. Some of his fellow teachers, new to the village and to such a climate of intimidation, used to break down under the stress and come to him in tears.

The movement saw the local authorities, modern or traditional, as "small reactionaries," much like the traders and rich peasants. Violence against them was all part of "pulling the weeds out by the roots."[40] Militias and party-guided peasant committees were supposed to become the organs of local governance as the countryside fell to Sendero, though they never got organized properly in Pomatambo for lack of recruits. In the meantime, the guerrillas banned all independent village authorities and killed several Pomatambans who held office. Still, the community's desire to run its own affairs was hard to overcome. The modern authorities persisted undercover, with their official stamps handed on in secret as officeholders succeeded one another.

Traditional leaders fared even worse. Since the *varayoq* system relied for its authority so heavily on trust, the climate of terror made it impossible to continue. Death threats from the guerrillas combined with growing mistrust among villagers to end the *varayoq* system in Pomatambo around 1982. This unraveling of age-old Andean structures took place across the highlands as the civil war raged.[41] Sendero's love of dramatic gestures was illustrated here. In many of the villages around Vilcashuamán, Senderistas seized the *varas*—silver-adorned wooden staffs that the *varayoqs* used to carry on formal occasions—and publicly burned them. This act struck at the heart of Andean community life. As the *varas* smoldered in the highlands, so did the customs and trust that held these hamlets together also go up in smoke. Pomatambans hid their *varas* for the duration of the conflict, but the damage to village life was already done.

No one was safe. The quickest way for the average Pomatamban to die was to be suspected of collaborating with the army. Senderistas darkly warned that "the Party has a thousand eyes and a thousand ears." The eyes and ears often got their stories twisted, or passed on accusations to settle old grudges. "People died because of false gossip," as Quintín put it. He knew firsthand the terror that could come from ill-founded suspicions. Once a militant told him that both his wife and his mother-in-law must be informers because they talked too much; they were both going to be killed, and his house would be turned to dust. Quintín, again pressed to defuse the situation, begged for their lives and paid a bribe of his last two hundred soles to win a reprieve.

He was one of the lucky ones. On another occasion, in the middle of the night guerrillas came to the house of a couple suspected of being informers. They shot both of them dead, leaving behind four orphans who ended up growing up in Lima. I met one of them, now an adult, when he returned to Pomatambo for a festival. He seemed to have prospered in the city and to be happy to reconnect with the village on his visits back. But he added that he never goes alone into his childhood home, still standing on the hillside with its red-tiled roof, because of the terrifying memories that haunt him.

While Sendero was terrorizing the peasantry in the name of a revolution gone awry, the army was matching it blow for blow, body for body. Indeed, as is usually the case, the army probably killed more people trying to suppress the insurgency than the insurgents did themselves. The army took over from the police in combating the insurgency after the growing threat to national security led to a declared state of emergency. Soldiers and Senderistas alternated in Pomatambo. The army had some advantages, however. While the guerrillas could operate safely only at night, the army could come during the day as well. Enjoying greater freedom of movement, soldiers came in groups of fifteen to twenty every couple of weeks. The army also drew most of its conscripts from the highlands, while many Senderistas came from the coastal cities. The altitude is punishing when you are unaccustomed to it. While many Senderistas gasped as they trekked through the mountains day after day, most soldiers could roam around as easily as the locals.

The army was as determined as Sendero to display the authority it claimed over the peasantry. Officers used to tell villagers not to believe Sendero's lies, and that the government in Lima was still the highest power in the land. To drive the point home, they showed much the same cavalier disregard for these humble people. Soldiers would come from time to time and ransack every house looking for Senderistas, weapons, or other evidence of collaboration. Those brave souls who refused searches—as was their right, since the soldiers did not have a warrant—were thrown to the floor and kicked mercilessly. Usually their belongings would end up smashed or stolen.

The army also acted brutally on rumors of collaboration. Every meeting of villagers called by Sendero had at least one informer who would later tell soldiers who had gone and who had said what. It was easy to get caught between the two sides. Roberta, a lively and talkative Pomatamban now in her seventies, said she kept her distance from Sendero's activities out of fear. The guerrillas hated people like her and started suspecting her of being an informer. Then the soldiers leveled the same accusation. They beat her and her husband and robbed them of clothes and cheese. "The soldier was a thief," she declared—in that sense worse than the average Senderista, who might be violent but usually did not take anything. On another occasion, a woman had lovingly raised a pet deer to maturity. She hid it whenever soldiers came into the village, but one day they found it on their way out and carried it off to cook.

Most deaths at the hands of the army happened in ones and twos. Supposed collaborators with Sendero were beaten or shot, usually in the middle of the night. Perhaps because the average army officer was less driven by ideology than by rage and pressure from above, some prisoners slipped through the cracks in moments of carelessness. One of Ignacio's neighbors, for example, was taken away by soldiers as a suspected Senderista but managed to escape. A couple of locals I know well were arrested but made their getaway while their captors slept. Pomatambans did what they could to frustrate the army's habit of making suspects disappear. Near the center of the village there used to be a narrow but deep hole in the ground. The locals filled it, lest the soldiers fling captives down the hole to their deaths.

Still, the killings continued, often for the most senseless of reasons. Going uphill once from Pomatambo towards Colpapampa, I noticed a cross in the stone wall beside a peasant house. I asked my friend what it represented. Apparently an old man had been sitting outside on the grass one day when a column of soldiers appeared on a low hill across from him. He got up and started walking back towards his house to get out of the way of whatever might happen. An officer shouted at him to halt, but he continued a few more steps towards the entrance. A trigger-happy soldier with a telescopic rifle promptly took aim, and the old man crumpled dead by the wall.

All these tragedies were in small numbers. But the worst single episode happened on October 22, 1986.[42] It was a little after sunset, and the community leaders and their families were at the center of the village making *chicha*, the highland corn beer, for a village football game. Some soldiers walked into the square unexpectedly. Uneasy though the villagers were to see them, the Andean impulse to hospitality prevailed and the guests were duly served *chicha*. Soon afterwards, the peace of the evening was shattered. A known Senderista, unaware that the army was about, suddenly appeared on horseback at the corner of the square. A torchlight beam fell on him. Then machine-gun shots rang out. He was hurled to the ground while his injured horse thrashed about.

Relishing their catch, the officers started interrogating the wounded Senderista then and there. Torture would not break his silence. Frustrated and suspicious that the villagers were in league with him, the soldiers then hauled seven of Pomatambo's most respected leaders out of the meeting hall. They were beaten, tied up, and subjected to a grueling overnight march to two other villages. They finally got to their destination, Parcco, a little before dawn in an appalling state. Other suspected collaborators were taken prisoner in Parcco, and a couple in their eighties were shot in their bed. After two more hours of merciless interrogation, the prisoners were taken out into the square at Parcco one by one, hacked, and shot. The bodies were burned. They turned up a few days later in a nearby ravine, where they had been flung. My friend's father, a schoolteacher of leftist sympathies, was among those killed; most of the rest of the family then took refuge in the city of Ayacucho. This massacre was the subject of hours of testimony to Peru's truth commission years later.

✦ ✦ ✦

The civil war went on for a few more years. By the late 1980s, the insurgency had spread to the cities. While Sendero's heavy-handedness had alienated much of the populace and made an outright victory unlikely, it had achieved a kind of strategic equilibrium with the state. Many of the shantytowns around Lima and much of the countryside in the south-central highlands were no-go areas dominated by Sendero. And confidence in the national government's ability to resolve the crisis and improve the lot of a war-weary country had plummeted. Some observers feared a collapse into even worse chaos.

In 1985, Alan García, the young and personable candidate of APRA, Peru's oldest and largest leftist party, won it the presidency for the first time. His moderately populist economic policies bore no fruit, however, and triggered hyperinflation. I once found a bank note for five million intis, left over from the time before a new currency was launched that knocked six zeroes off the old one. García's economic ham-handedness and his inability to end the civil war led to his leaving office in 1990 with an approval rating of just 5 percent.[43]

But 1990 also marked a turning point of sorts. The runoff round of that year's presidential election pitted the Nobel Prize-winning novelist Mario Vargas Llosa against a rising dark-horse candidate, the former agronomist and university rector Alberto Fujimori. Vargas Llosa, an admirer of the Asian Tigers and neoliberal market reforms, unnerved much of the electorate with the prospect of further belt-tightening. Fujimori presented himself as a moderate by comparison, a promarket reformer with a human face. Perhaps his greatest appeal to Peru's voters was that his was, quite visibly, a very different face from the rest of the country's political class. The son of Japanese immigrants, he offered an image of hard work and no-nonsense efficiency, and an alternative to the centuries-old ethnic tensions between the Spanish-descended coastal elite and the indigenous highlanders. He won the election handily. And on April 5, 1992, exasperated with a political impasse in the national legislature, he deployed the army in an *autogolpe,* a "self-coup," to dissolve the legislature, concentrate power further in his own hands, and write a new constitution.

The insurgency remained a threat, but a real breakthrough came on September 12, 1992, in one of those incidents that can change history in an instant. Abimael Guzmán, Sendero's leader, was captured. Had he been on the move in the remote highlands, as one might expect of a guerrilla chief, he would probably have remained free. But he suffered various health problems, including psoriasis and altitude sickness, that kept him in Lima. Detectives finally tracked him to a safe house in a comfortable part of the capital—a setting that did not go over well with some peasants who remembered his rhetoric about social justice and the poorest of the poor. "It was my turn to lose," he remarked matter-of-factly to those who arrested him.

Along with Guzmán, Peru's intelligence service also discovered computers and records of the names and locations of much of the leadership. The top echelons of the movement were rounded up within days, and Sendero collapsed like a house of cards. The army gradually took back the countryside over the next three years. The state's restored control of territory allowed Fujimori to target food aid and other spending to key zones like Vilcashuamán, in order to buy off whatever sympathy for Sendero might have lingered.

By my first visit to Pomatambo in 1995, the dwindling number of Senderistas were generally not going into villages any more. The guerrillas who had not already been captured or given up the fight typically roamed the hills, disoriented. In the late 1990s and early 2000s, a few die-hard Senderistas started telling peasants that they had learned their lesson and would no longer kill civilians. But it was too late to win back any sympathy.

Sendero's defeat ended the violence that had lasted nearly a decade and a half. In the aftermath, the peasantry in villages like Pomatambo were left to pick up the pieces of their lives. Ignacio, the former migrant whose plots of land had been reassigned by Senderistas, spent four years with relatives in the city of Ayacucho during the later stages of the civil war. When he finally got back to Pomatambo, he found himself with nothing. His land was his again, but his small house had been smashed to rubble. Almost all his possessions were gone, including his cows. He told me that life was just suffering now, that it only got "worse and worse." He was ashamed that he could not host his grown children in a nice home when they came back to visit.

Sendero and the army must share blame for the tragedies inflicted on Pomatambo during those years. Both mistreated these humble folk, whether out of relentless ideology, rage, personal grudges, or some combination of the three. Small wonder that on nights when either side seemed likely to come to Pomatambo, many villagers would sleep hidden amid the trees or down in the maize fields to minimize their risks. Quintín was like most other Pomatambans in taking advice from an old, wise peasant: *Ni con Dios, ni con el diablo,* "Neither with God nor with the devil." Any sensible person would keep some distance to avoid reprisals. And as his colleague Nélida pointed out, few really wanted to side with either Sendero or the government anyway, once they saw the true nature of each. She pointed out that both Senderistas and the politicians in Lima talked about values, but neither really practiced them. Only these simple people in Andean villages, the oppressed, really tried to live out what they believed. Amid their poverty, she insisted, they share with each other as the rich and the bloodthirsty do not.

In the early, heady days of the insurgency, some writers optimistically claimed that strong communities were resurgent because of Sendero. They read Sendero's rhetoric against the capitalist market as meaning that Andean solidarity was returning in areas of strong guerrilla presence.[44] But the experience of Pomatambo and villages like it makes it clear that the opposite happened. Not only were the insurgents' conduct and vision at odds with traditional Andean sensibilities. They also worked against the life of the community. Sendero sowed a climate of mistrust and damaged precisely the institutions and practices—the *varayoq* system and, to some extent, *ayni* and *minka*—that had sustained a genuine sense of community in places like Pomatambo. As one of the villagers taking a break from castrating pigs remarked, Pomatambo would have been finished if the violence had gone on longer.

From a long-term perspective, the Sendero years accelerated many of the changes that were already underway. The modern world had made inroads into the community by the 1970s. Sendero's own actions and the years of civil war just put more pressure on the fragile bonds that held Pomatambo together. A victorious Sendero would have remade the village and destroyed those bonds entirely. But even a defeated Sendero managed to wreak havoc during its effort to gain power. A movement declaiming against capitalist individualism helped erode some of Andean culture's strongest buffers against it.

The carnage left a deep impression on the peasant psyche. I shall never forget one night in 1995, sitting by the firelight amid the quiet of the countryside, listening as the people near me unexcitedly recounted their recent nightmares—a ghostly figure chasing one with a knife, for example—as if such nightmares were routine. The stress had driven many Pomatambans to drink. And strong drink it was: processed methylic alcohol bought on the market, not the mild corn beer of earlier days. Alcoholism was rampant for the first time. Some people paid workers with alcohol for odd jobs. Even one of the community leaders once came late to a meeting with me, staggering around the corner of a house, barely able to stay upright or form a coherent sentence because he had spent the morning getting plastered. When not drinking, he seemed to spend many of his days trying to find out why the latest shipment of food aid had not yet come. Fujimori's effort to buy off former Sendero strongholds with a mess of pottage was working. Meanwhile, agriculture stagnated.

Pomatambo did not fall apart entirely, of course. Some of the old norms and ideals remained in people's thinking in the mid-1990s. Now that peace was coming back, many of them wanted to rebuild within the old values. Towards the end of my first visit, some of the elders called villagers together to repair the meeting hall on the plaza. Half of it had collapsed after a Senderista bomb, and I could see some faded Maoist graffiti on the inner walls beyond the rubble. The rebuilding was not easy. There were no *varayoqs* now, only some concerned elders and others public-spirited enough to make the effort. A significant minority of people made clear that they would not join in. But basic Andean self-reliance and cooperation were present in enough Pomatamban volunteers. For several days, dozens of locals worked knee-deep in mud mixing adobe, pouring the mixture into simple wooden molds, and carrying dried bricks to the building site.

I left Pomatambo that time dismayed by the damage done to the fabric of the village and pessimistic about how many of the old ways could be recovered. Still, I was moved by the resilience of these people's spirit as they picked themselves up. They were going to take another crack at the world—though how much they could live on their own terms remained to be seen.

IV

Homeward and Hopeful

To mark the return of peace, Pomatambo adopted a community flag. The symbol is fitting: on a white background, two arms meet in a handshake of reconciliation. The flag does not come out often, but on the national holiday in July 2006 I saw it flying in the village square atop one of two tall flagpoles made of eucalyptus trunks; the red-and-white Peruvian triband flew on the other pole.

A few weeks later, the same square was the site of several days of activities for Pomatambo's annual village festival. The usually sleepy community buzzed with the merrymaking of hundreds of people, including countless visiting migrants and their city-raised children. It was for many the chief occasion each year to renew ties to their ancestral home and to indulge in the hearty feasting that has always been one of the peasantry's

Fig. 4: Young and old at the annual village festival

pastimes. Agriculture stops, and the days are given over to music, the running of bulls and horses, football games, and the like.

At the official start of the festival, a handful of locals gathered around a couple of musicians and a flag-carrier at my friends' house halfway up the hill. Plied with *chicha* and stronger stuff, I joined them. As the brass and wind notes wafted over the village, the growing crowd danced its way through the unpaved streets to the square, then to a grassy area overlooking the valley, where other groups converged from elsewhere in the village. When our group passed through the square, it drew near to a football game that had been underway among some youths from Pomatambo and neighboring communities. As we made our way along the edge of the square, a football too energetically kicked by one of the players rolled across the patchy grass and dirt straight through the feet of the moving crowd.

Some of the elders were outraged. The music did not stop, and the enthusiastic crowd kept moving, but some offended voices commented in Quechua. When their remarks were relayed to me in Spanish, I understood that they thought it quite wrong that the football players not only had kept playing when this miniparade appeared, but had also the temerity to kick their ball through the middle of it. Respect was not what it used to be.

No one was dwelling on that moment later in the evening, after a few more hours of drink and merriment had passed. But the football episode illuminated how much the community had changed in subtle ways over a generation. Enthusiasm for the village festivals remained strong, and with peace many of the old customs had come back. Even Pomatambans a generation or two removed from the village still had a place in their hearts for it. But the modern world was intruding in more ways than ever before.

Looking at the festival crowd, I could see that the average age of the village had dropped for those few days. During the violence, younger Pomatambans left in droves because they could adapt more easily to city life. The same happened in other communities. The middle-aged and elderly made up most of the village before long.[1] Even with the return of peace, agricultural stagnation and the economic draw of the cities still drove migration. Pomatambo now has few year-round inhabitants in their late teens or twenties. The complexion of the place changed noticeably when so many of them came back to visit.

Some older migrants returned too, of course, and I spent a while talking with one of them. He had left in 1972 and had since prospered in Lima with his own small construction business. He was comfortable but not rich, he told me. He tried to help his fellow Pomatambans by giving jobs to new migrants, and he hoped that after he retired he would be able to come back and do more for the community. Most Pomatambans who have left over the years still identify strongly with their home village; only some can afford to come back for visits.

People certainly do not come back to Pomatambo for economic opportunities. They no longer have to fear being shot by soldiers or Senderistas, and for some that is enough. But they usually make the decision to move home for sentimental or family reasons, not because making a living has become any easier here. Marta, for example, lived in Lima from 1971 to 1999, working odd jobs in a pharmacy and as a domestic servant but spending most of her time as a small trader. She came back occasionally to visit her aged parents, then moved back permanently to look after her mother after her father died. Otherwise, she said, she might still be in Lima.

Most migrants have stayed put in their new places. In the Ayacucho region as a whole, the urban population has grown from about a third of the total before the war to about three-fifths now.[2] Virtually every older Pomatamban mentioned to me his or her offspring in the city of Ayacucho or in Lima, even the occasional one as far afield as Argentina or Spain. Naturally they miss them, they told me, but these migrants seem to have settled into various odd jobs that pay them well enough to live day-to-day. Fortunato said his sons prefer Lima as long as they have the strength to work. Roberta's children visit her and send money to buy medicines. She has new huts for them to occupy if they move back, but she realizes that they probably never will. Now they are rooted in the city with their spouses and children.

For many younger and middle-aged migrants, their children, who have never really lived in the countryside, now tie them to the cities. Even in the family that I know best, a family that is strongly committed

91

to the well-being of the village, the children know the comforts of city life from infancy. Shortly before the festival, one of my friends brought her three-year-old son to Pomatambo. He had visited only a few times before. He seemed contented enough when I ran into them the day of their arrival, ambling across the wooden bridge into the village. But the next morning, I heard that he had wailed mightily in the night about the lack of electric lights and had asked when they were going home—to the city.

Migrants who return to Pomatambo rarely live there full-time. Many cycle back and forth between countryside and city, making money in seasonal work. Probably even more keep an unoccupied family home in the community but earn their main livelihood in the city. In a cash-poor village, this influx of even modest amounts of money makes a real difference. As of 2006, Pomatambo had its first three or four brick houses, all paid for by migrants or former migrants. Much of the money for community projects—like rebuilding the Catholic church—also comes from migrant donations. Migrants may be largely the poor of the cities, but they have surprising economic clout in the countryside.

Elsewhere in the Andes, one now encounters the same pattern of migrants moving back and forth.[3] Before, to be a villager meant to till the soil year-round in one place. Boundaries have become blurred now. Many migrants think of themselves as members of the village even though they patch together a livelihood between farming and city work. Perhaps this phenomenon is evidence of the migrants' empowerment and creativity. Perhaps it suggests a way to keep communities going by bringing in money from new sources. Or perhaps it just reveals hard-pressed people making the best of a dire economic situation.

Part of the reason migrants do not move back in droves and take up farming full-time is a shortage of land. Pomatambo is big on a map or from the air, but plots with good irrigation make up only a fraction of its area. Even with only a handful of migrants returning to farm, several villagers say that they are worried about population pressure. No one would deny a returning Pomatamban's ancestral right to land or hint that he or she had become an outsider. But among peasants who stayed and suffered through the whole civil war, there is a belief that their newly

returned neighbors are making life harder by taking land. Some relatives have argued over land rights, and many more low mud walls and
barbed-wire fences now surround some plots near the stream. The situation is not dire; by some measures half the agricultural land is still out
of use because of out-migration.[4] But experience elsewhere shows that
overpopulation and land exhaustion can dissolve a community quickly.
Sustainable land management requires trust and self-restraint. A village
reaches a tipping point as soon as every family feels pressed to wring
every bit of short-term gain from dwindling resources.[5]

That has yet to happen in Pomatambo. Much as before the violence,
tensions between old and new mostly stay below the surface. On one
level, migrants who come back and forth today have simply gained the
same horizon-broadening experiences obtained by the first generation of
pioneers like Amadeo, Fortunato, and Ignacio. Those experiences barely
matter to some older Pomatambans who have rarely left the village.
Roberta, for instance, told me that she did not really interact enough
with returned migrants to know how they thought about things. Others made the usual observations that the migrants have fewer children
and speak Spanish more often, or that they are more "civilized," in a
vague sense.

On another level, the new wave of migration during and since the
civil war has widened the chasm between old and new. New tastes
are manifest. One day I spoke with Mailo, a quiet young man in his
mid-twenties with a blue cap pulled down over his forehead. He had
become a capable musician despite problems with his eyesight. He had
not lived long in the city because he could not find work there, and
despite four years of schooling he found it awkward to speak Spanish.
He mostly used a violin to play traditional folk music from the area.
Most people his age can appreciate traditional music, he told me, but
they have acquired a taste for rock and other foreign styles during their
time in the cities. Indeed, changing music tastes and Western clothing fashions were mentioned often, with a tone of disapproval, by the
middle-aged and elderly.

Other Pomatambans remarked upon deeper clashes of outlook. Teo-
dosio, the elderly *varayoq* from long ago, credited returning migrants with

having more book learning. But he lamented that many of them seemed to have forgotten about old people and had no use for their wisdom. He had never lived outside Pomatambo, but others of the older generation who had done so shared his misgivings. Ignacio, for example, had migrated earlier and spent some time in the city during the worst violence. But he complained that when many new migrants come back, they lack a sensitivity to how the community operates. Some of the younger ones just want to grab power and do what they want, without holding the traditional assemblies to consult everyone. "They don't know to ask older people what they think," he said.

The clash also involves a sense of self. Víctor, a peasant now in his mid-fifties, spoke to me at length in both 1995 and 2006. He was among the group that talked about the violence during a break from castrating pigs. He is fond of reading and has fourteen years of schooling, much above the average here. But he also dislikes how most migrants and educated people think. They go along their own paths apart from the community, he said, doing everything just for themselves. This image squares with many observations from around the world. Plenty of people on the margins between rural life and modernity see progress as a move towards individualism. If they make that move themselves, many feel a lingering guilt about weakening their ties to the communities where they grew up. More traditional onlookers see them as self-indulgent, even unsavory, because of their norm-breaking and hardheadedness. As one anthropologist commenting on changing communities in rural Thailand put it, "in the course of such development 'nice guys' (as judged by the standards of village culture) often finish last."[6]

There is some truth in this perception. The more modernity makes inroads into places like Pomatambo, the more the norms of Andean life give way to what can seem like mere self-seeking. Of course, every coin has two sides. To those enthusiastic about it, such change releases a kind of pent-up creative energy. And many Pomatambans acknowledge that people coming back from the cities often have a strong work ethic.

Perhaps the most striking example of this new kind of Pomatamban is a young fellow named Alberto. He has spent much of his life in Lima, having left the village during the violence after his aunts died at the hands of Senderistas. Everyone who knew him described him as a hard worker. In my conversations with him, his energy level was apparent. He has a classic entrepreneurial personality and seems always to be on the lookout for a new opportunity. At the age of twenty-one, he had set up a barn to raise guinea pigs for sale (Andeans eat them as a delicacy, to the amusement or horror of outsiders). One day, Alberto helped me climb over the perilous ring of barbed wire around his barn so that I could walk inside and see his emerging business. The population numbered twenty guinea pigs and growing.

His biggest challenge doing business in the countryside, he told me, was a lack of money and other kinds of support available in Lima. He said that he had learned a lot in the city. It is a hard life without secure work, especially if you are alone, but you pick up good habits like saving money. In the villages, people quickly spend any cash they obtain because they can always rely on their own homegrown crops to live. In Alberto's conversations with me, the theme of changing the village so that a better future might be built kept cropping up. He hoped that his guinea-pig barn would inspire other Pomatambans to show more ambition. They need more vision if they are to improve their lot in life, he insisted. People like Alberto had to lead the way. If Pomatambans started raising guinea pigs for sale, he would happily serve as a middleman, because he knew where the markets were and how to reach them. One day, Peruvians working abroad in North America and Europe and missing their occasional serving of guinea pig might buy his product. He added that sometimes his sort of entrepreneurship provoked envy. "Even the walls have ears," he whispered to me somewhat conspiratorially as he described other business ideas he was chewing over.

My conversations with Alberto were all the more striking because he was such a novelty in Pomatambo. I had met villagers of an older generation who were obviously highly intelligent and possessed a good deal of initiative and desire to move up in the world. In a different society they might have gone into business. Yet Alberto was the first person I met who had channeled his aspirations into commerce so visibly. In some ways, the kinds of changes he wants to bring to Pomatambo represent a more typical pattern of rural change than what the Andean highlands have experienced so far. Instead of the partial modernization that arrives through education and expanded cultural horizons, Alberto's kind of modernization would be driven by economic opportunity.

Whether Alberto and those like him will get their way remains to be seen. They do have more prospect of victory now than ever before. Pomatambo's limited exposure to trade in the 1960s and 1970s was due to the difficulty of transport. My first visits in 1995 involved a bone-jarring six hours by bus on a dirt road from Ayacucho to Vilcashuamán, then a nine-mile trek over the hills and grasslands. The road to the village was a nearly impassable track. This has changed. The road from Ayacucho is still not paved, but it is smoother and has cut the journey down to a little over four hours. And since 1996, the dirt road to Pomatambo itself has been regularly maintained. In fact, the contract to maintain it and other nearby roads went in 1997 to a new business formed by six Pomatambans. Younger men, they entered a competition for the job and have since saved enough money to buy a truck.

During my stay in the area in 2006, I rode a motorcycle from Vilcashuamán to Pomatambo every day. The road was smooth enough that it took only about half an hour to go the nine miles—fast enough, depending on the hills and curves, to feel the icy cold of the Andean dawn working its way through my gloves. This was the dry season, but after a few days of rain the road revealed its drawbacks. Near Pomatambo, the surface turned to a reddish mud that would stick to the motorcycle wheels and end up gumming up the chain casing. One morning, a pebble got inside and promptly put enough tension on the chain that a bolt snapped. The specter of pushing the motorcycle all the way back to a mechanic at Vilcashuamán crossed my mind. But as soon as I walked into Pomatambo, one of the road-maintenance crew happily came out to help and, with rural ingenuity, repaired the whole thing with hardly any tools. Apparently the road often turns to mud in the rainy season, and there are days when even trucks cannot pass.

Despite those limits, the improved road has brought much more trade to Pomatambo. Without exception, the villagers told me that only good changes had resulted. Buses and small trucks come out, and Pomatambo has its own small weekly market, mostly attended by people from other nearby villages. Pomatambans themselves have started doing more of their own shopping at the bigger market in Vilcashuamán. The average person goes about twice a month, much more than before. Officially, there is even a long-distance bus service from Lima; the company's name, "Los Libertadores," is painted on a house in Pomatambo's cobbled main street. In reality, the bus drops off all its passengers for the area in Vilcashuamán; the drivers are nervous about the rickety wooden bridge into Pomatambo.

✦ ✦ ✦

Yet, as in the prewar years, no economic boom is driving change in villages like Pomatambo today. The most significant shifts are occurring in the realm of values and in mentality, shifts largely caused by exposure to the outside world and a loosening of social bonds.

Pomatambo's most pressing concerns are the social and psychological problems that stem from years of carnage, trauma, and displacement. Alcoholism became a plague in the mid-1990s and was worsened by the shift from home-made *chicha* to methylic alcohol paid for in cash. In the worst years, drink replaced work and food as the chief preoccupation of the most troubled villagers. The trauma also led to rises in the rates of wife-beating, child abuse, and death threats. Some of these problems have subsided because of workshops and assemblies, but they are still quite real. During my visit in 2006, Quintín had to perform CPR to save one victim of alcohol poisoning.

Family structure and norms of personal behavior have also altered. The displacement of families and the growing number of women who migrate have driven up the divorce rate. Because of family breakdown and deaths during the war, about a third of rural households are headed by a single parent. Generational differences have also come to the fore. Once I drank Coca-Cola in the small shop at the corner of the square with half-a-dozen youths in their late teens and early twenties. They were comfortable in Spanish and had a few years of education. Moving back and forth between the village and Vilcashuamán or Ayacucho is the norm for them, they said. One senses that in many ways the community has a weaker hold on its young than it did before.

Courtship, for example, is less structured. Marriages used to be arranged by the families involved; now they are up to the couple.[7] In conversation with the nurse at the village health post, I learned of other emerging challenges. Because Pomatambo has only a primary school, teenagers seeking secondary education have to go to Vilcashuamán or Pujas, both of which are too far away for daily trips. If they lack relatives there, they have to rent lodging and live unsupervised. The teen-pregnancy rate has surged in recent years. The nurse told me of one twenty-year-old in the area with three girlfriends in different villages, all fourteen or fifteen and pregnant. She found out about the situation when one of the girls reported to her that the boyfriend had beaten her badly during an argument up in the hills.

Several times I heard people—some rural, some urban, many not that old—decrying the moral decline of the floating youth population. Their lives are often marred by libertine behavior, uprootedness, and frustration at their lack of employment prospects. The city of Ayacucho was once quite safe, apart from the political turbulence. Now it has enough crime that you cannot walk at night outside the center, and taxi drivers refuse to go to some shantytowns. During my stay in 2006, a UNSCH student was murdered in a barroom brawl that was splashed in gory detail all over the most colorful tabloids. The worst of Lima is coming to the highlands.

I do not want to overstate the social problems of places like Pomatambo. The countryside is not the city, and youth with strong family ties to these villages do not suffer the worst effects of the former peasants' dislocation. The trends are troubling nonetheless. Imagine that the breakdown goes further over the next twenty years, without an improvement in economic prospects, and the problems of alcoholism and violence worsen. Imagine that governments in Lima keep doling out social spending where politically convenient, without an eye to building real local capacity. Such pressures risk turning places like Pomatambo—and, indeed, other rural backwaters across the global South—into something resembling the troubled and stagnant urban ghettos or Native American reservations in the United States. The values guiding what aid comes, and the direction of change in these communities as their horizons broaden, matter in profound ways.

These villages hang together as well as they now do, despite these pressures, because they still have plenty of backbone. For one thing, the *varayoq* system has been revived.[8] When I left in 1995, the gloom of mistrust hung over Pomatambo. I did not expect the traditional authorities ever to come back. But they did, in an unlikely turn of events that everyone agreed owed a lot to one woman.

María Gutiérrez was born in Vilcashuamán but lived in the city of Ayacucho for twenty-nine years, missing the worst of the violence. Now in her fifties, she came back to the area to be with her aged parents after her husband retired. Venturing into local politics, she worked on a variety of projects in the province and earned credibility with the peasants. Then she served as *gobernadora*—loosely, a kind of elected sheriff—from 2002 to 2004. When I interviewed her in 2006, I recognized a genuine commitment to openness and public service. By her choice, we sat on a bench in the courtyard of the municipal building in Vilcashuamán. Several times, she exchanged greetings in Quechua with familiar passersby; she even told one woman that she had heard about a problem she had, and then directed her to where she might go to solve it.

"Our communities have lost their customs," she told me, and she wanted to revive them. Since her mandate as *gobernadora* was the maintenance of public order, she began to work closely with the older generation. A few villages near Vilcashuamán brought back the *varayoq* system in the mid-1990s, but outlying ones like Pomatambo had not done so when she came into office. She encouraged them, because she felt that the traditional authorities had done a fine job before the insurgency of keeping order and resolving disputes peacefully. The modern authorities such as the village presidents had their hands full with other matters. Sure enough, Pomatambo chose a new *varayoq* in 2003, more than twenty years after the last one. Other villages did the same, and María Gutiérrez saw that holders of the post received an official credential. Not long afterwards, all the *varayoqs* of the area appeared in costume as part of a parade in the Vilcashuamán square. When they marched past, people applauded her for bringing them back.

The process of choosing a *varayoq* in Pomatambo today occurs much as in the old days. On the night of December 31 each year, the most community-minded villagers gather and deliberate about potential candidates, weighing their abilities and qualities of character. The choice is made by consensus, not by counting votes. Eventually they agree on a *varayoq* and walk to his house. They offer him a toast in honor of the occasion. The next morning, perhaps with a slight hangover, the new *varayoq* crosses himself and takes up the *vara* as symbol of his new office. In Pomatambo, this is the same *vara* that was hidden from the Senderistas during the violence.

As one older peasant told me during a break from building the new church on the square, the most important characteristic of a *varayoq* is that "he does his duty." This man had himself served recently as community president, the leading modern authority in Pomatambo, but he spoke of the *varayoqs*, with obvious warmth, as the most respected of all village leaders. While chewing coca leaves, he held forth to me about the many informal responsibilities of a *varayoq*, mostly involving the resolution of disputes. The community has a justice of the peace, too—that year it was Marta, the woman who had lived in Lima for twenty-eight years—but *varayoq* justice is the old Andean justice of norms and reconciliation, for those who want to appeal to it.

Two of the recent *varayoqs* gave me examples of how it works. One said that if a villager insulted someone or caused a fight, "we'd punish him so he would learn to live properly." A typical punishment would be having to spend all day outside with no lunch, mixing mud and straw to make adobe bricks. He chuckled over the image of such a forlorn creature mending his ways. Another *varayoq* explained how they dealt with disputes over damage to property. Sometimes a cow would stray into another farmer's field and trample the crops. The *varayoq* would impound the cow in a special pen encircled by a stone wall just off the square. He would bring the neighbors together and help them come to an agreement on what should be paid for the damage. Then the guilty cow would be released from jail, as it were. Once when we walked past the pen and saw that a dog had wandered in there overnight and died, my friend joked that it must have been locked up for eating a rooster.

Most disputes end up in front of the *varayoq* first. Only in graver criminal matters or conflicts that cannot be handled by gentle pressure and consensus do villagers resort to the higher authorities in Vilcashuamán. The system relies entirely on local norms and the conscience of the people involved. A *varayoq* cannot physically impose a punishment on an offender or force anyone to pay compensation.

Despite the loosening of some strictures in the community, the austere morality of the peasantry remains strong. One afternoon I noticed that my old and already battered motorcycle was missing one of its mirrors. As soon as Quintín heard about it, he concluded that the local children—who were always gathering around the motorcycle and touching it out of curiosity—had probably unscrewed the mirror as a toy, since no one else would have had any use for it. I did not much care, but I could tell from the severe expression on his face that his class would get a very serious talking-to. There are some things that one just does not do in an Andean village.

As enforcers of traditional norms, today's *varayoqs* have taken on much the same role as their predecessors. Fittingly, the first new *varayoq* after 2003 was Secundino, the son of Teodosio, the old fellow who had served as *varayoq* three times before the violence. Secundino has always lived in Pomatambo. He spent only two years at the village school, but unlike the earlier *varayoqs,* he speaks Spanish fluently. At forty-nine, he was also younger than one might expect for the post. He even spoke of himself matter-of-factly as among the younger cohort in Pomatambo. Likewise, the *varayoq* who succeeded him, Celestino, was only thirty-nine at the time. Celestino had six years of schooling and had lived in the city during the war. He hailed from Vilcashuamán but had settled in Pomatambo after marrying a local woman. The incumbent *varayoq* in 2006, Pastor, was only thirty-eight. The man had suffered greatly during the violence, being beaten brutally by both sides. He still has a crippled foot, a twisted left wrist, and damaged fingers—a microcosm of what the civil war did to pillars of the community.

The youth of the new *varayoqs* and their exposure to the world outside Pomatambo show how times have changed. The split between traditional and modern authorities is much less pronounced than in the 1970s. Of course there is still some rivalry. A couple of the modern officials told me in passing that their role is more important, especially in keeping order, because they have the state's coercive power behind them. And some returned migrants at first opposed reviving the *varayoq* system because they remembered it as backward. But such tensions have subsided. Indeed, Secundino stressed that the president and *varayoq* complement one another, and that people appreciate one another's viewpoints better than before. Most of the modern officials freely mentioned the *varayoq* among Pomatambo's many elected offices—fourteen in a village of two hundred people. The traditional authorities may have overcome the stigma of backwardness precisely because the men who have recently served as *varayoq* do not fit the old stereotype: they can speak Spanish and read and write, even though they stand for the traditional morality. They have caught up with the modern world without being of it.

The biggest challenge to today's *varayoqs* is not the image of the position itself. It is that a *varayoq's* power, while formidable, is less airtight than it used to be. It rests wholly on people's willingness to listen and be persuaded. The vast majority still respect the *varayoq* and what he represents. But it only takes a few willful or contemptuous villagers to undermine the whole system. The occasional drunk ignores reproaches more or less with impunity, and some villagers are hard to mobilize for shared duties like building the church or community hall. Quintín remarked with some sadness that the current *varayoq* found his duties frustrating because some people would not listen. At times he felt relegated to "the end of the line among the authorities."

In taking the pulse of Pomatambo as a community, we have to look beyond just how much authority such leaders have. More often, a real sense of community comes from daily habits, from how people work together to make a living under harsh conditions. Economic practices make up the texture of a village and shape the inhabitants' sense of themselves. Traditional forms of mutual aid like *ayni* and *minka* held Pomatambo together over the centuries. When they disappeared in the violence because of mistrust, the community seemed likely to unravel.

Fortunately, with the return of peace, Pomatambans have revived *ayni* and *minka*. Everyone senses a renewal of goodwill in the village, unlike the "sadness" of the mid-1990s. In August 2006, I attended a grand *minka* of the old style. A prosperous peasant was hosting a house-raising next to the cobbled main street. The concrete pillars and red bricks, still a novelty, provided evidence that some money had flowed in from the city. This *minka* was being held to finish the roof. The house became a hub of activity for a couple of days, with roughly twenty men at work. Even though this was a private event, two of the former *varayoqs* put in an appearance and helped.

Some of the women stood nearby singing a Quechua melody that alternated with long wails, apparently customary for a house-raising. The workers' ingenuity was demonstrated as they chopped eucalyptus trunks into perfect square beams for the roof, then laid smaller reeds over them to support the tiles. All this activity was punctuated by much chewing of coca leaves, friendly conversation, and drinking of *chicha*. When I handed the host three bottles of peach juice as a small contribution to the festivities, they disappeared for a few minutes. When he brought them back to pour me a glass, it turned out that the peach juice had been spiked with something stronger.

At lunchtime the long break came. It was time for Andean hospitality, which the women had spent most of the morning preparing. The food and the camaraderie are the only compensation the workers get, but they were contented to be there. It was a hearty lunch of rice with potatoes and purple onions in a spicy red sauce. The workers, their families, and neighbors all sat on a low bench around the perimeter of the big unfinished room on the ground floor. The house had modern bricks and would eventually have a concrete floor, too, but it had obviously been built for entertaining large numbers of neighbors the same way Pomatambans always had done. Its very layout was a sign of confidence in the spirit of community.

Past, present, and future came together in the festivities. As we settled after lunch into a well-fed rest and idle conversations in two and threes, Mailo and other musicians played traditional music on the violin and a huge box harp. As they knocked back a few more drinks, some of the villagers became loquacious. One of them proudly pointed out that *minka* dates back to the time of the Inkas, and that they were carrying the custom on today. Another said that this kind of work in common was just what Pomatambo needed to be more unified and get things done.

It is a good village, he remarked, with poor but good people who know how to pull together.

The story with *ayni* and *minka* is much like that with the *varayoq* system. All these customs have come back in recent years, and most of the time are as strong as ever. The house-raising was probably no different from a house-raising fifty years ago. When I asked people from Pomatambo or other nearby villages, nearly all agreed that things were right back where they had been. But when I pressed a few of them, I discovered signs of change that could bode ill for the next generation. One young fellow said that richer villagers and migrants still practice *ayni* and *minka,* but that it was obvious many of them would prefer a system in which the community demanded less of them. Another said that sometimes *minka* has become too expensive because hosts have to buy more meat in the market. Often they find it cheaper and easier to pay wages in cash. And Celestino, the second new *varayoq,* remarked that in some villages nearer Vilcashuamán, people will now build only for money, not hospitality.

Strong though the practices of community are in Pomatambo, the tide of history is running against them. The village is still immensely important to the livelihoods of its members, even with the recent expansion of trade. It is just as worthwhile to get along as it is to get ahead. Yet if the balance tips enough, if the cultural signals change a bit more, it is hard to imagine the *varayoqs* and the *minkas* playing the same role in a future Pomatambo.

Except for educated people familiar with trends outside Pomatambo, most villagers seemed not to worry about such changes. Celestino made a fairly typical comment when I pressed him. He said that he thought Pomatambo, unlike those villages that had abandoned *minka* for wages, could maintain its way of life. There was no threat to its customs, he insisted. If the community kept valuing those customs, then nothing should go wrong.

In some ways, such confidence was heartening. But it also made me wonder why, with the modern world pressing in on them, so many rural folk in villages like this are sanguine about their ability to go on as they always have done. There is, after all, no reason why in the long run the fate of Pomatambo should be any different than the fate of villages in other parts of the world that have already changed beyond recognition. Of course, this confidence could merely reflect a lack of awareness. But I eventually concluded that it has deeper roots in how these highland communities are now functioning, and particularly in what form their encounter with modernity is taking.

They do not see much of a threat because the balance of power is, in fact, still in their favor. Pomatambo today breaks down into three types of people—three cultural blocs and sets of attitudes, as it were. The largest bloc is still the traditionally minded. These people are more comfortable with Quechua than Spanish, if they speak Spanish at all. They have only a few years of schooling and often little experience of the cities. The community is their horizon, and they cannot imagine living outside all the duties and norms that bind it together.

The second bloc is made up of migrants like Alberto and others who have adopted the ambitions of city life. They would pursue business opportunities if more were available. They work within the customs of Pomatambo when they have to, but they would loosen some of the traditional norms if they could. With just these two groups—the traditional bloc and the commerce-minded individualists—Pomatambo would look like the usual landscape of modernization and community breakdown. The battle lines would be clearly drawn, with only the pace of change at stake.

But there is a third bloc as well, and it holds the balance between the other two. This bloc consists of those who are relatively educated and who float back and forth, usually only living in Pomatambo if they have employment teaching or the like. Some have leftist sympathies, though they might be better described as a populist intelligentsia, critical of the kind of modernization that Lima would impose on the countryside. They come from rural roots and remain strongly committed to these villages. Their ambitions focus on education and perhaps officeholding, not moneymaking. Despite their small numbers, they contribute much of the energy and initiative for new community projects. And when it comes down to commerce versus tradition, they usually side with tradition—or at least the spirit behind it. The wholly traditional folk in

Pomatambo do not perceive a threat to their customs because this crucial third bloc keeps it at bay.

Anyone with some schooling could be a quasi-intellectual of this sort, and I have found a few scattered among Pomatambo's farmers. Víctor would count as one with his fourteen years of education. But the most obvious examples are found among the schoolteachers. None of Pomatambo's teachers were born in this village, but they do come from similar rural backgrounds elsewhere in Ayacucho.

Quintín, for instance, told me that he takes pride in being the son of a peasant. His mother could not read at all. He had little good to say about locals who move to Lima and pretend to have forgotten their roots. He thinks of himself as first and foremost a Pomatamban because he lives here now, and he takes pride in being a Quechua-speaker. He called his village and his language "my life, my culture." The history of the area runs through his blood, and he identifies with the generations of honest and humble people who struggled against injustice. His allegiance goes back to the Peru of the Inkas, not the Lima bureaucrats he has seen making fun of Quechua-speakers. And these commitments are apparent in his daily life. He brings a contagious enthusiasm to any project intended to improve life in Pomatambo, and he is always involved in village decision-making—informally, because teachers cannot hold village-level office. He has always loved the Andean culture of participation. He fervently hopes that Pomatambo will maintain ancestral customs like *ayni* and *minka*.

Or take his colleague Nélida. Her parents drove mules, and she is the only one among all her siblings and cousins to become a teacher. She teaches her pupils to write in Quechua and to feel confident in their own culture before they master Spanish. Children must appreciate their own history, she insisted, starting with their pre-Inka ancestors and the glories of the Inka empire. If there were such a thing as an Andean nationalist, Nélida would probably be one. Yet her commitment to her people goes deeper than ethnic affirmation. Some of the commerce-minded migrants hold forth about the importance of Quechua and feel no need to hide their indigenous roots when they go to Lima. But for people like Nélida, Andean culture is not just a label of heritage. It is also a way of life, a set of values deeper than mere ethnicity. She told me that Andean culture has always been about hard work, a spirit of equality, and overcoming selfishness. She contrasted Andean values of solidarity with the "anti-values" of capitalism.

These rural teachers are not alone in their commitment to social justice and the spirit of traditional communities. The same outlook appears among some of the urban intelligentsia in the highlands, precisely because so many of them are at most one generation away from the peasantry. Take my research assistant in 2006, the nephew of the friend who introduced me to Pomatambo in 1995. He grew up in the city after his family left Pomatambo and has studied anthropology at UNSCH. But he comes back to the ancestral village often and introduces himself—and is accepted by locals—as a Pomatamban. Likewise, María Gutiérrez, the former *gobernadora* and reviver of the *varayoq* system, agreed that a lot of educated people in the area identify strongly with the villages. Her son, a lawyer, comes back often for festivals. And she told me of another youth who grew up in a village near Vilcashuamán, got to UNSCH, and after his graduation returned to his village and was duly elected as *varayoq*.

Perhaps none of this seems odd to people around here. As María Gutiérrez put it, they are "healthy folk" with a good sense of their roots. But it is not what you would expect in most parts of the world most of the time. Usually, the educated distance themselves from such traditional origins in order to side with one or another version of "progress." They resent age-old customs as suffocating and want to overcome "backwardness." Even those who do not go into business side with the commerce-minded individualists on moral and cultural matters.[9]

So why do many educated people in rural Ayacucho come down on the side of tradition and community? How do they end up holding the line against a capitalist modernity that elsewhere has made such villages unravel? Part of the reason, I think, is that after encountering the cities and higher education, so many of them find further upward mobility difficult. Latin America's old barriers of caste and ethnicity have largely dissolved, to be sure. So while some of these people experience discrimination, it is usually not intense enough to push them back to the countryside. Rather, the economic stagnation of the country—and the highlands in particular—means that opportunities to get rich in the normal ways are few. In one report on the Vilcashuamán area, most respondents, when asked who constituted the local upper class, pointed to salaried educators and other government employees, and maybe the occasional small innkeeper.[10]

There are no entrepreneurs on their way up in Vilcashuamán, because capable people here cannot make money. Since the capitalist economy does not offer enough outlets for their talents, most of them feel it is not their game. Instead they go into teaching, development work, or local politics. And the education they acquire, even after the end of Sendero, is heavily laden with Marxism. Even if they do not share all of its ideological precepts, they imbibe an intellectual culture of critique and opposition.

Imagine the Peruvian economy were booming. Educated youth in the highlands would probably have much less respect for traditional community life. If capitalism delivered—or at least convinced enough ambitious people that it *could* deliver for them—these villages would have more entrepreneurially minded smooth operators contemptuous of traditional morality. From the standpoint of peasants who value community, the lack of economic development so far has probably been a blessing in disguise.

But to put it this way raises more questions than it answers. To say that poverty has its benefits discounts the real material deprivation that people in Pomatambo feel. Moreover, this situation cannot go on forever. People want economic growth, and whether it comes sooner or later, economic growth tends to put pressure on traditional life. To get a better sense of how this might play out in Pomatambo, we have to look more closely at what development means to these folk, and how they think about its implications for their values.

Older Pomatambans who lived through the more peaceful times of the early to mid-twentieth century, before the modern world started pressing in on their village, look back on that era with great fondness. Today is better than during the civil war, they say, but nothing could have been worse. Their children and grandchildren can only compare today favorably to the carnage they witnessed. Conditions of life have not really improved much, of course. They use aluminum rather than clay pots now, and an NGO put in a water tank and a simple aqueduct a few years ago. These changes make life a bit easier. The rudimentary health post on the square now has a nurse most of the time. One day, I saw a peasant come in with his hand bleeding after he had cut it on a rusty tool. It is not sophisticated medicine, but he had the gash sewn up, and people could have colds and other problems treated for a token fee of fifteen to sixty cents. All these modest improvements are quite welcome. But the locals know how much is missing.

The development aspirations that these people have are quite typical. They told me that everyone should have good healthy food, clean paved streets, proper houses, bathrooms, kitchens, and so on. Those who have spent time in the cities appreciate the hospitals there. And the new solar-powered telephone in a shop on the square attracts peasants from miles around, since they have no other way to receive calls from relatives in the city.

They also want technical aid for agriculture. One day, when I was walking through the square, I struck up a conversation with a young farmer who had been working with his friend on an adobe and wood-beam house. I sat down with them, and we talked while passing back and forth a dirty plastic bottle with some dubiously strong drink in it. This fellow, Éder, said that they needed technical aid and public works so that they could make a better living and support their families. He also lit up at the idea of a small solar-ovens project that I was arranging. Other Pomatambans mentioned the need for better digging tools, better fences, improved cattle and crops, advice from agronomists, and so on.

For people with basically local horizons, they have a surprisingly clear sense of their comparative poverty. One of the *varayoqs* knew how staggeringly expensive it was to travel abroad, by the standards of his cash-poor village. Most of them also assume, wrongly, that the developed countries of Europe and North America are the norm rather than the exception in the world. One young man, curious about China, started off with the impression that it must be much richer than Peru—which, taking both countries as a whole, it is not. They want to catch up and feel that they could do so if given the chance. Those with a smattering of broader knowledge about Peru remarked that their country is not poor in any inherent sense; it just needs help to develop its capacities and the skills of its workforce. In this vein, a few Pomatambans mentioned their hope of building a small factory for cement, bricks, and plaster, if only they could get enough start-up capital. That way they could "get out of extreme poverty," as Fortunato put it.

Many of their aspirations are for the next generation. Some peasants in their sixties and seventies said that they are old now themselves, but that Pomatambo could be improved for younger people if enough projects were started. The most touching hopes were voiced by the parents of teenagers and younger children. One of the *varayoqs* has a son of about fifteen with a developmental problem of an unknown sort. He assumed that modern doctors could treat him if only he had access to them. Other parents complained of the shortage of educational materials. Those who follow what happens in the local school take pride in the teachers' commitment to education, but they know the obstacles presented by their poverty.

The hopes for a secondary school in Pomatambo are a case in point. The primary school has about sixty pupils, but for the majority who want to study further the only option is to move to Vilcashuamán or Pujas. Many do, but the cost and resulting social problems make it undesirable. In 2006, I met an education official from Vilcashuamán who had come to Pomatambo to assess the feasibility of building a secondary school there for Pomatambans and children of the nearby villages. It seemed likely to happen in the next few years. In the meantime, Quintín has lobbied unsuccessfully for a secondary-level distance-learning program to bridge the gap.

A secondary school would strengthen the community's influence over its young people. But it would not really counteract the pull of the cities. When I talked with the group that had been castrating pigs, our long conversation eventually turned to the aspirations of the young. A fifteen-year-old girl was sitting with them. She did not say much, but when asked she admitted that she would rather live in the city in the future. She had already spent a year studying in Ayacucho. Despite the elders' attachment to Pomatambo, they agreed that her choice was understandable. Their ancestors had all been farmers and herders. Nowadays, education held out new opportunities. The girl wanted to study medicine. She could be a nurse in the village, but the elders agreed on the advantages of working in a city, with its many different kinds of medical institutions.

An NGO report on the Vilcashuamán area confirmed that the vast majority of teenagers and twenty-somethings want to move out. It quoted a Pomatamban peasant: "Our young people are going. They all want to live in Lima. The migrants suggest it, but there's also no future in the community." People in other villages said much the same.[11] Often the comparison between city and countryside does not even involve education and opportunity, because earning a living in the city is hard, too. It hinges instead on basic conditions of daily life, like the lack of electricity in the countryside. The teachers, for example, are frustrated that they cannot draw on Internet-based material for their classes.

The lack of electricity is ironic, because along nearby hilltops you can see high-tension power lines bypassing the village. The electricity flows from one part of the country to another in a profitable trade that attests to the priorities of the government. Nearly half the communities in rural Vilcashuamán have lobbied heavily for electricity lines. A provincial politician told me that a budget had been approved and that electricity would be made available to these villages in the next few years. Most villagers expect it.

When electricity does come, it will be one of the biggest agents of change in Pomatambo since the school opened. Today, those who can afford batteries listen to small radios. A handful, including Fortunato and Quintín, have battery-powered televisions. But they can get only one television channel because of the mountains, and the battery imposes its own limit: to his exasperation, Quintín's television died in the middle of the last presidential debate. With electricity, exposure to the media will bring the outside world to Pomatambo in new and intrusive ways.

Here we come to a crucial point. How do these people see their presumed future? What do they imagine will happen when commerce and the media start pressing on them more intensely? What do they think it means to be fully modern like the people in Lima or the developed world?

Of the three blocs in Pomatambo, the commerce-minded migrants would most welcome such changes. They see the hustle and bustle of the modern world as liberating. They claim that Pomatambo needs their creative disruption in order to realize its potential. As we have seen, however, such people—at least for now—lack the influence and economic outlets to get what they want. The other two groups—the more traditional villagers and the educated but community-minded—see tradeoffs of gains and losses. They understand the appeal of the city if one can make a decent living there. But many of them, including some older returned migrants, feel freer and more at ease in the countryside. They can work and rest as they see fit, instead of having to earn wages and live hand-to-mouth. No one in Lima will give you anything if you need help, one old woman said. And those who know the values of the media are apprehensive. Quintín did not think anything good would result when most villagers, including children, started to watch the sort of salacious "false propaganda" that gets spewed over the airwaves.

The perception of the modern world as heartless and immoral is not limited to how peasants think about Peru's cities and media. It appears in how they think about the developed world in general. I vividly remember one conversation I had in another rural Ayacucho village some years ago. A handful of locals and a student from UNSCH were bouncing various perceptions of wealthy countries off me to see if they were true. A question came up in Quechua and was duly relayed to me in Spanish. "Is it true that the reason those countries are so powerful is because they get rid of useless things?" He paused. "That when you get to sixty years old . . ." And he made a cutting motion with his finger across his throat.

All those apprehensions struck me as oddly static, however. The cities are as they are, and other countries are as they are. But the idea that processes close at hand could one day turn Pomatambo into them seems harder for villagers to imagine. Even a teenager who studies in Vilcashuamán but chooses to come home every weekend told me that the peasants would never change their way of life. The threat of modernity seems to have made little impression on them. Only a few, like Quintín, sense that people's thinking can change in subtle ways over time. And he probably gets that sense more from his education and reading than from local experience.

All Pomatambans want development. They assume—with a confidence that is both heartening in its optimism and alarming in its ignorance—that development would leave their village more or less as it is. The cement factory, shops, electricity, and secondary school would supposedly all be seamlessly grafted onto a village of *varayoqs,* festivals, *ayni,* and *minka.* They want prosperity with their own values.

In a sign of how much the old values still shape the locals' priorities in development, most of the things they want are public goods. When I asked them about their most pressing needs, they mentioned paving the square and streets, improving the bridge into the village, rebuilding the village hall and church, funding the school, and even recognizing Pomatambo as a new district capital. Several were as dismayed about the backward image of the community as about the lack of household amenities like electricity and running water. Their development vision is community-centered. Values of hard work and cooperative self-reliance remain strong. No one suggested that a responsive government just ought to give handouts. Instead, they want aid to jump-start their own efforts, to build local economic capacity in agriculture or in new enterprises like the cement factory.

Part of this theme of self-reliance stems from a lack of confidence in higher political authorities. The more distant they are from Pomatambo, the less credibility politicians have. One of the recent *varayoqs* observed that the village has always had to rely on itself. Most decisions affecting it are made by community leaders and assembled locals. Education and health officials come out for brief inspections once a month at most. The police come even less often. Officers at the police station in Vilcashuamán told me that they only go to places like Pomatambo when the locals ask them to solve some otherwise unsolvable problem. They know that a deep mistrust lingers because of the civil war.

So Pomatambo really does stand alone much of the time. The credibility of local leaders is crucial because they have no resources behind them. Peruvian law says that village officials are responsible only for keeping a semblance of order, overseeing the rotation of communal land, and representing the village to higher powers.[12] The village has no budget of its own. It has no general funding from above and no way to raise revenue in such a cash-poor setting. When village leaders want to do anything more than just get by, they have to go hat in hand to the authorities in Vilcashuamán. People had varying views on whether the effort was worthwhile. Some said that the district- and province-level officials give a bit of aid now and then, and that they have all the power anyway. Others had little confidence in them. When Fortunato talked with me about his efforts to get electricity, he remarked with frustration that sometimes the higher authorities seem to want to keep outlying villages backward.

The poor performance of Vilcashuamán-level government is somewhat surprising, because there is plenty of civic consciousness here. Quintín reads multiple newspapers and seems to be always on the run from one meeting to another. María Gutiérrez's efforts to build local capacity also reveal real commitment. Such civic engagement and the participatory ethos of Andean communities show that areas like Vilcashuamán *could* have a vibrant civil society and responsive governments.

Why do they not? For one thing, district- and province-level political energy gets channeled in strange ways by badly designed institutions. Candidates for the Vilcashuamán council stand on lists put together by weak and fragmented parties. Whichever party wins the most votes, even if only a plurality, dominates the new government. The winning party in 2002 got 36 percent of the vote, and its replacement in November 2006 came in with just 32 percent.[13] No real consensus emerges from such elections. Moreover, the weak party organization in rural Peru means that aspiring leaders ally with parties based less on ideology than on personal ties. Quintín, for example, tried to venture into district-level politics for the first time in 2006. He could choose a party only by a rough guess of what ties would best help him to get anything done if elected. Electoral institutions fail to throw competing political visions into stark relief. Policy choices have a frustrating ad hoc quality and are characterized by discontinuity. As María Gutiérrez noted, an incoming politician finds it easy to undo the achievements of whoever came before and avoid accountability.

What about politics at higher levels? For the oldest villagers like Teo-dosio, political life beyond Vilcashuamán gets hazy. Their children and grandchildren, with more facility in Spanish and more exposure to the cities, do follow national politics. But even they see little link between realities on the ground and the parade of personalities in Lima.

The small exceptions here and there, such as they are, tend to confirm this dismal portrait of Peruvian politics. Despite Pomatambans' general skepticism about politicians in Lima, Fujimori is the least disliked of recent presidents. A fair number of them grudgingly respect him for stopping the violence. They also note a few visible benefits that came in the mid- to late 1990s: the improved dirt road, slight increases in fund-ing for education, food and milk for schoolchildren, some reforestation, and the like. Modest spending on the poor was one pillar of the effort to win back the countryside at the end of the civil war.

This aid yielded political dividends. Vilcashuamán district voted for Fujimori's reelection in both 1995 and 2000, as did most of the south-central highlands. The political approach behind these victories has been called "Fujipopulism." It used the windfalls from privatization of state-owned enterprises and tightened tax collection to finance new social spending. Aid was carefully targeted for political gain in the poor-est areas of the country, ranging from $20 to $60 per capita and peak-ing right before elections. The most important Fujimori-era rural-aid program was FONCODES. On each small project—such as building latrines and irrigation channels—FONCODES worked with a "nucleus" of handpicked local supporters. As a forum for grassroots participation, this model had its defects. The local committees were disconnected from other community leaders and one another and dissolved once their work ended. Thus, this kind of targeted spending did nothing to strengthen civil society, but it did serve its political purpose. It was always clearly identified with Fujimori himself, a kind of "executive philanthropy" that passed directly from the presidency to beneficiaries. And Fujimori acted the part, dressing up in Andean ponchos and pretending to bond with peasants at election time.[14]

Pomatambans today remember Fujimori-era spending, but not as having any profound effect on their standard of living. When I asked what the government had done for them, most villagers took some time before mentioning things like the very basic health post, a few more school materials, and the NGO-installed water tank. Their first response was usually a matter-of-fact "nothing." Indeed, even when technical aid arrives, it turns out to be poorly executed. One chunk of state aid in recent years has come through PRONAMACHS, a resource-management project that works with several villages including Pomatambo. According to a PRONAMACHS report that I acquired, its efforts had not impressed many. Peasants complained that many promises of aid had not materialized, that advisors did not respect them, and that the tools on offer were overpriced.[15]

We should hardly be surprised that this kind of aid brought at best minor and short-lived benefits. Policy choices in Lima over the last decade and a half have affected places like Pomatambo very little, because they have failed to engage the communities or to increase local economic capacity. Then again, they were never intended to do so. Viewed against the backdrop of the counterinsurgency and the pressures of national politics, it is easy to see that every such policy has reflected priorities in Lima rather than the real needs of the countryside.

Take Fujimori's paradoxical political style. On the one hand, it seemed ultimately democratic, in the sense that the president answered directly to the mass of voters through television and occasional elections. Fujimori enjoyed a fair amount of popular support most of the time because voters were tired of political gridlock. On the other hand, he coddled the armed forces, coopted or marginalized the opposition, and concentrated power in his own hands. His 1993 constitution, restoring democracy after his "self-coup," thinned out political participation, both in the national legislature and locally. It weakened regional governments by having their governors appointed from Lima. It also thwarted local officials who had run against Fujimori's slate earlier that year, by redesigning the tax system to cut municipal revenues by 79 percent. To replace local budgets, it set up a new fund to be doled out wholly at the whim of the president for political aims.[16]

One might ask if such dubious tactics really mattered, as long as they brought about a modest spending increase in the countryside. Perhaps the poorest of the poor need leaders just like Fujimori, a shrewd president who knows how to buy votes. That is what the poor have to sell, after all. Perhaps that is all one can expect from democracy: one wet finger determining the wind of public opinion, and one hand tossing out some coins. For a time, many Peruvians drew that conclusion. But two realities should give pause to anyone tempted to agree. First, aid given for political advantage has little if any lasting impact on local needs. Second, and more importantly, it is dangerous to entrust one's political fate to a leader who, when one scratches the surface, advances interests and ideals contrary to one's own.

For Fujimori was not just a self-seeking politician who could take the pulse of the electorate. Had he been so, his presidency might have illustrated the degradation of modern politics, but it would not have been harmful as such. Indeed, he would probably have thrown more money at the peasantry simply because of its numbers. To understand Fujimori and the distance between him and the mountain folk, we have to view his agenda from a broader perspective.

Fujimori's regime was typical of that era in Latin American and global politics. In the fevered days of market reforms in the 1990s, no-nonsense leaders like Fujimori came into their own across much of the world. Peru was not alone in losing what little democratic substance its institutions had had. Elsewhere, too, a pattern of "delegative democracy" prevailed: balloting every few years, and carte blanche in between for the president to carry out policies of his choosing. The president and his advisors were so-called "technopols" who could crunch the numbers of overall economic performance but also had the tough-minded political savvy to overcome opposition. Most politicians of Fujimori's ilk did not go so far as to suspend legislatures and rewrite constitutions. But they all put the niceties of democratic participation aside when it got in the way of their agenda.[17]

That agenda had little to do with backwaters like Pomatambo. The hinterlands just happened to have the votes, and those were attached to people poor enough to be won over by modest short-term spending. Peasants are right in concluding that one theme has stayed constant over the years: the highlands have never been a priority. The real agenda of Fujimori et al. was market-led development, which had quite different beneficiaries. Observers have noted that his presidency responded to expert advisors, international bankers, the export and finance sectors, and a network of political cronies. Unsurprisingly, his policies focused on efficiency as measured by macroeconomic indicators like inflation and GDP growth, not on equity across classes. The influential business interests around him tended to think of popular resistance to their agenda as mere "political noise" to be ignored or bought off. The moneyed classes had captured the state. They just happened to be a little more diverse than the old Spanish-descended oligarchy. Now their ranks included Asian immigrants and some provincial *nouveaux riches* who saw Fujimori as one of their own.[18]

Fujimori's allegiance to a small, prosperous, and hard-driving part of Peru's population was clear. Handouts to the poor fit into a larger political game that allowed the broader probusiness agenda to go forth. Peasants in places like Pomatambo were a means to an end, not an end in themselves. Small wonder that the inbred and manipulative practices of this political circle brought about its downfall as the new decade began. Fujimori only narrowly won a third term in 2000 amid allegations of electoral fraud. Then a video surfaced of one of his closest advisors attempting to bribe a legislator. As the opposition tightened the noose later that year, Fujimori resigned unexpectedly while abroad. He took refuge in Japan to avoid facing charges of corruption and brutality.

After a caretaker presidency, the 2001 election to succeed Fujimori was won by Alejandro Toledo, who had failed to defeat him a year earlier. The Toledo years offered still more evidence of the disconnect between Peru's political and economic elites and the rural poor. Personally, Toledo seemed very much a man of the people. He grew up in a peasant family that had moved to one of the northern coastal cities. In his teens, he had even worked as a shoeshine boy. Thanks to the help and encouragement of Peace Corps volunteers, he won a scholarship to the United States and eventually completed a doctorate in education at Stanford. Toledo's campaign played up this story of the poor boy who had made it. At last, the presidential palace in Lima would be occupied by a man who looked just like the highlanders and came from the same humble roots. Unsurprisingly, Vilcashuamán district went 74 percent for him in the 2001 runoff.[19]

In office, the story turned out differently. The new president's policies bore little fruit for those who remained poor. He carried on Fujimori's promarket policies, negotiating free-trade treaties with several countries and privatizing some state-owned companies. For the five years of his presidency, Peru had a high rate of overall economic growth: about 6 percent per year, with low inflation. Foreign investors loved the economic climate and poured money into the energy sector. As usual, however, this growth mostly remained in a few prosperous enclaves and did not trickle down. Toledo's approval rating sank to the single digits by 2004, and he faced protests across the spectrum, from teachers to coca-growers.[20]

Pomatambans told me that they had received less aid from Toledo than they had from Fujimori. The highlands slid further off the radar screen of Lima policymakers once the men with guns were killed or captured. The little aid that did come under Toledo fit the usual pattern. Consider the Juntos program, started in late 2005 for the poorest of the poor. It pays a modest sum of a hundred soles (about $30) a month to selected mothers of children under fourteen. Observers have noted political cronyism in its administration and the targeting of aid for short-term electoral gain.[21] As of 2006, thirty-eight Pomatamban mothers had qualified for support, which mostly pays for children's food, shoes, and clothing. To remain eligible, the recipients have to meet benchmarks for keeping children healthy and at school. Where household cash income averages only 150 soles a month, this cash handout undoubtedly makes a difference. But it is not so much. A teacher's salary is six to ten times that. Thirty dollars a month will not get you far in the cash economy.

When Juntos started, recipients had to pick up their cash in the city of Ayacucho, which meant that they spent a quarter of it on the round-trip bus fare. Now they can get it in Vilcashuamán. For a couple of days around the end and beginning of each month, a crowd of women in colorful Andean shawls snakes around the square and down one of the side streets, like a vast bread line waiting for a handout. Significantly, not many villagers mentioned it as a major form of state assistance—fewer mentioned it than the health post, for example, on which the same budget might more usefully have been spent.

Given their experiences, Pomatambans are disenchanted with the political class. Their frustration came out in the June 2006 presidential election. Most villagers hoped that whoever won would be better than

Toledo. The second-round runoff pitted two candidates against one another. One was Alan García, the former president who had left office in 1990 with a 5 percent approval rating. Despite his abysmal record, he had been his party's best bet to recapture the presidency. Against him stood a former army officer named Ollanta Humala. Countrywide, García triumphed 48 percent to 43 percent, with 9 percent of voters spoiling their ballots. In the southern highlands, however, Humala received an overwhelming majority. Vilcashuamán district gave 72 percent of its votes to him, 14 percent to García, and 14 percent blank or spoiled.[22] Since voting is mandatory, some of the blank or spoiled votes may have been gestures of protest against both candidates, though election observers have also said that the ballot is confusing to peasants who cannot read and have to rely on catchy symbols.

Most Pomatambans based their support for Humala on general impressions. He presented himself as the populist candidate. People said that they did not care for establishment politicians like García or Lourdes Flores, a probusiness candidate who came in third in the first round. Such figures knew nothing about poverty and were surrounded by millionaires who hardly wanted to share their wealth. Humala promised to pay attention to the poor and to spend much more on the countryside. His own history added to the image. He came from a family of ethnonationalist activists in Ayacucho, and like every soldier had slept in villages during the war. "He knows what it's like to suffer," they said. Humala had supposedly been involved in atrocities while fighting Sendero, but for Pomatambans that charge carried little weight. After all, no one from that era had clean hands, and Humala was running against the same man who had overseen the government's war effort from his presidential palace in Lima.

The victorious García enjoyed the confidence of few Pomatambans. The handful who had voted for him did so largely for random personal reasons, like good memories of finding work in Lima when it had a mayor from the same party. Most villagers had only bad recollections of his first presidency. They blamed him for the army's heavy-handed counterinsurgency strategy, including the 1986 massacre of local leaders, and for the hyperinflation of the late 1980s. Ignacio, for example, fumed at García as a "shameless murderer" because of how his incompetent policies had burdened the poor. He even insisted, a mere week into García's new term, that there were already signs of prices going up.

Few had faith that García would deliver development to people like them. They dismissed as "just talk" his promise to promote high-value export agriculture in the highlands. García had been newly incarnated as a moderate social democrat, careful and sober so as not to unnerve foreign investors. But the shift probably hurt his case with most Pomatambans, who remember him as quite changeable his first time in office. As if to confirm the usual pattern of Peruvian politics, the new president's approval rating dropped well below 50 percent within his first year in office.

The more things change, the more they stay the same. Andean peasants are understandably jaded about politics. They feel that despite all the sound and fury, no one really cares about them. Politicians come out to the countryside only at election time, spouting promises and "bringing a bit of bread." When they get into power they always forget the peasants, one of the road crew told me during the house-raising *minka*. The more the locals know about national politics, the more they affirm this conclusion. Quintín commented that the national budget has enough money to do more for the poor, but the high officials consume too much of it themselves. Nélida thought it ironic that the state supposedly belongs to all its citizens, while it really only serves the cities and ignores the Quechua-speaking highlanders.

This poor performance and unresponsiveness continue with each new generation. At most, the changings of the guard in Lima bring variations on a theme. When zealots do stir things up, as in the civil war, their efforts rarely reflect the values of the mountain folk. They impose one or another top-down vision, disconnected from the difficult but also very human reality of the rural poor.

Perhaps the saddest people of all in Pomatambo belong to the generation that first encountered the outside world in large numbers in the 1960s. That was a time of great expectations: that prosperity and opportunity were finally coming, that the political nerve centers were at last going to respond to the poor. Things were supposed to be so much better by now. As those now aging peasants look around at Pomatambo, they feel a profound disappointment.

One afternoon at Fortunato's home, I talked with him about all the changes of his lifetime, all that had and had not happened. We sat side by side on a bench covered with an old sheep hide. Just enough light came in through the walls of his humble adobe house to illuminate his lined face. He was tired and noncommittal. But one phrase stood out. A generation's frustrated hopes echoed in two words that rolled off his lips in Quechua-accented Spanish. He said them with no drama, just the stoicism and slightly plaintive tone familiar to anyone who has spent time among Andean peasants. *Olvidados somos.* "We're forgotten."

V

Peasantry of the Future

Fortunato's remark on feeling forgotten may have been a passing lamentation, but it was no less poignant because of that. Most of his fellow Pomatambans agree with him. The shortage of attention to Peru's rural backwaters has been both a burden and a blessing. Despite over four decades of rhetoric about developing the countryside, the policy of one after another government in Lima has added up to salutary neglect.

Sendero's efforts to remake these highland villages were far more intrusive than anything the state has undertaken. Sendero's radical vision would have turned a hearty fellowship into a joyless administered collec-

Fig. 5: Pomatambans at a village meeting to discuss a development project

tive. More harm was done to Pomatambo by the civil war—including the violence from both Senderistas and the army—than by generations of poverty. If outsiders who try their hands at changing the village have such effects, they might do better by leaving it alone.

The state's more or less hands-off approach has surely not been driven by any great sympathy for the Andean peasantry. These people continue to languish in poverty, with a host of daily deprivations and vulnerabilities that could easily be softened. They are simply not a priority for public or private investment. Very little aid has trickled in. Agencies may have planted a few trees, installed a water tank, and put an underequipped health post in an adobe building on the square, but the impact on the standard of living has been negligible. More prosperous parts of the world—even of the same country—continue to pull far ahead.

Peruvian governments have enacted countless laws dealing with peasant communities. They pay lip service to recognizing and respecting their way of life as "fundamental democratic institutions, autonomous in their organization, communal labor, and land use."[1] The rhetoric is belied by the form aid takes when it does come. The Juntos payments, for example, go to mothers in the hope of molding them—or rather their offspring—into productive and civilized citizens, by the state's definition. Rather than engaging the capabilities and values of the community, this kind of aid treats the community as more or less irrelevant to progress. The women who line up at the Vilcashuamán bank every month are seen as voters and as individuals with material needs. They just happen to live in villages. Give them a cash handout, along with some supposed benchmarks for how to raise their children, then monitor them every three months and see what happens. If the plan works, the children will be not only more capable and prosperous than their parents, but also a different human type. The village is neither part of the method nor part of the goal.

This is but one example, but it brings us to a broader issue. Take all the schemes that have been articulated for how to better the lot of the peasantry—the military government's, Sendero's, Fujimori's, García's, and so on. To be charitable, let us assume that all these political actors have had genuinely good intentions of bringing development to the poorest of the poor. They may have gone about it ineptly, they may have overlooked some details, and they may not have made it a high priority. But let us assume for the sake of argument that their hearts were in the right place. An inescapable fact remains. None of these visions came from the peasantry itself. Indeed, these efforts have been oddly disconnected from the lives and values of the supposed beneficiaries. The future is supposed to come despite these communities rather than in partnership with them.

When Peru's decision-makers survey the future of the highlands, they see it through this lens. They want to change the landscape of the countryside in order to bring to it economic dynamism. The optimists among them have as much go-getting energy as some of the would-be entrepreneurs among Pomatambo's floating migrants. They think they know the right policies to lift rural folk out of poverty and help them join the modern world.

In August 2006, I talked with one such optimist. Otto Castro Mendoza was at the time the *alcalde* (loosely, mayor) of Vilcashuamán province, with its roughly thirty thousand inhabitants. Now in his forties, he had been born in Vilcashuamán. After living in Lima from 1989 to 1992, he had come back to the area and had been in local politics ever since, taking office as *alcalde* in 2003. He had always been a member of the Popular Christian Party, a moderate promarket bloc. He had won that election with a respectable margin, doing somewhat better in the town of Vilcashuamán than in the countryside. His accomplishments in office so far had included setting up a technical institute in town, carrying out an archaeological inventory of the area for future tourism, and paving the way for rural electrification.

To prevent a return by Sendero or a similar movement, the *alcalde* told me, the province must offer people employment and opportunity. It needs improvement in education and health as well as technical aid to agriculture. Politics is both a science and an art; it is about finding new solutions to old problems and understanding what people really need. He said that he had kept in touch with the countryside by visiting outlying villages about three or four times each month. He added that he thought he was serving people by holding office, but that it was a drain personally. He could earn much more in business, after all, and sooner or later he would have to think of his future.

He explained that the most difficult part of his job was "developing the people—improving bad behavior," then launched into a litany of frustration. "They don't want to change themselves. They're not forward-looking, they don't have vision, they haven't traveled. They have everything here but they always look for the easy way out." To catalyze the area's economy, habits would have to change. The farmers needed to work more and not just count on getting by. "They're used to being lazy. They only work from eleven to three every day." Some of the same mentality of trying to get something for nothing lingered in town, too, he added. The townsfolk in Vilcashuamán pay no fees for water, which sets a bad precedent of getting things free of charge. The state cannot afford to pay for all the projects in the countryside that people want. If they need a school, for example, they should fall back on *minka* as a cheap way of building it. But that would not happen, because *minka* had died out and now people only work for cash.

Some of what the *alcalde* said struck me as odd. *Minka* had been largely revived in the area, for one thing. And if Pomatambans only worked from late morning to early afternoon, why was it so hard to find them at home after breakfast, when they went out to one or another task? The peasant ideal is for a married couple to rise early and go to the field to work. To delay is shameful, because you have to rely on yourself to eke out a living.[2] When I later mentioned this lazy and happy-go-lucky image of rural life to one of my friends, he laughed. He said it seemed a bit out of touch, like the visitor to the jungle who saw everyone snoozing during the daytime heat but failed to understand that they preferred to work at night when the temperature dropped.

But I do not want to dwell on how accurate the *alcalde*'s ideas about peasants were. Perhaps the fellow had had some discouraging experiences. More interesting were his plans for the future. With his hands clasped atop his spotlessly polished office desk, he eagerly laid out a vision, shared by many policymakers in the developing world, for how to jump-start the rural economy. Globalization and free trade would bring opportunity. Peru was debating ratification of a free-trade treaty with the United States that year, and the *alcalde* firmly supported it. Trade was the surest route to progress. It would bring down walls and do away with discrimination based on class or race or country, "because we're all human beings."

He argued that with the right kind of trade, rural Vilcashuamán could boom. It could find outlets to export agricultural products, and maybe bring in industry, too. Better education would give people marketable skills so that they did not have to move to the cities and find dead-end jobs as servants or become criminals. A flourishing rural market would let his constituents develop their talents. In an interesting twist on how many economists think, he added that development did not have to mean rural-to-urban migration. Capital could just as well come into the countryside. Along with export farming, for example, Vilcashuamán should develop its tourism sector. If they paved the road from Ayacucho and put in better infrastructure—hotels, restaurants, Internet access, a reliable water supply, and the like—tourists would flock to see the many ruins in the area. Tourism could generate plenty of income and employment here, just as it had in Cuzco.

Alongside trade and better infrastructure, the *alcalde* argued that education was the best way to move things forward. During the next twenty years, the schools need real reforms, he said. Today's teachers are not innovative enough; that is why Peru lags behind countries like Japan and the United States, and even Brazil and China. Better education adapted to the needs of the area would bring real economic payoffs.

Many policymakers agree with Vilcashuamán's *alcalde*. The idea of education as panacea has become popular around the world. In Chile, for instance, it has been a point of consensus between left and right as that country has experienced rapid growth.[3] If Peru and Chile had not been embroiled in a border dispute at the time, perhaps the *alcalde* would have mentioned Chile among the countries he admired. Wherever this focus on education prevails, the left supports it because the poor want education as a ticket to social mobility. The right likes it because a trained workforce is good for business. And having education as a priority means not having to tackle the thornier questions of rich versus poor, the power structure and temper of society, and the like. It is a win-win strategy, an easy way out, politically.

But the *alcalde*'s interest in education made sense for other reasons, too. As our conversation meandered through various topics, he kept mentioning the word "decentralization." He used the term in an unusual way. Against the background of everything else he said, I realized that he meant something more like *dispersion*. Trade and opportunity would disperse the benefits of the global economy even to poor and remote backwaters like Vilcashuamán. The market needs a way in to work its magic. The vision and the model are there for the taking and have already delivered success elsewhere. Apart from some tweaking of policies, the main obstacle is the hidebound mentality of peasants who cling to their ways and fail to embrace the ready-made solution to their poverty.

When he tossed around the world "decentralisation," it seemed off-key. What he intended was clear enough. But the word "decentralisation" usually conjures up quite another image. It means giving smaller units more control over what happens to them. It means moving decision-making down to local communities. In the highlands, decentralization would imply empowering villages like Pomatambo. But I realized that our *alcalde* could not possibly mean that. To empower villages like Pomatambo would be to empower people like Pomatambans. Still more alarmingly, it would be to empower them collectively, in their village assemblies, where their views would feed off one another. To empower backward people who lack initiative and only want to get by would work against progress. It would make it harder to adopt the ready-made models of market economics.

The *alcalde* struck me as a sincere man and an able administrator. I am sure he genuinely wants the best for the countryside as he sees it. Moreover, his views have a long lineage and plenty of support among other decision-makers across the global South. We have to take them seriously, for in many ways they are the prevailing image of the future. As an official in a poor and mostly rural area, he had translated the promise of market-driven globalization into its most popular form.

The *alcalde*'s vision of rural Vilcashuamán has support among some of his constituents, too. It mirrors the enthusiasm of Alberto, the would-be exporter of guinea pigs. The energy of some of Pomatambo's commerce-minded migrants would have plenty of outlets in the kind of market-driven rural economy that the *alcalde* envisions. And for people who find Andean village customs suffocating, the global market promises freedom—and a swift kick to their more lethargic neighbors.

But such supporters and would-be supporters are a minority. Most folk in the villages know all too well to be suspicious of outside modern experts who think that their habits need changing. They encounter them often enough and do not much like them. The outside experts admit as much. PRONAMACHS recently produced a report on why its projects in the area had not been more successful, and particularly on why relations with the locals were strained. More than a few passages dripped with contempt for the supposed passivity and poor organization of the villages. Without a market to drive output, the report commented, people lack dynamism.

But the report also quoted peasants from throughout the area: "Sometimes the experts lose control of their mouths and offend us, which isn't right." "They're highhanded. They don't greet you; you have to greet them first. They act as if they're in their own homes. They stay for a couple of hours then they go." "They're confusing. They humiliate us, practically calling us beggars when they say, 'You only know how to wait for help from institutions, but nothing about working.'"

The PRONAMACHS report offered suggestions for developing improved rapport with the peasants. Its authors no doubt took the problem seriously and wanted to make things work better. The report advised the organization's employees to tread more lightly. But it never stopped using words like *sensibilizar* (sensitize or, loosely, to make more conscious) to describe what they needed to do to the locals. Being more careful was a better means to the same end. Instead of proposing ideas themselves and provoking opposition, for example, they should plant those ideas in subtle ways so that the proposals, when they came up in village meetings, would seem more credibly to come from the peasants themselves.[4]

Now I know that working with the poor in traditional communities can be frustrating. We should not put undue blame on PRONAMACHS advisors or the *alcalde* or anyone else who expresses such sentiments. Sometimes inertia does need to be overcome. Sometimes a well-meaning outsider can only do what he or she thinks is right, even if it means trying to persuade a meeting of peasants to go in directions they might not go otherwise. That is ethically not vastly different from when a community leader tries to get a project underway against opposition.

Yet beyond these frustrations lies a deeper pattern. A common thread among those who want to catalyze this kind of rural development is that their desired model comes to these villages from the outside. To prosper, peasants have to join the outside world as it is. Their villages as they are today have little to offer in defining the model. They sit at the bottom of the world, the way up is clear, and moving up means moving away, in spirit if not in geography. Indeed, the habits—nay, the whole ethos—of these villages are part of the problem rather than part of the solution. Progress for peasants means overcoming what they are right now.

At the same time, the prevailing vision of the future contains an odd tension within it. On the one hand, it barely conceals a contempt for the poor of the developing world and insists that their whole mindset needs to be changed. On the other hand, it suggests that such people are a natural constituency for the global market economy. All human beings are *homo economicus* if you look at them the right way. They have a wont to truck and barter, to take advantage of opportunities in the market if conditions are ripe.[5] If they are set free by the right policies, if obstacles are removed, then even people like Pomatambo's villagers will take to the market economy like ducks to water. This tension between a disdain for peasants' backwardness and a confidence that such folk are really on the globalists' side after all does not mean that proponents of this vision are contradicting themselves. But it does mean that they have a peculiar image of the poor—as partly suffocated by circumstances and deluded about what they want, but also as lively producers and consumers and individualists if such distortions are removed.

Perhaps the best-known advocate in recent years of market-led globalization along these lines is Hernando de Soto. The Peruvian-born economist has become one of the most influential public intellectuals in the world. After receiving his education in Europe and making a fortune in business, he returned to Peru in the midst of the civil war. He entered the policy debate with two goals: making free-market capitalism a success in Peru as it had been in the developed world, and mapping a way out of poverty that could draw the poor away from Sendero's radicalism. His 1987 book was fittingly titled *El otro sendero* (*The Other Path*). His visibility grew over the next decade, and in 2000 he published a bestselling follow-up book, *The Mystery of Capital,* which put the issues in more global perspective.[6]

De Soto argued that the poor suffer because they are excluded from much of the capitalist economy. The market is not allowed to work properly for them. To make his case, de Soto focused on the so-called informal sector, the street peddlers and shantytown dwellers who make up much of Lima's swelling population. They are known for living outside the legal economy. They wheel and deal without permits or contracts, do not keep bank accounts or pay taxes, and erect their tin-roofed shacks on untitled land.

With a team of research assistants, de Soto delved into how the poor of the informal sector operate outside the law, and above all why they decide to do so. He found that to play by the rules would impose unbearable delays and costs. His team tested how long it would take to go through all the legal steps of registering a small business and found that it added up to 289 days and cost more money than many of the poor could earn in that time. To title land in a shantytown would take nearly seven years. In short, the informal sector operated outside the law because the law had too much red tape. The peddlers, shantytown dwellers, and under-the-radar small shops and minibus companies did get by. But without easy access to the protections of the law—especially contracts and property rights—they stayed mired in poverty.

By framing the issue in this way, de Soto challenged received wisdom on the left. For Sendero as well as for more moderate leftists, the key fault line was between rich and poor. The poor in Lima and elsewhere were poor because they were oppressed by capitalism. The market economy worked to keep them down, whether by intention or as a byproduct of other people's success. According to de Soto, however, the real fault line was not between rich and poor, but between legality and illegality. A few entrepreneurs of the informal sector were making a fair amount of money, for example, even though their energies were often frustrated by lack of access to the formal economy and its protections. Peru's red tape bred stagnation, cronyism, and bribery. The poor of the informal sector were discontented and found Sendero tempting not because they were oppressed by the market, but because they were denied full access to it.

In short, de Soto was saying that the poor needed more capitalism, not less. Like all human beings, they had an innate aptitude for commerce. By cutting red tape and redesigning institutions, a right-minded government could set their energies free and bring them into full economic life, benefiting everyone. Peru needed "a market and social revolution against economic poverty and legal oppression." That meant creating "legal systems where the assets of all citizens can be securely held and moved to their best possible use." The informal sector would be connected to the "oases of legality" and thus enjoy the same protections. Living standards would rise. This "other path" was the alternative to Sendero's class struggle and expropriation of wealth. The poor would come out of the shadows and join in global capitalism rather than stand by and resent it.

The argument about senseless red tape struck a chord with many of de Soto's readers. As in most developing countries, trying to accomplish even simple tasks in Peru can cause immense frustration. I experienced Peruvian paperwork firsthand during my visit in 2006, for example, when I had to buy a motorcycle to get back and forth from Vilcashuamán to Pomatambo every day. After asking around mechanics' workshops in Ayacucho, I found a battered but sturdy 1974 Yamaha. Doing the transfer turned out to be a headache. I learned that very few vehicles in Ayacucho have all their papers in order. The motorcycle was still registered to its original owner, who had long since died. The fellow selling it to me had a series of sales contracts linking various owners to one another, but none back to the original owner. A chuckling notary told me that to put things right would take a judicial process of several months. Eventually we just drew up another one of the doubtful contracts and got a notary's stamp on it to lend it an air of legality. Then I rode around for six weeks carrying the dead original owner's yellowed registration card as if he had lent the motorcycle to me. I resold it the same way when I left. No one thought the process at all odd.

De Soto's efforts did lead to some reduction of red tape in the 1990s. His Institute for Liberty and Democracy helped shape a range of Fujimori-era economic and legal reforms. (The Institute's prominence even led Sendero to bomb its offices.) According to de Soto and his circle of admirers, Sendero's defeat was largely on the level of ideas. Supposedly the poor had come to grasp that their best bet lay in entering fully into the market, not waging a war against it.

That version of history has its gaps. Sendero's defeat had more to do with its bloody excesses and the fortuitous capture of Abimael Guzmán and the rest of its leadership. Moreover, despite some deregulation, Peru's informal sector has not shrunk. The shantytowns and transactions at the edge of the law go on, and the poor still live in squalor. And most of de Soto's reform efforts focused on the urban poor, not the peasantry in places like Pomatambo. One would be hard pressed to find any aspect of rural life that has changed because of his "other path."

In thinking about rural development, therefore, de Soto's ideas are relevant not because they have effected change, or even because they represent a particularly active political movement. They clearly align with the vision of the *alcalde* and the would-be rural entrepreneurs, but circumstances have kept that vision mainly on the level of talk, so far. Rather, de Soto's perspective on the excluded and their needs is interesting because it represents the best face global capitalism can present to the poor of the developing world. It is a sincere, principled, and comprehensive model. And while it has yet to penetrate to most backwaters as policy, it will surely do so given enough time. In the world as it is, such a "market revolution" is the most likely way that the future will arrive in these communities and remake them. As a vision, it helps us throw into stark relief what is at stake.

So what *is* at stake? Despite the way de Soto and his fellow travelers frame their agenda, it is not just about making economic activity easier. It would also profoundly alter the texture of economic and cultural life. It would change how the poor relate to what they own, and how what they own fits into the global economy. In his two books, de Soto argued that giving people land title lets them engage in long-term economic planning. The untitled plots and huts that the poor own are not real assets that can be bought, sold, or mortgaged. An aspiring small-business owner, for example, cannot take out a loan because he or she lacks a convertible asset as collateral. The poor are left out of the fluidity of a modern capitalist economy because they cannot get the property they own to work for them. Yet their property is significant. De Soto estimated that the "dead capital" in Peru, in the form of extralegally held urban and rural real estate, adds up to $74 billion, far more than all the legally recognized property. And across the developing world, the poor have some $9.3 trillion of "dead capital" locked up in land and houses without clear title.

The idea of setting free this dead capital to empower the poor and jump-start the economy has percolated through Peru's political class. Vilcashuamán's *alcalde* seemed to take a page from de Soto when he held forth to me on the lack of legal title in his area. He said that many of his constituents buy and sell property by relying on wills and previous contracts to prove what they own. Without a unified land registry, they cannot fall back on an incontestable title if a problem arises. Few people even in the town of Vilcashuamán have straightforward property titles. According to the *alcalde,* that is why they do not invest in improving their land. They just subsist in their insecurity. If they had clear legal ownership, they could mortgage and sell their property more easily and generate capital for small businesses.

Nevertheless, efforts to carry out the de Soto agenda have been few and far between. Fujimori was sympathetic to the issue of private land title, but his government paid more attention to the shantytowns. Land tenure in the countryside rarely changed during his presidency. His land-titling program was primarily concerned with settling disputes concerning the boundaries of communities. It did not succeed in Pomatambo, the boundaries of which remain debated on all sides. Under the law, to settle those boundaries once and for all would require a two-thirds vote of the residents of both villages involved.[7] Mediating such conflicts was not a priority for the Fujimori government.

The most dramatic implication of de Soto's logic concerns titling individual plots *within* highland villages. No one thought it worthwhile in the 1990s to wade into this delicate and murky question. But the preferences of Fujimori and those around him were clear. If they had their druthers, agricultural land would be privatized. Two 1997 laws paved the way. State-owned land with farming potential was opened for sale to private investors, and it was made easier for coastal communities to decide by majority vote to break up their communal lands into individual plots. Doing so was supposed to encourage "the exercise of private initiative." Likewise, a program of surveying and titling rural land started in 2000 under the caretaker government between Fujimori and Toledo. It aimed explicitly at creating a rural market in land. Throughout these years, the language of private enterprise was applied more and more to the rural sector.[8]

Most highland peasants did not welcome these ideas when they got wind of them. A few Pomatambans had pushed for legally recognized private title during the violence, when people were coming and going and trust had broken down. But most locals believed that Fujimori's plan would have caused conflicts among neighbors. Land that had long been occupied and improved would be opened to all kinds of competing claims and manipulation. Remember that villagers already have *de facto* private ownership of houses as well as the most productive irrigated land. As long as they continue using it and stay on good terms with their neighbors, no one questions their ownership. Only if they move away for long periods or breach local norms might they have to appeal to legal title and outside authorities. Pomatambans felt that a concerted effort to register all land would cause more trouble than it would prevent.

That reaction was to a mild version of the land-titling agenda, which would only have formalized existing private plots. I suspect that if done in the right spirit, papering facts on the ground could do more good than harm. But the real threat to the community is from a much stronger version of the agenda, which would break up all communal land into private tracts. The community as a whole would own nothing except its meeting hall, square, and streets. This long-term goal lurks behind the "market revolution."

Pomatambans have never been faced with this possibility, but I did get a sense from other peasants of how strong the reaction would be. In 1995, even before my first visit to Pomatambo, I spent a day at Huanta, a town to the north of Ayacucho, attending a meeting of peasant leaders from several communities. The area is known for its intact Andean traditions and its strong peasant organizations. At one point, it led the way in setting up militias to counter Sendero's depredations and the threat of collectivization.[9] The meeting that day touched on many topics, but one of them was a tentative proposal from Lima to privatize community lands. The peasants in attendance murmured in disapproval once they understood what it meant. One of the first fears to arise was that richer villagers would take advantage of the land market to buy out poorer ones. Land ownership would become concentrated in a few hands, and poorer peasants would become landless.

Perhaps these fears were exaggerated, perhaps not. But studies have been done of what happens when agricultural land passes from communal to private ownership. On the one hand, privatization raises the incentives to adopt new technology. It can also lessen the ecological mismanagement of land—if the older community enforcement mechanisms have already broken down. On the other hand, privatization increases inequality. The gap between winners and losers widens, and the losers have less of a safety net on which to fall back. Fragmentation of communal land into individual plots also leads to a climate of individualism.[10]

Peasants who today live in communities with customs of mutual aid and a large portion of communal land are no fools. They sense that privatization would quite literally shift the ground beneath their feet. They foresee the insecurity that would result and how their way of life would change. The norms of Andean culture rest on an economic base that mixes communal land and individual plots.

I have seen firsthand the end result of a process of privatization. My first visit to the Andes in 1992 was not to Peru, but to Ecuador. I spent two months as a volunteer in a highland community composed of small-holders. They all spoke Spanish; as in much of Ecuador and northern Peru, Quechua had died out with an older generation. But the biggest difference, I was to realize years later, between this village and a village like Pomatambo was not in language. Rather, it was in how people related to one another.

This village had been fragmented into individual plots for some time. Everyone had some land, but rich and poor were clearly further apart than in Pomatambo. A more fundamental difference was in community spirit. People in that Ecuadorean village got together for meetings now and then and were perfectly hospitable and civil, but there was rarely cooperation approaching the level of *ayni* and *minka*. Plots were farmed separately. The level of trust was lower. One evening I was mulling over where to leave a couple of empty wire crates that had held seedlings for planting. Since a truck would come the next morning to pick them up,

I proposed to my host that we leave them nearer the dirt road than his house. "No, no," he exclaimed, gathering up the crates and trotting off to lock them away. "They're all thieves around here."

People experience the world and themselves through the texture of daily life. Reshaping their values requires only modest changes in how they make a living and how they think about what they own. If a government in Peru—or in any similar country, for that matter—vigorously pushed the privatization agenda, it would destroy the economic underpinnings of strong peasant communities. To do so against peasants' own misgivings suggests a rather cavalier attitude toward how the rural poor think and what they want.

But as we have seen, the neoliberal or market-revolution vision assumes that the poor will be better off in the long run. A more competitive economy, with "live" rather than "dead" capital, will raise incomes. And as for peasant values, well, they are part of the problem. An aversion to risk-taking and innovation prevents peasants from leaping into the future. If carrying out the neoliberal vision means riding roughshod over peasants' values for a while, so be it. Their computer-programming grandchildren will prove more enlightened about what had to happen.

This is roughly the argument made by politicians like the *alcalde*. It is also, of necessity, the kind of argument on which people like de Soto must rely when they run into the difficult fact that some—frankly, most—of the poor in the developing world are not really market enthusiasts. They must insist, in effect, that progress inherently involves overcoming the present, but the future thanks us for it.

As a vision, the "market revolution" is well-intentioned. De Soto and its other intellectual proponents advocate it because they find the ideas consistent and compelling. Among the political class, officials like the *alcalde* are close to realities on the ground. Their constituency is the rural poor. They translate the vision into the benefits that they think it would bring, if given a chance. And energetic, ambitious people like Alberto, the guinea-pig entrepreneur, share many of these assumptions about the best way for them to prosper and for those around them to escape stagnation. To doubt the likely effects of this vision on community values is not, by any means, to impugn the motives of those who now want to see it implemented.

137

All these thoughtful people take the countryside seriously. The mere fact that they reflect on how to bring rural folk into the global market shows as much. They could simply dismiss the peasantry and focus their energies elsewhere, after all. Many others do just that, including most of the powerful decision-makers in countries like Peru. One observer of Peruvian agricultural policy over the last two decades has noted, in this vein, that it has more or less written off small farmers. When it encourages agriculture at all, it focuses on the large export-oriented agribusiness companies, which are located mainly on the coast.[11] Ministers in Lima have assumed for half a century that economic growth will happen mostly on the coast and in more prosperous cities like Arequipa. The poor will have to move where the jobs are if they want to better their lot.

This neglect of the highland poor has driven the vast demographic shift of the last two generations. Few people abandon the villages of their birth for good unless they have to. All else being equal, those who leave during times of trouble come back once things settle down. But they see the development happening on the coast and in parts of the cities, and they vote with their feet. Since the most enterprising and talented have the most to gain, they are usually the first out in every generation. Migration drains energy from the countryside, and the vicious cycle of stagnation and departure continues.[12]

A common thread unites the well-intentioned vision of a "market revolution" and the out-migration driven by a less well-intentioned neglect of the countryside. That common thread is the assumption that progress for peasants means turning them into something other than peasants. The "market revolution" and out-migration differ only on whether peasants should stay put and turn into rural entrepreneurs, or move to the cities as urban employees instead. Either way, peasants must become something other than what they are now. The basis of their livelihood must change, and along with it their thinking and values. Only in that way can they take part in the booming globalized economy of the twenty-first century.

This assumption that progress means the disappearance of the peasantry's way of life is pervasive, but it does not get anywhere near the attention that it should. Some reasons are obvious. Politicians in a democracy—even a superficial one—would be committing electoral suicide if they told a large chunk of voters that a policy they support, if successful, would mean those voters' disappearance. And as we have seen, few Pomatambans fear that their customs are under threat today. They assume that they can have the goods of development without losing their way of life in the process. But if experience elsewhere is a guide, when global-market-driven change finally does come, they will have neither the time nor the power to do much about it.

There are also deeper reasons why this blithe acceptance of the peasantry's disappearance goes unexamined. In the second half of the twentieth century, the debate on all sides has been framed in ways that discourage the question from being raised. No major political force in Peru or elsewhere has imagined the economic future as anything other than an overcoming of the premodern. Rather than offering a point of departure and a moral reference point for how to build the future, the premodern is simply contrasted with the future. Modernity is just a process of creative destruction that turns the one into the other. And what is more premodern—more timelessly and placelessly premodern—than the clodhopper with his field and hut? Moreover, no major political force has had the peasantry as its core support base. Many activists have come from peasant stock, to be sure. But they have all been energetically on their way out of the peasantry, and usually they have seen their movement of choice as a faster way to get other people out, too. Sympathy for the clodhopper, as clodhopper, has been absent. For all these reasons, the peasantry presumably has to go, sooner or later.

In the earlier chapters of this book, I made a point of tracing these changes from the bottom. I wanted to show how they looked from Pomatambo, as outside political and economic forces exerted pressure on these humble people. Their values and hopes always seemed to be either ignored or under attack. Now we can begin to see why. Neither the Peruvian state in its various incarnations nor Sendero ever offered a viable model of development that built on the aspirations of the peasantry itself. In 2006, I put this conclusion to my friends in Pomatambo, and they agreed wholeheartedly. For example, when I asked Nélida which side in the civil war had best aligned with the values of the community, she swiftly said neither. "We don't go with either one. What we uphold comes from the Andes."

Not only did these formidable political forces fail to offer a vision that appealed to the mountain folk. Whenever they acted with any energy, they made clear that they were hell-bent on destroying the best of these communities. Traditional authorities were shattered, slaughtered, or undermined for long enough to do real damage, even though, against the odds, they have come back for now. The sort of community leaders who would be empowered if either the state or Sendero had its way would be unsympathetic to the traditional values of the village. And mistrust, whether arising through fear or through the insecurity of a competitive free-for-all, would unravel the bonds that have long held Pomatambans together.

I know that in leveling this indictment of left, center, and right, in defense of these villages, I shall tempt some critics to accuse me of exaggerating. This is all very well, they will say, but surely the picture I paint is too bleak. How much is really lost when these communities change into something more modern? Anyone who urges protecting them from the modern world must spell out what is worth protecting.

This challenge deserves a serious response. One way of getting at what is at stake when these communities break down is to look in the near distance—close enough that we are dealing with roughly the same people but in different circumstances. Let us look at the city of Ayacucho, now swollen to some one hundred thousand inhabitants. Earlier I mentioned the rising crime rate, the directionless self-indulgence of so many of the young, and the breakdown of families.

But take a more specific example within that city. In 2006, I met a Belgian-French couple, both devout Catholics, who had set up an orphanage in a forsaken shantytown on the outskirts of town. Of the twenty-five or so mostly young children living there, several were disabled. Most of the orphans came to this softhearted couple after being found abandoned in the street, or even in a garbage dump. Apparently many single mothers in the city do not have the support network that would allow them to look after their children and make a living at the same time, now that traditional support structures have broken down.[13] As many older Pomatambans said to me, in the city no one will give you anything. But in a village like theirs, one can count on the informal safety net of kin and neighbors for both material and moral support. Indeed, the family of migrants that I know best has prospered in the city partly because they have enough extended kin, who moved at the same time, to provide a formidable support network. Then, too, the ways of the village run in their blood still.

Perhaps the modern world does not have to be marked by children starving in the streets, or shantytown barroom brawls splashed over tabloid headlines. But the shift of atmosphere from the traditional village to the modern city or suburb is unmistakable. Older peasants see it in their encounters with the outside world, even if most of them hope to insulate themselves from it by staying put in the countryside and keeping up the old customs. And countless modern folk look back with nostalgia at what they or their grandparents lost and try to reconstruct fragments of it here and there. The breakdown of community is a lived reality in the modern age. The mere facts that some people welcome it because they prefer the individualism it releases, and that the odd intellectual or politician tries to define the problem away by sleight of hand, do not mean that the average person is going to stop regretting it.

If you take seriously the perspective of these Pomatamban peasants, where are you left? To preserve what is valuable about their way of life means trying to keep at bay, indeed to roll back, the forces that have pressed against them for three generations. It means an economic, political, and cultural project of restoration. Anything less and we lose for good, sooner or later. The hitherto defenseless have to go on the offensive. And given that the forces on the other side span the whole globe, the project has to be universal enough to meet them on their own scale. It must defend a way of life, not a patch of land, or a language, or a people. The true value of places like Pomatambo is not that they are *Andean* communities, after all, but that they are Andean *communities*.

I insist on putting the issue this way because to defend something else would be to misdirect our efforts. For example, suppose we set out only to defend Andean culture in all its uniqueness. That would imply that global capitalism offends because it wipes out cultural diversity. Thus, someone who sees diversity as the goal will focus on preserving and emphasizing signs of Andean distinctiveness. Whatever else changes, they will be told, the next generation must cling to and prove its Andeanness. And since the modern world honors people who prosper, Andeans would do their culture a disservice by lagging behind. Fast-forward a bit, and we shall find a mass of self-affirming Andeans who have embraced the "market revolution" and become fully modern. Andeanness would in this way get reduced to the kind of superficial identity-mongering that now happens in the West. We would have a Quechua version of MTV, and perhaps the occasional bronze-skinned businessman wearing a colorful poncho at a party in Miraflores.

Or suppose, instead of cultural diversity, we said that the key issue is to affirm a small-scale sense of place. Those who take this tack fall into two camps. One camp is exemplified by the well-known Colombian-born anthropologist Arturo Éscobar. A critic of the prevailing vision of development, Éscobar sees hope in "the defense of territory by social movements." In the rain forest and elsewhere, he says, people at the edges of the modern world are crafting new "place-based practices" that give them some breathing space. They mix and match in a sort of premodern and postmodern mélange, creating room at the margins for a "postdevelopment" diversity. Global capitalism, however, remains "this impossibly large monster than cannot be transformed."[14] Éscobar and like-minded souls, drawn largely from the ranks of left-leaning anthropologists, do not offer a grand transformative vision for the world as a whole. They just seek the nooks and crannies for more humane living.

A second camp of defenders of place includes agrarians like the American social critic Wendell Berry. Over the last few decades, Berry has written voluminously in defense of an older way of life rooted in the land, all while trying to live out the ideal at his farm in Kentucky. He and his fellow travelers declaim against the relentless pressures of agribusiness and other efforts to wring unsustainable or irresponsible profits from the ground. They call for the creation of sustainable, well-diversified small farms, farms that might even be worked by horses and in any case give back to nature as much as they take out. Their agrarian ethos is infused with a reverence for the soil and an appreciation of the habits of mind that come from close contact with nature.[15] They are more unapologetically traditional than Éscobar and the anthropology crowd, and often deeply religious. In practice, however, they have pursued much the same strategy. They channel their energies away from far-reaching political change and into small-scale experiments in community and sustainability.

To be sure, both these defenses of place—that of the sympathetic anthropologists and that of the agrarians—have much to offer. By stressing the values of small-scale lives and lives lived close to the soil, they highlight some common ground between Pomatambo, say, and humble communities elsewhere in the world. And unlike those who would be happy merely to celebrate a cultural distinctiveness on the surface, they do not pave the way for the yuppie with an Andean hat. But they are still too focused on the particular. A defense of place may have its parallels across cultures, but it hardly travels well. It is, by definition, defensive on a thousand disconnected fronts. It merely tries to stave off the encroachments of a world order that remains a "large monster."

Unfortunately, monsters have insatiable appetites. I am reminded of the guinea pigs that often run back and forth amid sprouts of alfalfa on the floors of Andean kitchens. Every week or two, the cook might bend over to pick one up by the scruff of the neck and send it on its way to the dinner table. If you are a guinea pig, it might seem a sound strategy to hide by scuttling around the cook's feet so that she cannot see you past her skirts. But you will not outsmart the cook for long. Sooner or later you will find yourself paws-upward in the roasting pan.

Any real defense of what is valuable in communities like Pomatambo has to go on the offensive. Instead of scuttling back and forth and hoping not to be noticed, the guinea pigs have to take over the kitchen and turn the cook into a vegetarian. A restorationist project worthy of the name would change the broader environment in which these communities exist. An effort to remake the global landscape must start by putting what is at stake in truly universal terms—terms not bound to one place, or even to one activity such as cultivating the soil. Only that way can beleaguered communities speak a common language, link up, and export their values into the larger, more modern society.

To restore a way of life is much like restoring a building or a piece of furniture. It needs restoring because it has become worn, layered over with encrustations, or battered by mistreatment. Restoration starts with a clear idea of the object's true contours and lineaments. Working from that idea, you can painstakingly strip off the encrustations, repair the rips and tears, and bring the object back to its full beauty and functionality. That restoration does not necessarily mean bringing the object back to how it was at some specific moment in the past. If you want electric lights in an old stone cottage, you have to put in the wiring unobtrusively. If an antique table will get a lot of daily use, you have to add an extra layer of protective varnish. But with careful judgment and some elbow grease, you will end up with something beautiful and functional in its original sense, yet also suited to whatever new demands might be put on it.

It is the same with communities like Pomatambo. Restoration will not mean returning them to a golden age when all was perfect. It will not even mean preserving all the details of their customs as they are now. Rather, it will mean pondering their most essential values and how they can best be expressed. Simply put, these communities have been settings in which people practiced—or at least aspired to practice—some important virtues. The ethos of traditional peasant life is one of no-nonsense self-reliance, austere morality, self-command amid adversity, duty towards kin and neighbors, generosity, hospitality, participation, and the anchoring of one's livelihood in an atmosphere of decency and fairness. These virtues have been universally valued among peasant folk all over the world. The peasant community and its customs reflected such virtues and created the conditions for people to exercise them. For all their imperfections, peasants have demanded of themselves and others more than modern society expects.

Looked at this way, the challenge has little to do with preserving custom X or place Y for its own sake. It hinges instead on strengthening peasant communities' abilities to persist as arenas for the exercise of important virtues. After all, is living properly not the highest worldly end for human beings? Since daily experience in peasant communities has been shaped by the processes of making a living, economic life must be arranged to serve this end. We must judge any change in economic practice against its effect on the community's ongoing ability to favor virtue over vice. People's material needs should be satisfied with an eye to their spiritual and social needs as well. And if empowering these people economically will help them defend their communities and add weight to their values, then economic empowerment they must have.

The prevailing model of progress tries to drag peasants into the modern world so that they can prosper. Along the way, other sorts of people gain power and profit, and the peasant gets killed off as a social type. We need to turn this prevailing model upside down. Concretely, this means figuring out how to bring prosperity to the peasantry, *as a peasantry.* In its most essential characteristics—in its qualities of character and its sense of how to live—a peasantry consists of much more than the millions who till the soil. Its sturdy virtues arose in an agricultural setting, but they transcend that setting. Prosperity will mean shifting the economic base of these communities away from just agriculture; let there be no doubt about that. But the peasantry should be able to recognize itself across future generations.

This is the project of restoration. This is the battle of ideas we must wage across the developing world. This is the alternative to the "market revolution" of de Soto and the world's powerful and jaded. This alternative can speak to the peasantry in its own language. It can become tomorrow's chapter in the story of Pomatambo, but it can also become tomorrow's chapter for communities like Pomatambo all over the global South. Nearly half the people in the world are still peasants. Modern capitalism and a self-absorbed consumer culture are closing around them and promise to consign them to the ash-heap of history. They can go quietly, or they can push back with the stalwart self-confidence of their ancestors.

✦ ✦ ✦

Our thinking about how to restore a healthy peasantry and the distinctive virtues supported by peasant life can connect with a long tradition of economic and political thought. The peasantry has had its admirers

145

through the ages. Many thinkers have praised the simple virtues of rural life, especially in contrast to what they have seen as the corruption and crafty self-regard of urban commerce. The great ancient civilizations, including the Roman and Chinese empires, rested on agriculture. The agrarian ideal is given voice in classic works from Cicero to Mencius.[16]

Until modern times, however, much admiration for the peasantry was either sentimental or understated because so much of what the peasantry represented could be taken for granted. Not until recently could anyone imagine a world in which most people were anything other than peasants. Only with the rise of the modern world and disruption of traditional ways did the outlook tied up with agrarianism come under attack. That attack in turn called forth efforts to revive older modes of economic life. By the early twentieth century, these traditionalist strands of thought and experiments inspired by them had cropped up independently across the world.

Thinkers writing three or four generations ago did not face quite the juggernaut of global capitalism and the intrusive vision of a "market revolution" that we face today. Instead of a global backlash against modernity, mostly they were trying to revive older economic models from the past of their own societies. But while they framed their causes in less universal language than we shall have to use today, their perspectives are still helpful. A glance back at these earlier ideas can help us better think through the contours of a global peasant-based alternative for our own time.

Consider the so-called "distributists," who wrote in England between the 1910s and the 1930s. Their leading lights included G. K. Chesterton, Hilaire Belloc, and Arthur J. Penty.[17] Chesterton and Belloc were prolific writers whose joint efforts led George Bernard Shaw to dub them the "Chesterbelloc." They and others in this loose movement printed pamphlets, held debates, and even founded an experimental community. The distributists put forth their ideas at a time in Europe roughly corresponding to what Peru and much of the global South are undergoing today. The standard of living was in the same range. Very traditional and very modern ways of life existed side-by-side in the same countries. Moreover, Europe in those years was in the midst of an intellectual and political ferment that has been unmatched since. All alternatives seemed to be on the table, from Stalinism to syndicalism to anarchism to fascism.

Most distributists were devout traditional Catholics. They shared the misgivings about modern economic life that were articulated in the 1891 papal encyclical *Rerum Novarum*.[18] Just as that text had done, they tried to stake out a "third way" alternative to both capitalism and socialism. Capitalism offended human dignity because of its cutthroat profit-seeking and exploitation of the worker. Socialism offended because it urged bitter class conflict and threatened to suffocate the individual in a state-run collective. Distributists felt that the most humane economic life was that of the small farmer and independent craftsman. Property, including the means of livelihood, whether land or equipment, should be widely distributed to avoid a dependence of individuals on either big business or the state.

The distributist vision rested on a clear view of human nature and what made for satisfying work. Rather than just a means to stay alive, work was a form of self-expression. People who worked under the right conditions could exercise their free will and faculties with a purpose in mind. To be free, responsible, and productive, one had to own the instruments of one's work rather than obey a capitalist or commissar. Distributists looked askance at arguments that the modern world enjoyed greater efficiency because of its large-scale economic arrangements. Those arrangements were dehumanizing and subordinated ends to means. "The one and only real type of efficiency," insisted Chesterton, "is the turnip-headed rustic left alone with his turnip."

Hilaire Belloc mapped out a distributist version of economic history to explain how the world had changed in the modern era.[19] He identified medieval Europe as the best example of a distributist economy. After the collapse of Rome, slavery had gradually died out. Feudalism had softened into a society of widespread small farms that paid only limited dues to the lord of the manor, and urban craftsmen organized in independent guilds. A common Christian worldview regulated economic self-interest. The monasteries with their vast lands helped stabilize the system and provide a safety net for the poor. According to Belloc, this happy state broke down during the Reformation, when Henry VIII expropriated the monasteries and gave their land to the aristocracy.

This gift to the already wealthy made them wealthier still. It upset the equilibrium of English society and put the peasantry on the defensive. Against their lords and without a powerful clergy to champion them, they had no way to resist the later enclosure of common lands and the gradual dispossession of the poor. The industrial revolution then burst upon this landscape, leading to the floating and exploited workforce of the nineteenth century. By his own time, Belloc argued, the modern world had ended up with an unsustainable mix of political democracy and freedom of contract, on the one hand, and an extreme concentration of wealth and economic dependence on the other.

Belloc predicted one of three outcomes. Capitalism might give way to a state-run socialism, which would be just as suffocating of freedom and no more equal in practice. More likely, it would evolve into the "servile state," which would revive a kind of quasislavery: workers would have a guaranteed income, but as a class they would be compelled by law to work. Or, to avoid either of those dehumanizing outcomes, people could choose the distributist route and get back their freedom.

The distributists never organized a political movement around this alternative. Indeed, they have been called "populist[s] without a people" because, at least in England, there was no real class of smallholders left to mobilize. At most they could hope to re-create one.[20] So they limited themselves to writing, and a few set up a model medieval-style village of craftsmen in Surrey. They also developed some policy ideas for distributist-oriented political parties to adopt. Most of these measures involved moderate efforts to tip the playing field against big business. They included providing tax advantages for small enterprises, restoring agricultural self-sufficiency, bringing back regulatory guilds, curtailing the use of machinery in dehumanizing ways, and so on. If useful technology like the railroads had to operate on a grand scale, then ownership should be broken up into small shares or handled cooperatively. Eventually, some distributist ideas found their way into the guild-socialist movement that arose after World War I, but few ever had much enduring political impact.[21]

Indeed, these economic traditionalists believed that their vision could be realized only over the long term, not in a sudden political rupture. Belloc remarked, for example, that for most people a transition to h capitalism to socialism was easier to grasp than a transition back to distributism. "If modern capitalist England were made by magic a state of small owners, we should all suffer an enormous revolution. We should marvel at the insolence of the poor, at the laziness of the contented, at the strange diversities of task, at the rebellious, vigorous personalities discernible upon every side."

The distributists had counterparts elsewhere in the world in those decades. In China during the 1920s and 1930s, the so-called "last Confucian," Liang Shuming, tried to set up village cooperatives in Shandong. His movement for "rural reconstruction" offered a third way against both capitalist Westernization and the class struggle of the Communists. Liang hoped to build in those villages a type of development compatible with the Confucian spirit of emotional and ethical harmony. While the West was burdened with a dehumanizing urge to wring ever more material goods out of nature, China stressed the adjustment of one's desires to the needs of coexistence in a community.[22]

In India, Mohandas Gandhi similarly put forth an economic model centered on the villages. True independence from the West meant recovering the face-to-face scale and simple practices of premodern life, he taught. Even if some new technologies had their use, people lived best when they were self-sufficient. Real human satisfaction came from tempering one's appetites, not building ever more machinery to churn out consumer goods. Gandhi insisted that sustainable peace and equality could only flourish with a return to the villages.[23]

These are just a few examples of economic traditionalist thought in the early twentieth century. The emphases of these schools differed somewhat—the distributists stressed property and the dignity of work, Liang ethical harmony, and Gandhi a tranquil self-reliance—but they had obvious common ground. Of course, they also all failed. The distributists never made political headway, and some of their flirtations with other antiliberal movements of the era got them into trouble. Unfairly—but effectively—many liberals accused them of fascist sympathies. Liang lost because World War II shut down his rural reconstruction work; following that, the struggle for China came down to the Communists versus the Guomindang, neither of whom had any use for him. And the Indian independence that Gandhi's activism helped bring to fruition turned out to be, as he had warned beforehand, "the tiger's nature without the tiger." The new Indian government came down strongly in favor of industrialization and bureaucracy.

But this general current of thinking continued even into the late twentieth century, albeit with a shift of emphasis. Perhaps the best-known voice of alternative development in recent decades has been that of the unorthodox economist E. F. Schumacher, author in 1973 of the bestselling book *Small Is Beautiful*.[24] Influenced strongly by Catholic economic thought, he nonetheless chose to emphasize the Buddhist and Gandhian elements of his thinking. Schumacher held that "man is small, and, therefore, small is beautiful." A staunch opponent of environmental destruction and abstract corporate planning, he called for a return to sustainable technology, humane work, and small-scale economic units. Schumacher's followers have included the defenders of "place-based practices" and local economies.

In many ways, Schumacher and those inspired by him fit into the same tradition as earlier critics. Much of what his followers have said since the 1970s would be recognizable to, and applauded by, the distributists and others. But the reverse is less true. Schumacher's followers are culturally quite different from the likes of Belloc and Chesterton. As Schumacher himself did, they steer clear of traditionalist language. They find it alien, because most of them are fully products of late-modern Europe and North America. They have more in common with the hippies of the 1970s than with the catechism-reciting Catholics of the 1910s. Many of them no doubt accept the mainstream liberal charge that the distributists were quasifascists. They lament the direction of the modern world, but unlike the traditionalist thinkers of the past, they do not instinctively look back to older affirmations. Their critique of corporate capitalism rests on a general sensibility about the modern world, not a system of belief that transcends time and space.

Yet all these modern efforts to revive a "third way" alternative to capitalism and socialism that is grounded in small communities have been sympathetic to the peasantry. Unsurprisingly, they have seen in the traditional peasant both an exemplar of a humane way of life and—where the peasant still survives—a potential supporter of its restoration. The portrait of Pomatambo that I have attempted to paint shows that they have been right. There is plenty of confirmation that the peasantry wants neither a capitalist free-for-all nor an intrusive state. Eric Wolf has called peasants "natural anarchists" who are attached to the independence of their communities. His fellow political scientist James Scott has identified a "moral economy of the peasant" that emphasizes solidarity and security.[25] Few observers of peasant life buy the idea that peasants are closet individualists just waiting to get a crack at capitalism.

Of course, those political scientists who have a soft spot for peasant communities—contrary to the tastes of most of today's intelligentsia—focus on some features rather than others. Scott, for example, highlights the peasantry's attachment to a secure subsistence and its resistance to governments that try to micromanage local life. But he also peppers his writing with warnings not to idealize the past. He sees insecurity and powerlessness when communities break down, as do Schumacher's followers and others on the left, but he does not frame the problem mainly as one of traditional versus modern culture.[26] The same could be said about some pro-peasant Marxists, including in the Andes. They regret that communities unravel and inequalities grow as capitalism expands. But they see the suffering of the poor through the lens of class, and they think that history's inevitable direction means that they must push through capitalism to the other side. In their eyes, the efforts of traditionalists to resist capitalism, or to preserve or restore older types of community, is mere nostalgia—a distraction from the socialist struggle.[27]

That sort of narrow focus on power, poverty, and insecurity misses the point. Traditionalist currents of economic thought, dating back to the early twentieth century, have painted the most complete picture of what has gone wrong and what is worth defending. We could flood the rural poor with baubles, weave the most generous social democratic safety net under them, and write into law a full range of liberal rights for their benefit. In one sense, they might then be better off than living in squalor and getting thrashed by soldiers or guerrillas. Yet we still would not have preserved or restored the conditions for a deeper human flourishing. For in the end, a development alternative true to the spirit of these communities is about much more than relieving deprivation and vulnerability. It *is* about that, and it would provide such relief more reliably than recent governments have done. But ultimately it must seek to maintain a worthy way of life and set of virtues and offer them anew to those who have lost them. That end is connected to economics, but lies beyond it.

Taking up the traditionalist banner thus means stressing the centrality of values in this alternative. Yet the battle of ideas is at the same time intertwined with a very real, high-stakes struggle over power and interests. We should give the benefit of the doubt to those advocates of the "market revolution" who genuinely believe what they say and do not stand to gain much personally one way or the other. But enough other powerful and advantaged people do stand to profit from this prevailing vision of the future. Thus, to resist it means, in the long run, mobilizing the peasantry to push back against those who would gain at its expense.

Whose power and interests are at stake? Who would gain from eroding the solidarity of peasant communities and breaking up their communal property into legally titled individual parcels? First, an overbearing state would benefit. As Scott rightly points out, modern states have undertaken massive efforts to bring order and legal regularity to unruly parts of their territories and populations. The more states break down customs and solidarity, the more easily the authorities can penetrate such little communities.[28] Depending on the nature and purposes of the state, this may be a good or a bad thing. Second, the wealthy would benefit by bringing the poor into capitalism and deflecting their discontent from its inequalities. Even de Soto, amid his main argument about how the poor would benefit from titling their land, remarked in passing that when the poor have even a little property, they accept much more readily the legitimacy of the property ownership of the rich. Whether that is a good or a bad thing depends on how you see capitalism and the inequalities within it.

The "market revolution" would benefit some of the already advantaged in even more profound ways. Let us look more closely at what would happen if, as de Soto proposes, all the "dead capital" of untitled property were turned into "live capital," that is, were made into fully convertible and mortgageable assets. De Soto acknowledges that while live capital allows a person to pursue new opportunities, the risk of forfeiture is the other side of the coin. Fair enough. But he seems blind to the power dynamics involved. Giving the poor full access to the capital market also means giving the capital market full access to the poor. It cuts both ways. And which way it cuts for each individual will depend on personal circumstances. Some people are much better situated than others to take advantage of this fluidity. An enterprising fellow like Alberto the guinea-pig trader would probably do well, and even if he did not do well the first or second or third time around, he would bounce back easily.

Others would do less well. I heard the story of one of them in July 2006. Without realizing it ahead of time, I managed to arrive in Vilcashuamán at the opening of the Vilcas Raymi festival, when the two very basic inns on the square were completely full. After more than an hour of asking around for accommodation, I was put in touch with a middle-aged woman who lived a couple of blocks away. She offered me a room. Her two-story house was old, mainly adobe and wood but with a concrete extension.

When I talked with her the next morning, I learned that she had been deeply in the red for years. The extension had been done by a barely competent builder in cahoots with a bank that had been the subject of countless complaints. To pay the builder, she had taken a loan secured against her house—one of the few in town with clear enough title—with a usurious interest rate that she still did not fully understand. The balance was growing, and short of the bank being shut down for its misdeeds she had no way out. When I read through her loan contract, I found it flawlessly crafted in the best of modern legalese to close all loopholes.

Maybe the woman had made a bad decision, and maybe the bank had pushed the limits of the law and business ethics. But de Soto and other enthusiasts of bringing "dead capital" to life underestimate the vulnerability of the poor. The more fluid a capital market, particularly when a large part of the population is ill-equipped to play its games, the more quickly wealth sloshes around and concentrates. Advocates of the "market revolution" have to admit, if they think about it, that their vision accepts that this will happen. Even in the developed world, most small businesses fail and millions of homes are foreclosed every year because of economic pressures. The present global recession, which started with a subprime mortgage crisis in the United States, highlights these vulnerabilities in stunning fashion.

The market revolutionists never say so publicly, but their kind of progress means letting such no-longer-dead capital flow out of the hands of people who are not shrewd or talented enough to use it efficiently, and into the hands of the enterprising and experienced. A few smallholding peasants will become prosperous exporters of cash crops, with tractors and hired hands. Most of the rest, sooner or later, will join the rat race as propertyless employees, prodded by a necessity that the "turnip-headed rustic left alone with his turnip" does not sufficiently feel. The advocates of this change will defend it as progress, because the national income will go up. After all, the former clodhoppers will be able to spend their precarious wage packets on apartment rents and televisions, will they not?

History has already witnessed something eerily like this hemorrhage of property out of the peasantry. It happened in England from the sixteenth to the nineteenth centuries. In the Middle Ages, villages had had plenty of common land for pasturage and gleaning, quite like the communal land in places like Pomatambo today. A web of customs regulated its use. With only small plots of their own, the poor relied on the commons to supplement their subsistence and see them through hard times. Then the great landowners discovered that land could be farmed or grazed more profitably if enclosed in large tracts. They hired lawyers to disentangle old feudal titles and convert custom-bound manorial property—i.e., the commons—into their own unencumbered private property. The so-called enclosure movement made it impossible for many of the poor to survive by farming and forced them into the cities as a cheap workforce at the mercy of emerging industrialists.[29]

De Soto mentioned the European enclosure movement briefly in his second book. His position was clear: enclosure happened in another era and was about dispossession, not giving the poor clear legal rights. He insisted that Europe's sin a couple of centuries ago had nothing in common with an effort to bring "dead capital" to life. In democracies today, even in the developing world, the poor have real protections that would prevent such abuses from happening.

In the most limited sense, he may be right. Usually the "market revolution" will not involve men with guns forcing peasants off their land to benefit developers, though just that has happened in rural China in recent years. But even without force, and with perfect legal clarity and attention to the niceties of ownership, the same massive transfer of property would produce a similar increase in vulnerability. In effect, it is the enclosure movement all over again, on humanity's last frontier. The global financial sector salivates over the prospect of getting its hands on the informal assets of the poor. The $9.3 trillion of extralegal property across the developing world adds up to a large enough injection of wealth to give global capitalism some much-needed extra vitality for a generation. The shaved percentages can buy plenty of penthouses in New York and Hong Kong.

✦   ✦   ✦

So far we have seen what is at stake in this choice between the "market revolution" and an alternative founded on the essence and aspirations of the peasantry itself. It is a conflict of values and a conflict of power and interests. But an inevitable question arises. Why should the outcome of this struggle, in this generation and this kind of setting, be any different than it has been in the past? From the enclosure movement all the way to the roaring globalization of the late 1990s, global capitalism and the liberal ethos have won one after another battle. Even if half of all living humans are still peasants, and even if they draw a line on these issues, will it not be their last stand?

This question breaks down into two parts. One, which I shall defer for now, is really about whether we can put together a workable strategy that can succeed against powerful opposition. The other, which has to come first, is about whether our agenda can be framed in a more compelling way now than it was in the past. I think it can be. The same ultimate principles are at stake in places like Pomatambo today, as in the early twentieth century when the distributists and Liang Shuming and Gandhi were writing. But because of our time and circumstances, we can now connect more issues and put the challenge in more universal terms. The countryside of the global South is a fine initial front for this battle of ideas and interests. And a long tradition of thought from all over the world is enriched by being updated and applied in this setting. Things converge around this compelling alternative for four reasons.

First, places like Pomatambo are both traditional and poor. This obvious fact may seem unimportant, until you reflect on how difficult it would be to construct an alternative economic vision among those who are either traditional and rich, or poor and not traditional. Take many self-described cultural conservatives in the West today. If they read the likes of Belloc and Chesterton—which few do—they agree with most of their complaints about the breakdown of personal morality, the crassness of public culture, the loss of faith, and so on. As soon as they stumble across passages critical of capitalism, however, they become uneasy.[30] Western cultural conservatives, by and large, are comfortable enough that a disruption to the capitalist economy would inconvenience them. I am sure that some of them would stand on principle against interest, if it came down to it, but it is not easy to do. In the global South, however, the poor and the traditional overlap. They thus have much more freedom to imagine alternatives to capitalist modernity that are informed by traditional values.

Second, an alternative that speaks to the entire global South, and can meet the present world order on its own scale, must be thoroughly universal. The essence of these villages *is* universal, in the sense that we find the same virtues and habits of mind among peasants everywhere. Yet that common essence takes different forms depending on local customs and social arrangements. Take land tenure, for example. Much has been written on how property rights and the village commons vary across cultures.[31] The English distributists saw economic traditionalism as relying on the ideal of the sturdy and self-reliant smallholder. Most Andeans would put more emphasis on reciprocity and communal land. Liang and Gandhi might say that land tenure is beside the point, and that attitudes to nature and desire count for much more. Seeing these different approaches, it is easy to neglect the forest for the trees. Having to offer a viable alternative across cultures, across different peasantries, means having to step back and think hard about universal common ground. We can do this today more easily than could like-minded people a century ago.

Third, the global South is non-Western. In the West, the battle between tradition and liberal modernity is already long over. Liberal modernity won. But as Belloc argued, it did not necessarily have to turn out that way. He reminded his readers that much of history consists of political choices and chains of consequences. If England's monasteries had remained intact, for example, perhaps the smallholders would have enjoyed more bargaining power and social hierarchies would have flattened even more. If the industrial revolution had originated in a more equal society, he suggested, it might have brought only widespread prosperity rather than a century of dispossession and squalor. Maybe the guilds would have ended up overseeing the new technologies for the benefit of the many rather than the few.[32]

If Belloc could muse on fanciful alternative histories of England, how much more could one imagine for a place like the Andes, with its legacy of an interrupted Inka civilization? An idealized image of what the Inka empire could have become without the Spanish conquest has persisted over generations. Even many peasants think that modern technology falling into the hands of Europeans and not Andeans is an arbitrary twist of fate.[33] Such speculations and mythmaking never get one very far, and liberal modernity has become truly universal anyway. But the residual association of global capitalism with the West may open up a bit more psychological space for peasants in the global South to imagine other trajectories of development.

Fourth and finally, the global South is very poor. It is all very well for intellectuals and the mildly discontented in the developed world to ponder more humane alternatives to the prevailing image of the future. They are universal issues, after all. But comfortable critics in the North gravitate to niche experiments that might change a bit at the margins and add up only over the long run. The severe deprivation and vulnerability of people in the global South, particularly in the countryside, lend more urgency to such questions. They experience in vivid ways the failure of the present model to deliver benefits to them, as well as the shortcomings of that model whenever it starts intruding into and disrupting their way of life. They have urgent needs that they rightly expect any alternative worth its salt to meet within a generation or so.

For all these reasons, drawing our battle lines in the countryside of the global South makes good sense. Doing so means turning upside down the mental map of progress. Usually the North leads the way and foreshadows the future of the South. The traditional ways of life that linger in the South are seen as worthless and doomed. But framing the issues as I have done here means taking a long, hard look at precisely what the prevailing model of progress writes off. The truly humane alternative exists in a microcosm in these poor and traditional communities. Like an old house destined for restoration, they need new wiring and insulation, but the bricks are already there.

The peasants might find this observation heartening. They have something to offer the future after all. But the idea that political momentum comes from a solid tradition might not surprise them greatly. Observers of peasant movements have long said that the greatest energy and moral tenacity come from traditional norms and myths of the past, not from wholly new, invented ideologies. And such movements succeed if they are given the structure and clarity of direction that they need to accomplish the purposes of the moment.[34]

So if we can translate the aspirations of people like Pomatambo's villagers into concrete action on the ground, perhaps there is hope yet. Perhaps the forgotten of the modern world can take a stand and win. In the next chapter, I suggest what taking a stand would involve.

VI

Building an Economy of Values

Enthusiasts of the prevailing development model have an easy task. When prominent businessmen, politicians, and their intellectual hangers-on debate economic policies, they do so from a position of strength. After a century of what they call progress, the world today operates in their interest. They can afford to pick this or that policy in a spirit of experimentation. Errors may lower the growth rate a bit, shift benefits and burdens in unexpected ways, or lead to a change of presidents or prime ministers if they rub enough voters the wrong way. But from their perspective it would take unimaginable catastrophe for the pillars of the global economic and political order to crack, let alone crumble. Even the current global financial crisis and recession, for all the hand-wringing they have caused, hardly add up to a mortal threat to

Fig. 6: Old customs, new materials: a house-raising party

capitalism itself. The regulatory adjustments that will follow are minor in the grand scheme of things. They aim at reinforcing the system and correcting some of its short-term excesses, not at drastically changing its beneficiaries. When you sit at what you have convinced yourself is history's end, policy choices are mere details. The persistence or doom of your whole way of life does not hang in the balance.

For those on the other side of the modern world, the stakes are much higher. A peasant who struggles at the edge of subsistence may well have his or her survival at issue when facing a choice between this or that plan for rural development. If peasants go out on a limb with an experiment of their own, they assume even more risk, and there is little chance that those in power will come to their aid if things go awry. The pressures the modern world exerts against traditional communities are formidable and relentless. Pushing back against those pressures rarely stands much chance of success. If the peasants get it wrong, as they often will, the next generation will yield even more ground.

In other words, no one should lightly propose that peasants or other vulnerable folk fight an uphill battle. The challenge I outlined in the previous chapter is an appeal to the doubly powerless. They are poor and have few resources to mobilize on behalf of an alternative. But that alternative is their best chance of obtaining a rising living standard. Culturally they are on the run, dismissed as backward by all the spokespersons of our apparent future. But they should try not only to defend the values of duty and community, but also to export them to others who have forgotten them. Looking at the world as it is, this may seem an odd set of battles to pick. Yet given the direction of that same world, I would insist that unless fought, these battles will simply be forfeited.

The alternative I propose has two parts. On the one hand, it seeks material prosperity for the countryside of the global South. On the other, it aims to work within the deepest values of these communities, and to lend them economic and political weight so that they can reshape the broader world. The first goal, economic development, is the simpler to judge and is easy to delineate. When I asked Quintín what he thought a development path true to Andean values would look like, he stressed that it would furnish all the usual goods: employment, education, electricity, transportation, and the like. Nélida said that it would deliver those goods better than the present sort of development does, and it would adopt useful practices wherever in the world it could find them. They both added that the spirit would be different, though. People would live and work together in harmony and mutual respect. No longer would greedy and powerful decision-makers be allowed to grab more and more for themselves.

Neither Quintín and Nélida nor the ordinary peasants in Pomatambo have an aversion to modern comforts. They would all like to live in houses with tiled floors, electricity, and running water. They would like to walk and drive on paved streets. They would like to stay up in the evenings without inhaling smoke and wearing out their eyes by candlelight. The highland folk are no different from those housewives in Europe and North America a couple of generations ago who longed for refrigerators and washing machines to ease the drudgery of daily life. One can look at the modern world critically while still appreciating the material blessings it has brought.

An Andean development, or a development in tune with peasant values anywhere else, is still development. For the poor in such places to enjoy such comforts will require all the technology and infrastructure that made them possible in the developed world. To pretend otherwise, or to deny these people development out of some romantic attachment to the rustic and primitive, is silly, arrogant, or both. So while the spirit of these communities should be preserved, development necessarily implies a broadening of their economic base. Without new material support, their traditional way of life long founded on agriculture will die out. The goal, therefore, is to bring a new, more developed economic base into harmony with an age-old pattern of human decency. The former must serve the latter instead of overrunning it.

More than a few thoughtful people in recent decades have tried to judge and craft contemporary practices according to older wisdom. But they have done so more in politics than in economics. Modern admirers of the ancient Greeks, for example, sometimes wonder what the active citizenship of the small city-states might look like today. In a much larger and faster-paced society, what kinds of political institutions and civic learning might favor the political virtues that Aristotle, say, would recognize? Professors of political philosophy often banter about such questions.[1] Even the odd political activist, frustrated by the passivity of the modern consumer-voter, dreams of reviving long-dead kinds of civic energy.

Such musings rarely go anywhere. Modern idealists hardly ever get to redesign political institutions, even on a small scale. Even if they did, institutions are only as good as the powers, interests, and values that flow through them. More fundamentally, it is well-nigh impossible to revive old practices of citizenship in a vacuum. The political is but one dimension of people's experience. A city-state, town meeting, or academy for training engaged citizens would still operate in a global economy and consumer culture that would work at cross-purposes with it.

For most people, particularly humble folk like those in Pomatambo, the demands and habits of making a living daily shape their sense of self. Yet efforts to apply older economic wisdom to the modern world have been remarkably few. Most readers of the political classics or religious texts would say that too much has changed to draw any useful comparisons. Beyond vague exhortations to honesty and goodwill, they rarely even try to translate the ethos of an ancient or medieval economy into guides for action in a high-tech capitalist world.

Mapping out a vision of tradition-grounded development in a village like Pomatambo means undertaking this kind of task. It is made slightly easier since our point of departure is a manageably small-scale setting, with many traditional structures and practices still intact. It is not like trying to restore ethical order, in one fell swoop, to a global economy most of whose central actors have never known anything other than disarray and self-seeking. Yet, the guiding question is the same regardless of scale: how do we arrange economic activity so that people will continue to practice the old virtues more often than not?

The answer has several dimensions. Economic activity breaks down into what we might call practices and powers. People are shaped by the organization of work and consumption, by the nitty-gritty of how they make a living, navigate risk, and weigh pressures from other people and the scarcity of resources. At the same time, any economy has structures of power. Specific institutions and people own the raw materials and equipment, and they make decisions that shape the use of society's wealth. Those powers stand behind one or another set of values and priorities. Any alternative development model, therefore, will have to address both the tone of economic practices and the distribution of economic powers.

We must work with three strategic goals in mind. The first is to enhance the *economic* capabilities of the world's poorest. Delivering prosperity will win any alternative some real credibility among people living in dire poverty. The second is to strengthen the best of the community's *cultural* practices. The habits of life that promote the traditional virtues—understood as broadly as possible—must be maintained, reinforced, and where necessary revived and exported. The third is to translate these economic and cultural efforts into networks of *political* power. Only an alternative with political teeth will ever be able to shape a larger environment hospitable to its diffusion.

Along with taking into account these three strategic prongs, a successful alternative has to be adaptable. The first experiments in villages like Pomatambo will start modestly, and because they build on familiar local strengths will be the easiest to plan. If those experiments succeed, then the alternative will have to make the leap into redefining the policy options at the national level. Finally, with enough economic and cultural weight behind it, a global movement could bring pressure to bear on the present order. The more ambitious the scale, the more adaptable the strategy has to be. That the entire project is an uphill battle I do not deny. But enough of a lived alternative lingers in these forgotten villages to give us a starting point. As Belloc wrote of the distributists' own idealistic efforts nearly a century ago, "there may be embers aglow here and there, sufficient to start the small beginnings of a flame."[2]

One starts with the embers of tradition and community, scattered here and there, because doing so takes nothing for granted. An alternative development model such as I will suggest here cannot count on the generosity of outside actors to get it on its way. Nor can it hope for a sudden change in the broader economic and political environment. Rather, it has to build on the resources and experience that the traditional peasant communities already possess.

It is a truism in some alternative development circles that the best place to search for ways to lift a poor community out of poverty is in the practices that already help it subsist. The peasants living in Andean highland communities are certainly creative agents of their own survival. Anthropologist Anthony Bebbington, for example, has noted the many ways they keep their heads above water by mixing agriculture and migrant work. They are not just passive victims of the state or market. Against the odds, they have kept their communities viable. They have made the most of the limited options available to them.[3]

An alternative model would have to provide more of what the peasants already want. Most of them say first and foremost that they need technical aid for agriculture. In the PRONAMACHS report, the locals were said to have asked for irrigation technology and the like. They were tired of promises of equipment and technical advice that never arrived. When peasants can afford even basic new inputs into agriculture, they embrace them eagerly. Pesticides, fertilizers, and the other gains of the green revolution have raised agricultural productivity around the world. In Ecuador, for example, Quechua-speaking peasants with access to such new techniques have found no conflict between them and the values of their communities. Indeed, some have seen raising agricultural productivity as the best way to reduce out-migration, which they know is the greatest eroder of indigenous culture in the long run.[4]

The *right* kind of simple technology can work wonders. The most community-friendly development efforts pay attention to appropriate technology. One well-known Peru-based NGO, PRATEC, has tried to revive centuries-old Andean terracing and cultivation techniques, on the grounds that they are both culturally authentic and ecologically better suited to the terrain and soils.[5] In a very different setting, the Amish of North America screen out modern technologies that would disrupt their way of life. Getting around in horse-drawn buggies rather than cars, refusing to hook up to the electricity grid or to take part in medical insurance schemes, among other policies, are intended to preserve among them a humble self-reliance. They accept what they judge to be useful and harmless, like plumbing and even generators, but they always judge technology against the independence of their communities and their religious commitments.

Of course, when it comes to appropriate technology and its effects, traditional peoples in different parts of the world draw the line in different places. But unlike in the mainstream of fevered consumer society, they typically at least weigh the implications of new technologies seriously. Any alternative has to draw on such best practices.

Technology must also be cost-effective. Because of a "demonstration effect"—imitating what one sees among the world's wealthy—the poor of the global South often want to run before they can walk. Many times in Pomatambo, for example, villagers asked me how they could get expensive electronic equipment like laptop computers, photovoltaic panels to charge them, and so on. With some initial reluctance, they understood when I explained that such goods could hardly be a priority use for the limited money they might scrape together or attract from donors. Instead, I helped them build a prototype solar oven from wood, glass, and steel sheeting, and got them the materials to copy it for each household. The ovens cost very little, but experience elsewhere in the world had shown that they can heat water and cook food without women having to collect firewood or monitor a fire. Moreover, the ovens are easy to build locally and require no outside maintenance or expensive replacement parts. Simple technology builds local capacity; expensive technology stimulates a slide into dependence.

All these points about appropriateness are obvious to anyone who has spent time in peasant villages—and who does not stand to profit from selling inappropriate goods to them. I raise these observations here partly to highlight them, but also because they point to larger issues. A spirit of creative self-reliance and self-consciousness about development choices, where present, are resources on which to build. But they are not part of a larger strategy; they tend to be ad hoc and disconnected. People think at most one step ahead of how they are already subsisting. They take opportunities when they arise, but they lack a clear blueprint for innovation and reinvestment. They do not coordinate among themselves across communities and different parts of the world. They lack a vision of future prosperity to guide and inspire each step within a longer-term effort. Even communities with a consistent and explicit worldview, like the Amish, tend more to react to new challenges—such as an innovation that they must adopt or reject—than to seek them out.

The best example of this short time horizon is the pervasive failure to address head-on the question of agriculture and what comes after it. Peasant communities have always had their economic base in farming and livestock raising. The texture of daily life is so wrapped up with the soil that few can imagine being a true peasant without continuing to scratch one's living from it. For now, this need not matter much. Agriculture remains backward, with plenty of room for new technical inputs to raise productivity enormously. Even today, some 80 to 90 percent of agricultural production in the Vilcashuamán district is for subsistence.[6] If a generous donor dropped a couple million dollars of agricultural aid into Pomatambo, the locals could become extraordinarily rich farmers by present standards. Thus, understandably, they think of agricultural development as the obvious route to prosperity (aside from leaving the village altogether and taking up urban employment).

But in the long term, this way of thinking will not do. The agricultural horizon has to be crossed. More efficient farming will not raise living standards very far beyond a certain point. Modern farmers in the developed world can make a comfortable income if they stay a step ahead of the banks and the regulators. But they amount to only 2 to 4 percent of the population of developed countries. Highly efficient agriculture cannot employ many people, and an agriculture of middling efficiency cannot support the full range of industries and services that the poor universally want.

Keeping a close attachment to the soil and a humane scale of food production make sense, for the sake of both a sturdy self-reliance and peace of mind. But as even most hard-core agrarians will admit when pushed, the right kind of village can keep the best of that way of life even if most of its residents are not farming most of the time. In short, it is useless to deny that both labor and capital inevitably will move out of agriculture—in the narrow sense of people living mainly by sowing and reaping—over the next century. This will happen everywhere, including in Pomatambo. For the community to persist in a recognizable form rather than withering to a handful of cash-cropping tractor drivers, it will need a new and diversified economic base. But that new economic base will have to be built within the values of the existing community rather than in a way that is at odds with them.

You cannot fake such a new economic base. For instance, Pomatambans talk often about gold and other mineral deposits that they think lie nearby. Some of them imagine enriching the village by taking up mining, much as the Senderistas proposed years ago. The authorities in Vilcashuamán talk of mineral wealth as well, despite ambiguous evidence that it is extensive.[7] But counting on windfalls—which, by their very nature, are few and far between and tend also to be swiftly exhausted—from mining or other sources makes little sense. Only a true, sustainable diversification of production will save communities such as Pomatambo from oblivion. They need increasingly sophisticated manufacturing and a full range of services to employ people and make life attractively comfortable.

Much the same warning applies to tourism, another pet vision of the provincial authorities.[8] The Vilcashuamán area has plenty of natural and historical tourist attractions. When the infrastructure is in place, it will probably get a fair number of visitors from all over the world. Such tourism could be channeled in sustainable ways and provide one long-term source of employment. But expectations should be circumscribed. Tourism-based economies tend to be one-dimensional and, obviously, create dependence on outsiders. The most prosperous tourist destinations in the world have diversified economies as well—think of Venice or the Cotswolds. Furthermore, since most villages around the world have little tourist potential, the rare one that does will offer few general lessons for how to develop.

In a poor country with many corrupt decision-makers, grand ideas about tourism also tend to channel state funding in bizarre directions. In 1998, one of Fujimori's cronies convinced him to pay for an asphalted runway at Vilcashuamán so that well-heeled tourists from abroad could stop there en route from Lima to Cuzco. At one mile, the runway is long enough for a huge cargo plane. But it has never been used. The company that lobbied for it went bankrupt and failed to put in place the rest of the necesssary infrastructure. For the same cost, the road could have been paved from Ayacucho to Vilcashuamán.

Somewhat more promising than tourism is craft production. This involves simple technology and builds on traditional capacities. Many villages near Pomatambo have recently started working with Chirapaq, an NGO founded in 1986 by a young peasant woman from Pujas. It has received some aid from the Netherlands but relies mainly on local resources. In 2006, I met a Chirapaq representative when he came to Pomatambo to lay the groundwork for local activities. He explained that Chirapaq sought to transmit to children the old skills of ceramics, sculpture, and weaving. In one moving image, he described a scene of offering coca leaves to neglected elders as they are invited to join in and pass on their otherwise soon-to-be-forgotten knowledge. Chirapaq aims eventually to sell some craft products abroad and generate income, all while carrying on local traditions.

This kind of craft production has its appeals. People across the spectrum—from María Gutiérrez, the traditionally minded former *gobernadora,* to Alberto the guinea-pig entrepreneur—spoke to me of it with enthusiasm. Like tourism, such revived craftsmanship could generate some income while keeping local traditions highly visible. It could help locals become more savvy about economic outlets for their products. But as a development path, it has built-in limits. In the Vilcashuamán area, for example, little traditional craftsmanship has survived: primarily carpentry, masonry, and weaving, all for the household or fellow villagers. It is dying out because when peasants can afford factory-made clothes and other products in the market, they usually buy them instead.[9] If craft products cannot hold their own on quality and price, then they have only one niche left to occupy. They will be exotic exports to the developed world. The Ten Thousand Villages store chain, for example, prospers by mediating between village craftworkers and well-heeled consumers. The demand is there and will continue. But such exports do not offer a well-diversified economic base for these communities.

Real diversification means engaging in wholly new lines of activity that take advantage of modern technology and can hold their own within larger economies of scale. Usually light industry comes to the countryside when outside entrepreneurs smell a profit. If good roads and shipping connected rural Vilcashuamán to the global market, low labor costs might well attract factories. But those outside entrepreneurs would hardly be bringing the alternative development model that the area needs. They would hasten the demise of old community structures and empower new people quite at odds with traditional values. Villages like Pomatambo face a Catch-22. They lack the capital to finance an economic breakthrough on their own. The infrastructure that would attract outside investors is missing, and if they did arrive the type of development that would follow would destroy the community's way of life. There seems no way out, no way to give the village a diversified economic base on its own terms.

✤　✤　✤

To approach this challenge, we should start by looking more closely at the most obvious obstacle: lack of capital. If these people had more money to invest, they could launch any number of new economic ventures without having to answer to anyone but themselves. At present, only teachers who draw a state salary even have bank accounts. Other villagers have no contact with financial institutions and very modest cash reserves. They own only what they see around them and use to subsist. If a typical Pomatamban household sold all its most valuable moveable property—its livestock—it would get a few hundred dollars. Private maize plots and dwellings might net a few thousand dollars per household at most, but only another subsistence farmer from the area would have any use for such fragmented strips of land. As a sign of how cash-poor Pomatambo is, the state decided appropriate compensation to the whole community for the 1986 massacre and other atrocities was only $30,000. Life is cheap here. At that rate, future Peruvian governments might think they can shoot their way across the highlands rather inexpensively.

Not all people connected with Pomatambo live at the edge of subsistence. Many migrants with jobs in the cities do have modest savings. But, as in most communities like this one, such assets do not find their way into local investment. Very few highland migrants anywhere in Peru acquire enough wealth to finance ambitious ventures in the agricultural sector. Few would choose to do so if they could, because of the lack of infrastructure and an unpredictable market. Highland agriculture does not make economic sense to anyone with capital to invest. Besides, an influx of private money from rich migrants tends to cause tension. Peasants used to subsistence often have what has been called "an image of limited good," in which sudden wealth is assumed to come at the expense of others.[10] Private investment in agriculture would also disrupt the complex web of reciprocity and custom that holds these villages together. For all these reasons, migrants and others with a bit more money than average limit their spending to building better houses or buying consumer goods from the cities.

It seems safe to say that the capital needed to diversify the economic base of these communities will not come from the locals themselves. The local economy needs new inputs. Now, advocates of the "market revolution" have a couple of easy answers to our problem. They think that the best way to bring capital to the countryside is to make the countryside profitable for capital. One way or another, the world's businesses and wealthy investors must find it more lucrative to carry on their trade in these areas than in others. Perhaps they must find buying up land and installing huge agribusiness complexes easier and cheaper than it is now. Or perhaps they must find that the locals will work for lower wages because they need cash or because subsisting on their own is made more difficult. If this standard approach to attracting capital does not work, then the "market revolution" advocates have a backup strategy. They will make so-called "microcredit" loans, without collateral, to the more enterprising locals so that they can start small businesses. Even if only a few of them succeed, their small concentrations of wealth will snowball and make the market grow.[11]

Both of these approaches are at cross-purposes with our goal. Making the countryside attractive to capitalism means changing the countryside to suit the needs of others. In practice, it also means more vulnerability, more inequality, and more unraveling of communities. And while the microcredit route is gentler, it still bypasses traditional community arrangements. It hopes to miniaturize capitalism and turn a few peasants into entrepreneurs. Either way, the movement is away from traditional values and toward market values. The peasantry is supposed to conform to the prevailing style of development rather than the other way around.

So while we need an infusion of capital, we have to think very carefully about whence it comes and with what strings attached. Quality of capital matters as much as quantity of capital, so to speak. Money is power.

One anthropologist has noted that the influence of the aged in traditional cultures is often strengthened by their ability to bequeath property crucial to subsistence.[12] The logic extends far beyond that example, though. Put capital in individual hands, and it will behave individualistically. Reward capital for efficiency alone, and it will serve no other masters. Capital owned or managed by individuals who are oriented solely to the market—whether by taste or by dire necessity—will dissolve these communities more than it will strengthen them.

We come to an inescapable conclusion: the only way to add capital to these local economies without undermining the communities is to make sure that the capital stays in community hands, in one form or another. Such capital will respond to a wider range of calculations beyond efficiency, including the values of the community itself. It can be the lifeblood of an *economy of values*. The greater economic weight of community capital will also give more bargaining power against outside actors. The poor acting as individuals in the market have short time horizons and too often succumb to their vulnerabilities. The same is much less true of a permanent association that has to deliberate on its investment choices and can be bound by rules of its own making.

Enthusiasts of the global market economy as it now exists will scoff at this idea. They will say that it makes no economic sense to hold capital collectively. Only individuals have a real incentive to put their wealth to the best use. Communities like Pomatambo would make decisions on irrational grounds and in response to political pressure. Even if new ventures owned by the community did not fold, they would still lag far behind businesses run by individuals with a beady eye on the bottom line. The market enthusiasts will go on to say that in the unlikely event community capital were managed efficiently, the focus on efficiency would make its decisions no different from the decisions made by an outside investor of the usual type. In other words, either community capital stagnates, or it behaves in a way that makes the community capital label meaningless. Better to stick to the current model.

This criticism has grains of truth, but only a few. The performance of an investment depends on how it is managed, not on who gets revenue from it. Look at all the world's university and foundation endowments, for example. And between stagnation from sentimentally or politically driven mismanagement, and an obsession with profit above all else, lies a whole spectrum of approaches. But the best response to this criticism is to consider examples of how something like community capital has worked in practice elsewhere. One would be hard-pressed to find traditional villages that have had capital invested in modern economic ventures. But other lessons abound. Cooperative and community-based enterprises have flourished elsewhere in the world when they have been set up carefully.

Perhaps the best-known case of such an alternative business doing well within a larger capitalist economy is Spain's Mondragón cooperatives.[13] These cooperatives started in 1956 in a small city in the Basque country. The idea came from a Catholic priest who had fought on the Republican side during the Spanish civil war and then settled in the area. Mondragón began humbly, with fewer than twenty men who pooled their resources to start a cooperative and provide employment in a depressed region. Over the next half century, it grew beyond the wildest dreams of its founders. It now has split into over a hundred specialized cooperatives with thirty thousand employees, and it collectively makes up one of Spain's largest corporations. Most of its production is industrial. Mondragón makes a large proportion of Spain's radiators and washing machines. It has even set up a credit union to finance expansion and a polytechnic to train workers.

Throughout its expansion, Mondragón has stayed true to its cooperative principles. It accepts no outside capital, instead making do with reinvested profits and modest buy-in contributions taken from employees when they start their jobs. Over the course of their employment, workers build up retirement accounts that collectively provide a huge pool of long-term investment capital. Pay differences among employees are kept within a range wide enough to reward hard work but narrow enough to preserve a spirit of equality. Workers elect the umbrella corporation's governing board, which in turn appoints lower-level managers.

Mondragón has attracted praise from enthusiasts of cooperatives on both left and right. Some socialists have pointed to it as an example of a successful business built on worker ownership and workplace democracy.

One does not have to have shareholders and a layer of overpaid managers to run an enterprise efficiently. Some Catholic traditionalists, including admirers of the distributists, have seen it as a kind of third way between a soulless competitive capitalism and a top-heavy state-run economy. Close observers of Mondragón say that it has performed better than most producer cooperatives for several reasons. In part, they credit the strong heritage of equality and associations among the Basque people. Success also comes from Mondragón's design. While top management ultimately answers to employees, who have a stake in both their own work atmosphere and the bottom line, line managers are given enough leeway and responsibility to keep the shop floor running well. Mondragón also benefits from having built up a large pool of capital. Workers can cash out their accounts only when they leave, which discourages short-term speculation. The credit union and polytechnic also provide long-term support for Mondragón's expansion.[14]

Mondragón is not perfect, of course. With the more competitive global market that began to appear in the 1980s, it has faced internal struggles over how to balance worker participation and social objectives on the one hand with a more "businesslike" focus on efficiency on the other. Sometimes those struggles have been openly debated, sometimes not. At the same time, hard-core Marxists who see industrial relations only through the lens of class conflict think that Mondragón paints too rosy a picture of cooperation. They highlight the hierarchies of expertise and status that persist within these ostensibly worker-run cooperatives. They try to dispel the optimistic "myth of Mondragón" and call for union-centered activism against the business class instead.[15]

A more mixed view of Mondragón suggests that it does some things well, others less well. It has held its own and even expanded in a competitive environment, proving wrong the naysayers who insist that cooperatives always underperform. And it has balanced high employment and a decent return on capital by tweaking the time horizons of its members. But according to this view, Mondragón offers only limited lessons for cooperatives in general, and hardly any for how to run an economy along cooperative lines. It has been parasitic on the surrounding capitalist economy in Spain, copying innovations that arise in the pure free-market sector rather than developing its own. This parasitism supposedly comes from the very time horizon that keeps Mondragón stable in the first place. Since workers have to approve new ventures democratically, and they have all their savings in one basket and cannot withdraw them at will, they block many innovations as too risky.[16]

I bring up the example of Mondragón not because I think the model can be transplanted wholesale to the countryside of the global South. Mondragón has always been mainly industrial and urban, without close links to traditional communities. And while the Basque country in the 1950s was poor, it was far more prosperous than places like Pomatambo are today. Rather, Mondragón matters because it demonstrates two things. First, it highlights the importance of designing an experimental enterprise carefully in order to balance efficiency and participation, to adjust time horizons, and to provide the supporting institutions and growing pool of capital necessary for expansion over the long term. Second, it makes clear that capital held and managed collectively, with an eye to a range of social goods alongside rate of return, can flourish even against stiff competition from mainstream capitalism.

If cooperative enterprises financed by community-owned capital were to succeed in the Andean highlands, they would provoke an interesting dialogue with the enthusiasts of the "market revolution." Such people cannot justify suppressing or unduly hindering enterprises that are voluntarily organized and operate within the law. To do so would violate the liberal principles they espouse. Indeed, they cannot even offer much of a critique of such enterprises. Remember, they have always based their arguments for privatization, titling extralegally held land, and the like, on efficiency. All else comes second. If these community-oriented experimental enterprises were to stay afloat and grow amid competition, then by definition they would be economically efficient. And if capital is being used efficiently, then the market revolutionists have no grounds for complaining that it is ultimately owned by a group rather than by individuals. After all, if such enthusiasts really favored individual over collective entrepreneurship, then they would complain when corporations drive small proprietors out of business. They do not complain—far from it. For them, capital is capital, profit is profit, and growth is growth.

The only real motive for objection, if anyone dared to raise it openly, would be that they prefer capital in some hands rather than others. Perhaps they think that progress demands the disempowerment and dissolution of backward traditional communities like Pomatambo. Or perhaps some shrewd and ambitious souls prefer to deal not with communities and cooperatives, which have too much bargaining power, but rather with more vulnerable smallholders. Only time will tell. The proponents of the market revolution would have to reveal their priorities in due course.

Before going into the details of how community-owned capital might be managed in these villages, we have to return to a more basic question, one that I have bracketed so far. Where can the poor raise the significant capital that would allow them to have something to manage in the first place? The answer will be different in each area, and Pomatambo's likely solution may not travel well. But by looking at this community more closely, we discover some useful lessons.

One day in August 2006, I went on a long hike guided by Pomatambo's fortuneteller and old mountain hand. It took a gasping climb of about four hours from the village to reach the top of Hatun Cruz, the highest mountain in the area. On the way we passed through slope after slope of what I learned was Pomatambo's pasture land. It adds up to as much as six square miles on a map, but the sheer size only becomes clear when you are trudging through it on foot. Cows dotted the landscape. Apparently some families leave them for months on end. The cows become so accustomed to their grazing grounds that if they are taken down to the settlement and escape, they find their way back uphill. My climb was exhausting but well worth it. The summit had crumbling stone ruins and revealed a vast panorama of rural Vilcashuamán. I realized that the terrain before my eyes was, in a real sense, community itself. Five-sixths of the land is communally owned by each of the various villages. In Peru as a whole, peasant communities occupy some 89,000 square miles of territory.[17]

The common lands make up a vital part of the village economy, alongside the rotated tracts and irrigated private plots. In the parlance of resource-management experts, the pasture lands are held in a "common property regime." All inhabitants of a particular village can use its common land for grazing their own animals. They own the resource jointly but benefit as individuals when they use it. The grass belongs to everyone until it goes into the cow's stomach. This arrangement sets common property apart from a corporation or a cooperative, in which individuals pool their assets to generate a common profit. All over the world, common property of this sort has to be managed carefully to be sustainable. Its users have an incentive to pasture as many of their animals as possible, while the community needs to impose some limits to avoid exhausting the land. Traditional customs of land use have always filled this role.[18] Of course, villagers exploit pasture land unevenly. Those with more livestock naturally gain more from it because they have more mouths chewing the grass. María Gutiérrez told me that this inequality has sometimes been a sore point for poorer peasants around Vilcashuamán.

Despite their imperfections, the common lands continue to serve these communities well enough. For our purposes here, however, they have unrecognized potential. Looking at them from the summit of Hatun Cruz, I appreciated that they are the single largest asset of each of these villages. They are already a vast reserve of collectively owned capital, which over the centuries has yielded a modest but steady contribution to the livelihood of its owners. The community has real weight for its members in part because it stands behind this part of their subsistence. The common lands are the embodiment of community.

Unfortunately, this vast reserve of capital is also wholly undiversified and bound to agricultural stagnation. To finance the growth that could broaden the community's economic base, the communal lands would need to be converted into more flexible investment capital. This would amount to changing one form of collective wealth into another. Loosely, "common property" would turn into "corporate property," an endowment, or a stake in social enterprises. Profits on that capital would feed back into the community economy. For social critics who think that the very cycle of capital and profit is part of the problem, this approach may seem misguided at first. But capital in a technical sense is nothing more than a pool of wealth that supports productive activity. Call it what you will, but all societies need it in one form or another. In the modern world, capital lays communities waste and deforms the human experience only because it behaves so one-dimensionally, with no regard for broader social goods. Capital owned by and anchored in peasant communities like Pomatambo could behave quite differently.

The question then becomes one of *how* to convert common property in land into investment capital that can support a wider range of enterprises. I do not for a moment propose simply selling off the communal land en masse to generate cash. There are legal obstacles to doing so, as we shall see, and probably no buyers. Moreover, such a risky strategy would be foolish. But the villagers have other ways to leverage underused pasture (or rotational) land into a community-owned capital endowment. In the simplest terms, they must find a way to increase the output on that land, then channel the extra earnings into a new pool of investment money.

Some modest experimentation would let them do so. Take the problem of an economy of scale. Even if technical aid for agriculture poured into Pomatambo, the fragmented plots now under cultivation hardly lend themselves to innovation and use of machinery. And Sendero's threat to collectivize individual parcels of land was disastrously at odds with peasant values. On a chunk of the underused communal land, however, experimental techniques and machinery could dramatically raise output. There is ample precedent: the Inka empire accomplished some of its greatest feats of agricultural productivity—through irrigation, terracing, and the like—on state-owned land at the margins of these villages. You can still see abandoned terraces throughout the area.[19] One way to manage this experiment is for a few innovation-minded farmers to set up a cooperative that leases a section of the underused communal land from the village. The farmers would have leeway to experiment and to use any outside aid to best effect. Terraces could be built or rebuilt, and high-value export crops and hybrid strains could flourish. Perhaps Pomatambo could start selling specialty crops to the city of Ayacucho, for example. Such new crops would not compete with subsistence agriculture, which very likely would persist for a long time as a safety net.

At the same time, the rent or profit-sharing on that land would give the community as a whole a revenue stream that could flow into other kinds of small enterprises. This is the origin of a new type of community-owned capital. Small beginnings can have a major impact over time.

Eventually small enterprises financed by this capital could manufacture agricultural tools and simple consumer goods. Even peasants who mainly stuck to farming their own plots would gain the opportunity to earn a cash income through part-time employment in cooperatives.

Both the new forms of agriculture and the emerging nonagricultural sector would be organized as social enterprises. The peasants joining those enterprises would organize themselves democratically and cooperatively, drawing lessons from Mondragón and elsewhere. And the community, through its endowment or a cooperative bank, would hold a significant equity share in all of them. The village would retain its economic weight despite modernization. Its part-ownership of these new enterprises would allow it to share in economic growth and to bring its values and priorities to bear on decision-making. Energetic fellows like Alberto would have plenty of opportunity to prosper. We should not deny them that opportunity, hinder the release of their talents, or treat them as opponents of a cooperative economy. Quite the contrary—such entrepreneurially minded folk have much to offer the future. But through careful design of institutions, we can make sure they prosper within rather than outside the old values. This arrangement of cooperative enterprises and community-owned capital may be the closest analogy, under modern conditions, to the traditional village economy.

Legally, such an experiment would be easy to start in Pomatambo. Peruvian law gives peasant communities "legal existence and juridical personality." With the democratic consent of their members, they can enter into contracts, own property, and even set up businesses. While they cannot sell communal land, they can assign its use to their business partners in exchange for payment.[20] The exact rules for community enterprises have shifted over the years, but ample room for such experiments has remained. Given the entrepreneurial language of the statutes and the general priorities of the Peruvian state, it is clear that the aim has been to promote more conventional kinds of small business. Yet those laws can be used for many purposes, including empowering traditional communities and maintaining their basic values.

Of course, peasants elsewhere might look enviously at Pomatambo and other highland villages. They might say that what I propose could work nicely for communities lucky enough to have a huge reservoir of common property to leverage into a pool of capital. But what about villages where today the only land is in tiny private plots, with no room for experimentation? I do not deny that Pomatambo has it easy in some ways. Less favored villages would have to hunt for other sources of start-up capital. Where migrants have cash and nowhere promising to put it, a credit union could pay them a modest return based on a stake in a local cooperative. Or outside donors, instead of microlending to many vulnerable individuals, could endow a capital fund in one or more communities that would finance new cooperatives that agree to abide by a community-oriented business model. The source of capital would vary, but the purpose would not. Whether the start-up capital comes mainly from communities, individuals, or donors, the cooperatives it finances would generate a stream of revenue. Careful reinvestment would let it grow over time. How well favored a village is at the outset would affect only the scale of the first experiments.

My goal is not to lay out a one-size-fits-all blueprint for how to start a virtuous cycle of community-based growth. Rather, it is to point to different components of an alternative development model and how they might interlock. Independent enterprises, cooperatively organized, would have many of the habits of self-reliance and reciprocity that peasants have long practiced. The investment of community capital endowments in those enterprises would replicate the economic weight that traditional communities have had in the livelihood of their members. People merely need to make the leap of imagining that such communities can own moveable property, directly or indirectly, and that community property does not have to be only in land.

If a spiral of growth financed by community capital got underway, a host of ripple effects would follow. For one thing, relations among villages in the Vilcashuamán area would improve. Nowadays there are arguments about land boundaries. Even in the last decade, Pomatambans have ridden on horseback, ready to fight, up to the pasture land disputed with the neighboring village of Huaccaña. As the civil war wound down in the mid-1990s, community leaders apparently even urged migrants to move back so that Pomatambo would have more bodies to do battle.[21] This is a kind of tribal warfare for the twenty-first century. Furthermore, when a smattering of aid arrives from NGOs, villages cannot cooperate to use it. The PRONAMACHS report abounded with examples from all over rural Vilcashuamán of peasants speaking ill of their neighbors in nearby villages or complaining about having to work with them.[22]

If several villages in the same area started experiments in community-based growth, these tensions would very likely subside. The first enterprises should not be joint ventures among villages, because of the arguments that would disrupt them. But investment capital is inherently more fluid and mobile, more deterritorialized, than the pasture land over which these villages are now fighting. A formidable intercommunity banking network could emerge to finance development. Deterritorializing community capital would eventually lead to a more vibrant regional economy. To realize economies of scale and create markets for their products, these new cooperatives would have to network with one another across community lines.

These ties would alter the psychology of peasants who now like to insult their counterparts over the next hill. The founding father of sociology, Émile Durkheim, observed a shift in what binds people together in different periods of history. In simple villages, everyone is more or less the same. This sameness holds each community together but also means that it is self-contained. No larger unit bridging communities lasts long. In more complex modern societies, people have a wider range of occupations and lifestyles. Because of the division of labor, however, these different people have to depend on one another. Ties are weaker, but they can also radiate across wider areas.[23]

The strategy of community-based development I am proposing here would keep intact the old village solidarity as much as possible. But the economic networks among cooperatives would create new horizontal ties crisscrossing the countryside. They would replace the mostly defunct barter arrangements that used to link villages at different altitudes. At present, Pomatambo and its neighbors have hardly any economic relations. Subsistence agriculture is self-contained in each village, and the state and the occasional NGO deal with each one separately. Greater interdependence would help these communities realize what they have in common. They would have a stake in getting along. Growth would create a vibrant economy throughout the district and province. Whether in intent or just in effect, the government so far has pursued an approach of divide-and-conquer in the countryside, and consequently these villages have far less political influence than their population would suggest. An alternative economy, by weaving a network among them, would create a regional bloc with substantial bargaining power.

Perhaps a decade or so after the start of the experiment, half of the new productive activity in Vilcashuamán's countryside could be arising within the economy of values. A few more years, and that proportion could be higher. If the experiment got this far, it would already have achieved a good deal. Living standards would be rising, growth would be happening in a framework of community values, and the peasants would have more of a voice than they now enjoy.

But if allowed to continue, this model could have even more far-reaching impact. Remember that the point of this alternative development strategy is to bring prosperity while also strengthening traditional values. It is not to close off self-contained small economies, as some of the defenders of "place-based practices" might desire. Where self-reliance can help participation or nurture an experiment, we should welcome it. But traditional communities have always suffered from having all their eggs in one basket. The rudimentary local safety net meant individuals almost never starved before modern times; yet entire communities sometimes starved when hit by crop failures or other disasters.

The community endowments and cooperatives I have proposed would not be at risk of starvation. But they would still rest on too narrow a base for the long term. Imagine that hundreds of villages all over the global South, with thousands of cooperatives, took up this strategy. They would prosper and sustain their values. But they would still live on the defensive within global capitalism. They would surrender the largest economies of scale to more conventional kinds of businesses, and they would suffer more acutely from local and regional economic downturns.

So how might we build longer-range networks and economies of scale while remaining true to the community-based model? At the outset, a community endowment would be able to invest in only an experimental farming cooperative, village workshop, or the like. Its revenue and capital would remain modest until quite a few of those small businesses were flourishing. But as the investment pool grew, it could be diversified beyond a circle of local enterprises. Perhaps half of the medium-term revenue could flow into a kind of parallel global economy that would bind these local experiments together. Communities that prosper and want a more secure return on surplus capital could invest it in cooperative start-ups in other villages. In the long run, a village like Pomatambo could own shares not only in local enterprises, but also—directly or indirectly—in cooperatives all over the world. Add in the mobilization of modest individual savings through community-based credit unions, and we should have quite a pool of money.

This strategy would stimulate broader access to capital, economies of scale, and diversification. But it would offer all these things on terms very different from those of mainstream capitalism, and in a way less disposed to the excesses that caused the latest global financial crisis. This parallel global capital market would be controlled by the peasantry and people close to it. They would be investing their money with people like themselves, with a common purpose and networks of trust, rather than just adding it to the global juggernaut that now bears down on them. The community-oriented capital market would be informed by their values and could develop clear guidelines for what kinds of enterprises it would underwrite. For the first time in modern history, the world would have an ever larger pool of capital sloshing around among cooperative enterprises and helping to finance the right kind of prosperity.

In the later stages of this trajectory, the poor of the global South would enjoy the economic dynamism that advocates of the "market revolution" and microfinance now promise them. But it would be a much healthier kind of dynamism. Enthusiasts of today's global economy want to pull the poor into capitalism cutting them loose from their traditional moorings in the process. Their kind of prosperity for the poor would mark the final victory of a soulless global order, as the last bastions of tradition run up a white flag. This alternative instead starts from the values of the poor. It aims to catalyze a virtuous spiral of growth within a parallel economy that blends efficiency and a decent way of life. Every advance in the "economy of values" would mean an inroad against global capitalism, a slow but relentless displacement of it from below.

For that displacement to happen, the economy of values will have to stay the course. A strategic thread must run all the way from the first farming cooperatives and workshops to the point, a generation or more later, when this alternative economy is large enough to begin reshaping the contours of world order. That strategic thread requires an overarching vision and sensibility, of course. But it also requires careful design of the rules and incentives that will shape how these community endowments and cooperatives act. After all, if a light manufacturing workshop that starts today with a handful of young peasants succeeds, it will still exist, in a grander form, forty years hence. We have to make sure it operates in the same spirit, rather than turning into a narrow profit-seeking corporation that goes over to the other side of history.

In effect, we need a new model for how to shape decision-making by economic actors. Liberal states today tread quite lightly, preferring to let individuals and firms pursue their narrow self-interest. Supposedly, their exchanges in the market serve the public good via the "invisible hand." Liberal states usually intervene in only two cases. They pass laws against abuses and dishonesty; within the space untouched by those laws, anything goes. And when the pursuit of self-interest produces so-called "externalities"—side effects, such as pollution, that harm other people—then liberal states may tweak the incentives that shape behavior, perhaps by imposing taxes or granting subsidies.

Some thinkers lately have proposed slightly different ways to deal with problems generated by narrow self-interest, such as pollution or the exhaustion of common resources. Peter Barnes, in his book *Capitalism 3.0,* proposed "propertizing the commons." Air and water, for example, would be treated as the common property of the public. Polluters would have to buy the right to pollute. Along with rewarding a lighter environmental footprint, this reform would also raise revenue to finance public goods and pay dividends to all citizens.[24]

Whatever the merits of Barnes's proposal on one level, his approach misses a key point. Current liberal practice and these moderate reforms both lack imagination. They try to spur better behavior from individuals and firms by shaping the environment in which they operate. Either some activities are marked off as completely out of bounds, or the costs of doing business are changed so that the bottom line is affected. Unsurprisingly, this habit of mind appears in present policy debates over how to respond to recent mismanagement of the financial markets. The overriding motive of each economic actor is taken for granted. It is to pursue narrow self-interest, or to get the maximum profit from one's transactions. In the big picture, capital will flow to wherever it can get the highest return from the most efficient activity.

If you care only about efficiency, then that is your model; nothing needs changing. But the economy of values I have outlined here rests on a wider range of priorities. Efficiency is a very important one, but alongside it we have to weigh the effects on community cohesion, work practices, sustainability, and above all the cultural signals sent to people over time. By and large, these are not the kinds of goods that can be preserved or strengthened by regulation or by putting pressure on the balance sheet. Those tactics are blunt instruments that may even work against the spirit of traditional decency by favoring those who have a knack for ferreting out loopholes.

The best way to serve all these deeper ethical goals is to broaden the motives of the people who choose where society's investments go. In other words, we must target the decision-making itself rather than just its context.

To illuminate the issues, let us imagine the simplest solution, which I shall call "the virtuous millionaire." Suppose most of a society's wealth were in the hands of ethical and public-spirited people. Each of them would decide separately where to invest. They would seek a decent return on their investments, but they would also ponder the effect of their choices on community solidarity, cultural atmosphere, and other such ends. Efficiency and ethics would be seamlessly interwoven, without regulatory interference from above.

Where premodern societies worked reasonably well, they often had enough people like the virtuous millionaire. Traditionally educated landed proprietors were bound to the religious and customary norms of their societies. For all their imperfections and the real exploitation that often happened, such people were more likely than today's investment bankers to look beyond narrow economic self-interest. Such societies had collective versions of the virtuous millionaire as well. Monasteries in medieval Europe and the *waqf* endowments of the Islamic world managed their wealth for social purposes like charity and education. They made decisions freely, without the distortions that overregulation can create, but with an eye to much more than a quarterly profit report.

For the economy of values to work, it will have to replicate the virtuous millionaire as best it can. And that virtuous millionaire cannot die or acquire vices as soon as he becomes a billionaire. The economy of values must be saturated with capital that is (1) fruitful, (2) independent, (3) well-distributed, (4) diversified, and (5) managed according to a comprehensive set of values. It will be *fruitful* if it goes into productive enterprises and grows over time at a rate at or exceeding the growth rate in the mainstream capitalist economy. *Independence* of decision-making by each endowment and cooperative will allow flexibility and boldness in adapting to circumstances. A broad *distribution* of underlying ownership will uphold a decent spirit of equality and ensure that the benefits of development reach the neediest. *Diversification* of investments will even out risk and secure the patrimony of the world's most vulnerable people. And, not least, economic decisions made according to deeper *values* will reinforce those values, both because people would practice them year after year and because more financial weight would be added to them in the world at large.

Most of these goals could be built into the charters of endowments and cooperatives at the outset. Institutions can bind themselves in ways that individuals, whatever their good intentions, usually cannot. But the economy of values will need more if it is to gain ground over a few decades. For one thing, these economic networks can flourish only if cooperatives and endowments can work easily with one another. Upon establishment, therefore, they must all have charters that promote collaboration. The likeliest way to accomplish this is by setting up a global NGO to devise a common organizational blueprint, navigate the legal constraints that vary across countries, and ease the founding of new members of the network.

Based on participatory processes that reflected people's thinking and experiences on the ground, such an umbrella NGO could also certify each new enterprise. This certification process would enhance trust among members of the network. To belong to it in Ayacucho would mean the same as to belong to it in Addis Ababa. Certification can also discourage defection by marking off clearly which kinds of behavior and business models fall within, and which fall outside, the economy of values. An enterprise that defected to a more conventional business strategy of narrow profit-seeking could be decertified. Losing access to much of the economy of values would be swift punishment for defecting. Such a threat would discourage selling out. Even if it did not, it would neutralize such an enterprise's ability to poison the rest of the network.

Alongside certification, the umbrella NGO could also play a crucial role in raising capital to get the cycle of growth underway. It could help raise initial funding from sympathetic donors, set up credit unions, and the like. As an entity ultimately responsible to the peasantry, it could also set up the infrastructure necessary for the community-oriented global capital market in the long run. It could connect communities and cooperatives needing start-up funding with those seeking a secure outlet for their extra capital. By ensuring transparency and consistency, it would help networks of trust to develop.

Some observers sympathetic to local economic alternatives might balk at this global network and capital market. They might fear that it diminishes the local independence of precisely the communities it aims to help. But I would insist that one does not lose anything by connecting communities to one another. To be sure, we might harm them by connecting them to the *wrong* kind of economy, as the market revolution proposes to do. But by connecting one community to another with much the same goals, we would only multiply their strengths—and, in the end, make it less necessary for them to deal with the devil on the devil's terms.

Moreover, it matters greatly how the global network and capital market function. By its very nature, the umbrella NGO would tread lightly. It would connect localities and independent cooperatives, not supplant them or lock them into one organization. No community or cooperative would lose the ability to make its own decisions about economic activities or partnerships. On an economic landscape tilted toward some fairly basic ethical commitments, they would have full freedom of movement. The umbrella NGO would be a well-designed clearinghouse of resources and information, so that the thousands of decentralized decisions by its member enterprises would be more rather than less responsive to a values-driven vision of development.

This parallel economy will grow more quickly if it also feeds as much activity as possible back into itself. All these enterprises will have to buy from and sell to the broader market. But they should give preference to one another where possible. Imagine a coffee-growers' cooperative that can contract with a transport cooperative to take a shipment of beans to a cooperative processing plant, which in turn could sell it to a cooperative wholesaler abroad. The enterprise charters and cross-investment channels can be carefully designed to favor these alliances where they are economically viable, without dictating the business choices of each cooperative. Efficiency could still be promoted by competition among cooperatives trying to fill the same niche. The richer and more diverse the parallel economy becomes, the higher the proportion of its activity that could stay within.

Let there be no doubt that, in the long run, the strategy is to colonize ever more economic space and thereby peacefully displace the one-dimensional market. Close the circuits of collaboration where you can, to reinforce the unique pattern of decision-making, benefit the like-minded, and discourage enterprises from leaving. Open the circuits where you must, to meet your needs or to capture more resources from the mainstream economy. Mainstream businesses will deal with you when you make it worth their while, even if doing so strengthens an experiment informed by very different values. Capitalism has never lacked defectors.

As a vision and strategic roadmap, the economy of values occupies a distinct space. The differences with the one-dimensional economy of global capitalism are clear. Capitalism rewards the relentless pursuit of efficiency. Over time, wealth gravitates towards those who push other considerations to the margin. According to the defenders of this model, it is well that those other values get thrust aside. The market is self-correcting, they aver, and eventually it raises living standards for everyone. The distribution of wealth matters little, if at all, so long as absolute prosperity increases. The economy is about consumption, not power or values, and it can serve consumption best when left to its own logic.

The economy of values is not only a challenge to one-dimensional capitalism, however. It also contrasts with other failed alternatives to capitalism. State socialism, for example, identified the problem with capitalism as basically a lack of democratic control. It broke down the boundary between economic and political life by bringing capital under state ownership. The socialist alternative was just as modern as capitalism itself, however. In lieu of private investors, it simply installed a layer of bureaucracy. Either way, traditional folk lost control over their own lives. Dignity, ordered liberty, and community ended up in retreat under socialism just as much as under capitalism.

Much gentler has been the defense of local economies that Schumacher and some on the radical left have advocated. Recent experiments inspired by "place-based practices" have included farmer's markets, local credit unions, and voluntary local currencies that support regional economies and small businesses.[25] No doubt we can learn from some of their ideas in designing an economy of values. And they should welcome this kind of experiment, because virtually everything they want has a place within it.

But I think the movement to re-create humane local economies is incomplete on two counts, one strategic and one substantive. First, a defense of place is inherently limiting. Whatever forms such a defense of place takes, it targets only one aspect of capitalism: its size and uprootedness. While walls can make good defenses, they also limit the imagination. The defense of one or another place does not help one to reconquer the world, in the sense of building a larger political and economic environment that works with rather than against these communities. An alternative should not have to exist on the sufferance of the larger society. To put it bluntly, the local-economy enthusiasts are not aggressive enough: they cede the global high ground a bit too easily. Occasionally they say that local economies in different parts of the world could collaborate with one another in loose alliances or networks. But their strategy does not involve a clear, *universal* model for a worldwide parallel economy, which is the only hope for displacing the monster of one-dimensional capitalism.

Second, the local-economy movement has serious problems with substance. I suspect the timidity about a global strategy starts here. The contemporary left, of which this movement forms one strand, is profoundly uncomfortable with any talk about universal values, about cross-cultural truths of the human condition. Its social base is not in the global South; it is among comfortable moral relativists in Europe and North America. Indeed, traditional communities around the world often strike such people as too hard-edged, too constraining, too demanding on their members. Since traditional folk tend to see values as true—as requiring assent rather than invention—the contemporary left is instinctively ill at ease with them. It will usually defend them against encroachment by global corporations, which it loathes, but it will not come out and baldly declare that the traditional peasantry is right and the modern world is wrong. Without such unapologetic clarity, the local-economy movement cannot hope to mobilize the large and promising social base among the rural poor. It also has a hard time justifying anything more ambitious than niche experiments here and there.

Compared to the local-economy movement, the traditionalist critiques of capitalism in the early twentieth century were closer to the mark. They discerned a deeper truth behind the traditional economic arrangements they wanted to defend or revive. They also said quite bluntly that their alternative would empower the right rather than the wrong kind of people. But I part company with the distributists in drawing different conclusions about strategy. Since they thought the basic problem with capitalism (and socialism) was the concentration of economic power, they wanted to disperse property among smallholders. Those like Penty who admired the medieval guilds thought that reviving them was the best way to assure economic justice. Their hearts were in the right place. But to define the problem as one of how many people own what, or what structures can keep an economy in just equilibrium, misses the point. It makes too much of power and structure as a way to get at morality. It usually ends up prescribing institutional arrangements that are too rigid to travel well, to withstand economic pressure, or to drive future growth on their own terms. The distributists were not moral relativists, as some critics of capitalism are today. Their critique was all the more powerful because of its underlying universalism. But the structures and patterns of ownership they defended were still too bound to time and place.

In short, capitalism is too narrow, socialism is too top-heavy, the contemporary left is too defensive, and the early traditionalists were too static. Only the economy of values, as I have outlined it here, gets at what is arguably the deepest issue: the motives behind decision-making. You can have all the freedom, equality, independence, and adaptability you want. You just have to design institutions so that economic actors must weigh a range of ethical goals. Viewed in that light, it makes sense to start the experiment in communities like Pomatambo, where people still do just that. They retain most of the traditional view of economic life as intertwined with ethics, community, and culture. Choices made by them collectively, in a well-considered way, will reflect those values. To empower them is to empower tradition. The social and economic base to challenge modernity's ills is already present, if you know where to look.

At the same time, places like Pomatambo have a substantial reserve of wealth that has yet to be enclosed and fragmented. Throughout most of the developed world, such property vanished with industrialization. It persists tenuously for a minority of the peasantry in parts of Latin America, Africa, and southern Asia. In China, rural land has been owned by the state and assigned to villages for the last half century. Such underlying common property might give some leeway for community-based economic experiments there. But China's villages have been collapsing from outmigration and agricultural stagnation. Common property itself is under siege, too. The "market revolution" is targeting it ever more directly, including through recent proposals for privatizing land title. Whether the Chinese peasantry will be able to push back and decide its own fate remains to be seen.

Where unenclosed traditional communities like Pomatambo still exist, they are the last surviving remnants of the precapitalist economy, of the old commonwealth. The common property we find there remains infused with social and ethical expectations. It has not become wealth for wealth's sake, as the market revolution threatens to make it. The right people possess this wealth already; they need not acquire it before they can start working with it. Far better to start building our alternative where such value-laden common property still survives than to try to conjure it out of thin air. We do not have to re-create a peasantry from scratch, as the distributists hoped to do in England in the 1920s. Why not enlist what is left of the world's peasantry to fight for itself while it still can?

Unlike other alternatives to capitalism, moreover, the model I have proposed would have plenty of entrepreneurial dynamism. It would aim not merely to defend a patch of ground, but rather to grow and occupy ever more space in the economy. The endowments and cooperatives would have enough incentives to achieve efficiency that they would pursue new opportunities. If directed properly, community-owned capital can finance well-paid and fulfilling employment. It can also channel resources to strengthen rather than undermine these communities. Pay your employees and members decently, structure work so that it affirms human dignity and solidarity, and give capital first and foremost to those on the right side of history—these are the mandates.

Running a business ethically along these lines is expensive, to be sure. After deducting all the costs and avoiding unsavory practices, the rate of profit might well be lower than for a conventional business in the same place but with no goal beyond narrow profit-making. But there would still be some profits, and what those managing the community endowments do with them will make a huge difference, strategically. For the economy of values to flourish, it will need more than just to make ethically informed choices about where capital goes and how it is used. It will also need a decent cumulative return on capital so that it can grow.

The obvious way to assure an upward spiral of growth is by reinvesting profits in the network over several decades. Such disciplined reinvestment means having the parsimony of an eighteenth-century Calvinist, not because anyone should be a tormented miser but because the only way to displace capitalism is to outperform it. Such reinvestment is fairly easy to do as a technical matter. Endowment and enterprise charters could require it from the start. And in trying to outgrow mainstream capital-ism, the economy of values has a key advantage: It would be mainly the affair of the world's poorest people and areas. All else being equal, return on capital is usually higher where there is less of it floating around. This parallel economy could thus outpace its rival for a long time, thereby expanding its share of global wealth and power.

It bears stressing that disciplined reinvestment does not have to mean shortchanging the peasantry or keeping living standards artificially low. The twentieth century abounds with examples of state socialist regimes that squeezed farmers to subsistence to fund industrialization, cavalierly promising that it would pay off for everyone eventually. The economy of values, by contrast, would be managed by peasants and those close to them. They would ensure that the cooperatives paid their members well and that rural infrastructure really benefited their communities. The strat-egy of reinvesting profits only applies after such legitimate expenditure is deducted. But after taking that duly into account, it must be stressed that reinvestment is crucial. Most peasants have the plain common sense to know that too free and shortsighted a payout of gains would work against their interests in the long run. Less reinvestment would slow down the overall rate of growth in the economy of values, making it harder if not impossible to displace one-dimensional capitalism.

More concretely, consider how this argument might be put to peasants in a village like Pomatambo. They now have community capital locked up in land. That land helps support their livelihood in a modest way, yield-ing up dividends in kind. It is also the embodiment of their community and shapes their lives in ways that most of them generally endorse. If the market revolutionists get their way, sooner or later that capital will flow out of community hands, and the community will unravel as well. Peas-ants will have neither a secure livelihood nor their present way of life. Capital will fall into the hands of an entrepreneurial and investor class. Economic life will be arranged to maximize return on that capital. Its new owners will pat the peasants on the head and tell them that they are getting a good deal anyway, because outside capital is financing economic activity that pays their salaries and builds infrastructure. They will be told that the profits rightly belong to the employers and investors, and that they do not need a share of the profits for their living standard to rise, for that is a byproduct of profit-making.

If Pomatambans and people like them want to defend their interests and values, the best way is to make sure that their community has plenty of economic weight behind it. The economy of values would provide that weight. Growth within it would give its members added bargaining power. They would oversee their own endowments and enterprises, and economic decisions would reflect a wider range of values than any capitalist entrepreneur would weigh. Moreover, community-owned capital would finance at least as much economic growth as the capitalist entrepreneur would. It would pay peasants' salaries and build rural infrastructure. Indeed, it would do more of these things and better, because of the guidelines about how it is to be used. Efficiency, dynamism, and spillover effects are all built into this model.

It is worth recalling that in mainstream economic thinking, profits are usually seen as a payment to capital for its use. So in this case, if profits do not go back into the experiment, where else could they properly go? In many instances, the start-up capital financing the economy of values would be the unenclosed common property of these villages. It would be the physical embodiment of traditional life, as it were. Growth of community capital is a growth of community power. It follows that peasants might think of profits not as something to pay themselves as short-term dividends, but instead as an ongoing investment in a future hospitable to their own way of life.

✦ ✦ ✦

So far I have dwelt on the economic dimension of the alternative, but the cultural dimension matters just as much. The economy of values would rest on the traditional virtues even as living standards rise. Just as economic growth without values offers more of the same sterile modern world, so would traditional practices without growing economic clout be a dead end. By advancing economically and radiating out in all directions, this experiment would strengthen and multiply the social networks of traditionalists. In today's world, generally speaking, the more liberal, secular, and mercenary you are, the wider your geographic horizons. The economy of values would offer a material base for an alternative, more ethical, global civil society. After all, economic development is always a means to an end.

In some ways, this aspect of the experiment would replicate globally what Liang Shuming tried to do in China in the 1930s. His "rural reconstruction" movement put together a network of adult-education institutes, rural credit unions, county fairs, and the like. It hoped to show by example a Confucian alternative to Westernization. Peasants would prosper, but they would also learn the skills for a vibrant new civil society.[26]

What I propose would have more global reach because it would not depend on appealing to any one civilization's heritage. It would, of course, build on the most intact traditions of our time. In areas like the Andean highlands, for example, the old ways persist as a point of departure. The schoolteachers and people like them, with their energy, critical spirit, and sympathy for the rural poor, could bring their formidable mobilizing potential to bear. In its early stages, the economy of values would link these most promising islands of resistance. Once it had shown it could deliver real development, even modestly, it would spread elsewhere—including to those parts of the global South, like much of the Chinese hinterland, that now seem defeated by the "market revolution." The clarity and vigor of an alternative on the march would impress all onlookers.

In economics and culture, this momentum would rely on no outsiders. It would arise from the efforts of those who chose to participate, and it would affect mainly them. I am merely proposing a framework and a tool kit that will help those efforts get underway, and above all multiply their effects. It is not a blueprint to be imposed politically on villages like Pomatambo; they have had enough of that. Beyond an early stage, however, some of this alternative's momentum would have to transfer into the political realm. The foundations laid in civil society can support a much more far-reaching change in the political environment. Indeed, the alternative must engage other political forces in the long run to accomplish its ends.

But one might ask why we need a political agenda at all. Why not be content with a strategy of steady displacement? To be sure, the most crucial victories will come early, simply by getting things moving in the right direction economically and culturally. Those gains alone would improve the lives of the rural poor. But even with such successes, the alternative would still be swimming against the tide. The largest concentrations of economic, cultural, and political influence in the world would remain on the other side of history. You do not have to be paranoid to foresee that if the economy of values gains ground, influence would be brought to bear against it. It would be slowed down if not rolled back.

To keep opposing pressures at bay, therefore, we have to match the economic and cultural confidence of a reinvigorated peasantry with political power. Moreover, fully realizing the vision means restructuring the broader economic and political environment. A world hospitable to these values must restore real local political participation and rein in the pressure exerted against these communities by the mainstream economy. Purely voluntary efforts in civil society will not be sufficient. We need the state. Policies must change from grudgingly allowing the alternative to actively encouraging it.

The details of this political agenda will vary from country to country. Peru, for example, offers some advantages, given its present political landscape. It may not at first seem a likely setting for restorationist, peasant-based politics, if only because it lacks a powerful indigenous movement. Unlike in Bolivia, Ecuador, and Guatemala, Peru's peasants rarely mobilize along ethnic lines as Quechua-speakers.[27] But this may also be a strength. The alternative is not, after all, ultimately about any one culture. It is a universalist, not an ethnic, vision. So Peru may prove a fine setting for putting the values of the peasantry into more placeless language. Whether or not this alternative ever passes through a phase of being called "the Peruvian model," it should surely not be called "the Andean model," in an exclusive sense. It should speak to everyone.

Another Peruvian advantage involves the electorate's alienation from political institutions and elites. The broader public—not only the peasantry—feels excluded by an unresponsive national government. Politicians engage voters only superficially. Most parties are weak, short-lived, and revolve around personalities rather than visions.[28] In such a political landscape, a party with a confident traditionalist base could rise very quickly. It could occupy a third of the political spectrum, perhaps more if it reached out successfully to the cities, where so many displaced former peasants now live. Furthermore, Peru's disarray of political forces and the state's haphazard relationship with any one of them opens up room for vigorous policy initiatives. If such a traditionalist party won a national election, it could carry through major reforms by working with its already solidified base in civil society. If it delivered real benefits to the countryside, it would ensure its electoral good fortune for the long term.

Even without a clear political victory, greater influence over the state would still help the alternative gain ground that it could not occupy just by relying on civil society. At a minimum, a more sympathetic government in Lima could expand space for these rural ventures. It could enhance the legal machinery that traditional communities could deploy on behalf of their values and interests. In parts of the world where such communities have even less recognition, governments could give them full legal personality and the right to start economic experiments.

Greater political power would also make possible far-reaching institutional reforms. In recent years, Peru has been beset with all manner of proposals to change how the levels of government relate to one another. Some ideas have dealt with redrawing regional boundaries, others with clustering provinces and the like. Toledo's government made some halfhearted efforts to decentralize, but without real transfers of power to lower levels of government. One small party in the 2006 presidential election, the Decentralist Coalition, called for devolving functions further to strengthen participation.[29] But all such proposals remain disconnected from the lives and values of the people who could most benefit. For all the modernizers' talk about democracy and civic participation, they ignore what lies right under their noses. Hardly any of them genuinely respect and want to build on the age-old participatory practices of the highland communities.

To tap the peasantry's potential for civic engagement will require more avenues for local political participation. Such grassroots democracy can serve as a skeletal support structure, so to speak, complementing the circulatory system of the economy of values. The twentieth century everywhere concentrated power in the hands of technocrats out of touch with the peasantry. By giving real authority to the local, district, and provincial levels, we could bring decision-making much closer to these people. The nearly sixty villages in Vilcashuamán already manage most of their own affairs. But the influence of rural folk on higher levels of government remains limited. As we saw earlier, most Pomatambans see higher authorities as uninterested in their needs, even disdainful of them. If we extended the peasant culture of participation upwards, we would see provincial peasant assemblies with real debates in Quechua. These people could at last feel that they own the political institutions that affect them.

The best way to make these smaller units of government matter is by giving them more power. Let them make more spending decisions, for example. The national government today, even after deducting costs that could not be decentralized—defense, debt service, and the like—controls some four-fifths of remaining public expenditures.[30] The *alcalde* told me that Vilcashuamán province now has an annual budget of less than $400,000—about $13 a person—out of which nearly half goes toward official salaries rather than infrastructure and basic services. Ideally, a shift of much spending authority to the community and district levels would coincide with a substantial transfer of state aid to these newly empowered communities. Perhaps a third of the national budget could flow to these local governments as block grants. A formula could give them at least a share proportionate to their population—if not much more, based on their dire need.

When I casually broached this idea in 2006, it got warm responses from peasants who now feel forgotten as well as from locals across a wide political spectrum. Even the *alcalde,* for all his misgivings about the peasantry, welcomed the prospect of block grants. He did so because of a desire not so much for rural civic engagement as for simple efficiency. He thought that much as in a market, people know their own priorities more accurately than do officials gauging them from a distance.

Along with the economic clout that community endowments would have, such local political empowerment would shore up the importance of these villages. Many observers of traditional life say that communities have hung together over the generations because of poverty. They shape the boundaries of subsistence and offer a rudimentary safety net.[31] As they prosper, the pressures of poverty will no longer bind them together in the same way. As living standards rise, the relevance of the communities to daily life would benefit from political reinforcement. Those villagers who used to care about the community as a support network in poverty might come to care about it as a channel for services instead. Channeling a chunk of public spending through them will raise the stakes of civic participation.

I am confident that Pomatambans offered such responsibility would handle it in the right spirit. When they go hat in hand to the district and provincial authorities, they are usually asking for public goods for the community—precisely the things that block grants would give them the discretion to buy. Even today, they favor spending on the community over spending on short-term individual consumption. In the days leading up to the village festival in 2006, for example, I told a couple of the village leaders that I wanted to make the gesture of a small contribution toward the feast expenses. They mulled it over and said that it would do more good in the long run to apply the same amount towards the new church roof they were struggling to build.

Moreover, strengthening local decision-making now would empower the right kind of people, the people committed to a restoration of the old ways. Among the questions to ask of any decentralizing proposal are whose voices it would amplify and what values they have. The traditional authorities and people like them still enjoy plenty of influence in villages like Pomatambo. Giving block grants to the community would mean the community, led by its most esteemed members, could decide what to do with those funds. Power would shift away from those who are good at begging from suit-clad technocrats and politicians in town, and towards those who live the ethos of community every day. Imagine the respect with which visiting experts would treat the peasantry if people like the *varayoqs* held the purse strings on local projects.

An enthusiastic modernizer will protest that this is a recipe for stagnation and corruption. How could such benighted folk manage development funds when they lack expertise in and knowledge of the larger economic and political picture? Well, for one thing, we should not underestimate the intelligence of these highlanders. No dimwit would ever get to serve as one of the traditional authorities. Peasant leaders are acquiring more

education each decade, anyway, and the tasks involved require no technical expertise beyond what can be contracted from outside. Moreover, the
cultural norms of these communities work against corruption because
they urge public-spiritedness and frown on lying, cheating, and stealing.
Indeed, because of their credibility with most peasants who are not part
of the modern world, the traditional authorities may have *more* room to
take bold initiatives to improve their villages.

In any case, one learns by doing. If leaders lack all the skills to manage
development spending themselves, it is because up to now they have not
needed them. Empower the villages, and they will elect leaders who either
have those skills or will cultivate them very quickly. This decentralization would also reverse a sad trend of the modern era. Ambitious people
with political know-how tend to move out of the peasantry—out of the
working class in general—rather than stay and fight on its behalf.[32] The
capitalist economy and top-heavy states co-opt them. With more decisions happening locally, more of them would stick to their roots—and
their influence would grow.

What would all these changes mean in the medium term? Imagine
that after a generation or so, the various prongs of the alternative had
advanced on the economic, cultural, and political fronts. Living standards
for the world's poorest would be rising. Communities that have long
rested on agriculture would be diversifying their economic bases while
staying intact. Their networks would be radiating out into a parallel
economy of values. Precisely the people who have now been written out
of the future would have renewed confidence and the weight to assert
themselves politically. Above all, the slow slide into oblivion of the best
of traditional life would have been arrested.

Taken together, these gains would add up to a remarkable accomplishment. A secure perimeter would have been established around the
alternative. The incursions of the "market revolution" and other pressures against traditional life would have been slowed, stopped, and partly
reversed. The world's economic, cultural, and political elites might feel
the ground starting to shift under their feet.

But erecting a secure perimeter would still not mean victory. Much
more would remain to be done. All the groundwork laid up to that point

would simply have paved the way for a far more profound and enduring shift in the contours of the global order.

VII

Dawn over the Andes

This has been a book about the peasantry, its experiences, and its hopes. In the story of this one Andean village we see some of the most pressing issues of our time brought down to a human scale. The poorest of the poor feel buffeted on all sides. The economic growth that enriches the world's fortunate has not percolated down to these backwaters. Most politicians, businessmen, and their fellow travelers dismiss peasants as contributing nothing to development. The few who pay more attention, like Fujimori and de Soto, want to remake the countryside so that the fevered energies of the market can penetrate remote hamlets. At the other end of the political spectrum, radical movements of the left, like Sendero,

Fig. 7: Sunrise on the road between Pomatambo and Vilcashuamán

have preached revolution. But it has been a revolution that proposes to shred the social fabric of these villages and install grim cadres.

Either way, peasants have every reason to suspect that they are doomed. No future on offer includes them. Both right and left claim to offer prosperity, but at the price of wiping out most of what has made the lives of rural folk decent and fulfilling. On its present track, history promises peasant communities only oblivion.

The alternative I have sketched in this book takes peasant values seriously as a point of departure. I am not a peasant. I can hardly pretend to get inside their heads and express all of their thoughts. And I put what is at stake in different language than an Andean farmer would use: doing so is the only way to connect these people's suffering and dreams to the larger forces that surround them. Yet I believe that they would find the kind of diagnosis and vision put forth in these pages more recognizable than what has been thrust at them by mercenary politicians and militants with guns and little red books.

This alternative aims to give them the best of both worlds: economic justice *and* traditional values. The economy of values would relieve severe poverty. It would also empower these villages rather than ripping them apart. And it would do so while helping them to stay confidently within the solid tradition of small decencies that has served them so well through the centuries. In short, the alternative is about the defense of communities.

For the modernizers who dominate the political and intellectual mainstream, communities can persist in the future only as hollow shells. They will make no real difference in how people live and work. The great-grandchildren of today's Pomatambans might have a vague fondness for their ancestral village. They might come back for the annual festival, and they might even wear old-fashioned clothing now and then for novelty's sake. They might proudly note their Andean heritage when asked about it by friends or coworkers in Miraflores, Miami, or Mumbai. But such "Pomatambans" would be a wholly different breed from today's mountain folk. Community for them would be but a place and a name, not a spirit of duty and sense of belonging.

Our alternative would try to avoid such a future. It would build another one aligned with the best of the past. Community is an ethos, not an identity. What makes Pomatambo worthwhile is a self-understanding that comes out in a hundred gestures of daily life. That self-understanding used to appear in villages all over the world. In some, it has disappeared in recent generations. In others, it hangs on here and there, mostly among the old and the insular. In villages where it still holds strong, a mere defense of place will just delay its vanishing. Only by going on the offensive and changing the broader environment in which these villages exist can we hope not only to preserve this way of life where it now survives but also to restore it elsewhere. It must be put in universal terms in order to grow economic and political teeth. Better to export these values as placeless than to lose them and end up with ties to place in name only.

If it gains ground, the economy of values would go a long way towards accomplishing this end. It would bring the right kind of prosperity to the poor and the traditional. It would expand their political influence in many countries whose governments now disdain them. The networks of cooperation on which it rests would bring like-minded people and communities together, as they try to live out an alternative vision of the future brimming with modernity's best technologies and capabilities, yet without the cultural and spiritual collapse.

In mapping out this future, I have focused on the world's most vulnerable and down-to-earth people. The economy of values will resonate with them most of all, simply because they have been neglected the most and have concretely the most to gain. Any alternative to the modern world that passes lightly over their needs deserves to fail. But whatever the benefits to these folk, the ethical commitments behind this vision hardly stop with them. People far more comfortable than they have every reason to doubt the sanity of much of modern life. One can have a full stomach and still be dismayed by the unraveling of decency and the flattening of higher aspirations. Consumerist excess and the rule of mercenary souls do no one any good.

I am a deep traditionalist, both inside and outside villages. I shall not dwell on those broader issues here because I have already written about them at length in *Beyond the Global Culture War*. Suffice it to say that even though the rural poor will rightly see this experiment as mainly about their needs and their values, it is also just one front in a much broader struggle over what kind of world civilization we want.

Gaining economic and political ground within countries like Peru will help the alternative prosper. Yet it is easy to imagine the economy of values stalling and stagnating at that point. Worse, it could be rolled back under pressure from the world's power centers. Only a change in the character of the global economy as a whole could really secure its gains. Moreover, true human fellowship around the world will require overcoming the development gap between North and South. Even in the best scenario, the economy of values could bring only a substantial rise in living standards and a modest narrowing of that gap. Closing it will eventually mean a more level playing field, along with well-directed North–South aid for infrastructure and the like. It bears noting that aid would have more effect if it flowed into a flourishing economy of values, with a strong civil society and local participation, rather than through today's top-heavy and unresponsive governments.

That more ambitious agenda must await a shift in the global constellation of interests, institutions, and policy priorities. Such a shift will occur only if this movement can transmit its momentum to a global political agenda at the right instant. That global political agenda could have many possible venues, depending on the shape of world politics a generation or two hence. Today, we have no global institutions directly responsive to public pressure. Perhaps the sort of people who now shape world events will see fit by then to create some for their own ends. If they do so, then the movement could fight its ultimate political battles within those global democratic institutions, in the name of older values that otherwise would be written out of the future. If such institutions do not then exist, perhaps founding them could become one rallying cry for the movement. In the meantime, it will have to find other pressure points.

Whatever the form global political engagement takes, it must pass through some obvious stages of maturation. By networking across borders, the economy of values would create a parallel civil society. That civil society would be made up of the traditionally minded and would help them overcome their now quite narrow horizons. The younger generation has a role to play in building people-to-people contacts. The cooperative networks could become pathways along which youths move as they seek training and indulge their wanderlust. Better to circulate from one community to another, as journeymen did during the Middle Ages, than to feel one has to abandon community altogether for the turbulent insecurity of the cities. Youthful energy and idealism need a healthier outlet than today's one-dimensional global economy can offer them. The economy of values can provide a different and more humane way up, so to speak. Whether such young people travel and work elsewhere for one year or several, or even if they settle outside the village of their birth, they would always be a net gain to this network of communities. They would transmit best practices wherever they went. And they would build long-distance ties that, over time, would weave around the world a more elastic extension of the fabric that now binds peasant villages together.

This alternative global civil society might be slow in coming, but when it came it would carry immense weight. These networks would help the kind of people now dismissed as backward and irrelevant gradually to become the base for a global political alternative. This very long-term approach has proven its worth many times before on a smaller scale and across the political spectrum. On the left, the Italian Marxist Antonio Gramsci long ago outlined a strategic "war of position" that guided so-called Eurocommunists for decades. It involved making peaceful inroads in key institutions of civil society such as universities, unions, and the media in order to broaden the radical support base over time. On the right, American conservatives over a generation have built an entire network of think tanks, foundations, and media outlets to advance their challenge to the liberal-centrist establishment.[1] Whatever their more visible victories, neither the Eurocommunists nor the American conservative movement would have had much influence without their bases in civil society.

Traditionalists have never been quite so adept at long-term strategy. As the experiences of the distributists, Liang Shuming, Gandhi, and others show, they have usually fallen back on self-contained experiments that have plenty of symbolic value but little staying power. Such tentativeness has many causes, I suspect. Traditionalists often lack the no-holds-barred relentlessness of the Marxist left and promarket right. They also peg their experiments on restoring one or another practice in one or another place, rather than offering a model for export. And, not least, their experiments hardly ever build in enough momentum to grow of their own accord.

The alternative I have sketched here has by its very nature both the universality and the drive to grow that those earlier efforts lacked. When it comes to the requisite relentlessness, I trust we can be as hardheaded as we need to be when faced with certain obstacles, now that we know from a century's experience how unyielding they are. And we can do so while remaining true to the basic ethical considerations that move us in the first place.

What would a transition to more global political assertion look like for this movement? Or to put it another way, what might we see in the phase between the achievement of noticeable economic and political clout in countries like Peru, and a more far-reaching rearrangement of global institutions? Perhaps the most obvious change would involve forming political alliances across borders. As I suggested in the previous chapter, a party committed to economy-of-values principles could occupy plenty of space on the political spectrum in any country where existing parties are weak and unresponsive. Given enough economic weight and clarity of purpose, this movement could give rise to such parties in at least a third of the countries of the developing world. Separately, they could accomplish all the gains outlined earlier in the book. Together, they could do still more. The time would be ripe for what we might call a Traditionalist International: an alliance of traditionalist parties or blocs across all countries where they have gained a toehold.

A Traditionalist International would help advance this agenda in several ways. Smaller and newer parties could learn from the successes of their counterparts elsewhere. They would also have an explicitly global vision to spur on their mobilizing efforts, so they would not seem merely to defend one or another backward enclave. Still more importantly, gains by the economy of values in some countries would make it easier for political leaders elsewhere to advocate policies helpful to it. They could point to rising living standards to prove that the alternative was already working for real people. They could also counter some of the pressures that now work against experimentation. Any government today that unnerves global power centers with unorthodox talk stands to lose foreign corporate investment. Such a threat keeps most vulnerable Southern governments in line and stunts the imagination. If the economy of values were flourishing elsewhere, such experimenters would have somewhere to turn. A policy environment less servile to one-dimensional investors might well drive some of them out. But if designed properly, it would also attract a growing pool of values-driven capital to balance the loss. Voters would feel freer to choose.

And the voter base is there. A proven economic alternative and the security of cross-border alliances would release its inhibitions. If a well-considered economic policy that blended social justice with a traditional sense of decency and community were put up to a vote in the developing world, it would win by a landslide nearly everywhere. Voters in places like rural Vilcashuamán would line up in droves to mark their ballots for a political option that really spoke to them.

While the peasantry will shrink somewhat over the next generation—because of migration to the world's swelling cities—this voter base will not disappear. After all, every new urban migrant is but an uprooted peasant. Most such migrants would probably have stayed in the countryside if it had offered more economic opportunities. By building rural prosperity, the economy of values would allow these hard-pressed and uprooted people to think about going home again. And even if they do not go home, the alternative has plenty to offer them. One in seven human beings today lives in an urban slum.[2] The shantytowns of Ayacucho and places like it need economic development of the right kind, not the haphazard eking out of a living that one sees among displaced people today. Community capital endowments and a growing network of cooperatives could raise employment and living standards there just as well as in the villages. The economic model transfers well across the rural–urban divide. Circuits of trade and investment could bind city and countryside together, all within the framework of the economy of values.

Here I know I shall run into a major objection. Some skeptics will ask, what about the developed world? You can build all the support you like in the villages and shantytowns of the global South. Perhaps such folk will go along with you for a time. But you will find it hard to make any inroads in the North. People in North America, Europe, Japan, and other enclaves of prosperity will never buy into this vision. At first, it will probably not even make sense to them. And when they do grasp what is at stake, they will dismiss it as backward-looking or even sinister and oppressive in its attachment to tradition. Moreover, even though the wealthy countries make up but a small fraction of humanity, they have most of the power. Your alternative will remain confined to the poorest countries. In the long run it will wither, because the more ambitious global restructuring it needs to survive and triumph will not occur.

I do not deny that a critic could make this case. All these challenges will need resolving. I readily admit that an alternative confined to the global South cannot win—or, at least, it cannot win fully enough to satisfy anyone deeply committed to it. The way this trajectory will unfold is uncertain, and some of the assumptions made by such critics may prove to be wrong. But let me do my best to suggest a way out.

Beyond any doubt, the North has hardly any reservoir of traditional communities like Pomatambo. Without that lived experience, we thus lack raw material for this experiment in the most prosperous parts of the world. For the same reason, this alternative will not immediately resonate with many people. Community is for most Northerners either a place name, an identity with little real content, or a nostalgic image of something that their grandparents had. For many of the most energetic and driven souls in those societies, traditional settings are an evil. They see them as dampening self-expression and crushing people who would otherwise be free to move up in the world. In short, the North seems already to have succumbed en masse to the misguided myths of modernity. Views to which only the powerful and outward-oriented subscribe in countries like Peru have become, in these climes, the reigning orthodoxy.

If we scratch the surface, however, we find discontent even within the North. Only a small chunk of the populace eagerly embraces liberal modernity and feels free and fulfilled within it. Most Northerners feel a growing economic insecurity in the midst of the rat race. They also sense that something deeper is amiss in how people relate to one another and in what their public culture really values. They have been pummeled for a couple of generations with a set of ideas about traditional life and its shortcomings. But for all the defects of the past, those ideas have come less from ordinary people's experience of the past than from how modernity's salesmen like to portray it. That many folk have absorbed such ideas is a misfortune, but their conversion to the modern world runs less deeply than some observers might think. I admit that what I have proposed in this book might be greeted coolly by many people in the developed world at first. But that reaction is mainly a product of relentless, decades-long propaganda, along with the lack of a visible, lived alternative.

Even with all these obstacles, the economy of values and the defense of community life would appeal to some Northerners. Look at the edges of the political spectrum in the developed world even today. Thoughtful souls among both cultural conservatives and economic leftists voice many of the same misgivings about rampant consumerism, the erosion of human decency, and the vacuity of modern politics.[3] They may have different idioms and different bedfellows. Yet they could talk to each other a good deal more than they now do. If a real alternative started flourishing elsewhere in the world and was offered to them, they would have plenty to discuss. We might even imagine them overcoming some of the present barriers to political action. After all, when it comes down to it, most people take more interest in how changes will affect their quality of life day-to-day than in what political labels might get disrupted in the process.

Political realignments do happen, even in the North. In the United States, for instance, a party sympathetic to both economic justice and traditional mores could sweep a national election. Today's entrenched political classes on both sides have managed to prevent such upheaval—and limit change to the superficial—simply by drawing the partisan map so that voting blocs congeal along lines more to their liking. Much of the electorate has to grit its teeth as it chooses between voting against its values or against its economic interests, or not voting at all. Such a landscape is inherently unstable, especially when the assault on both cultural and economic decency intensifies with each passing decade. The generational pendulum also swings. By most accounts, the so-called "Millennial Generation" of young people born in the 1980s and 1990s already shows signs of greater idealism and civic engagement than their parents.[4] They provide fertile ground for new ideas.

Any alternative coming from within the North will inevitably be moderate, simply because of the narrow range of experience most Northerners have. Even if they do gravitate to a mix of economic justice and traditional mores, they will hardly come close to the clearer break with political convention that people in the countryside of the global South would support. But such a realignment in the North would still make for a more receptive landscape. Conversations between North and South could happen then in a way they cannot happen today. Even a modest increase in thinking about what traditional communities were about, and what we have lost, could go a long way toward letting an alternative gain ground globally.

Moreover, because of their relative prosperity, many Northerners are open to a spirit of experimentation. Voluntary communities, social enterprises, cooperatives, and the like are easy to set up in the developed world. Enough idealists would surely want to set up Northern branches of the economy of values once it started gaining momentum in poorer parts of the world. It could make inroads in the North even if the most influential layers of society looked askance at it.

There is evidence that Northerners by and large would want a different way of life if they could have it. A generation ago, an American named Luke Lea commissioned a Gallup poll of his countrymen. He asked if they would be interested in living in a society that moved most of its factories to the countryside so that people could work in them part-time and spend the rest of their time in part-time agriculture. Two-thirds of respondents said yes. Such decentralization would allow people to rediscover a fairer and simpler lifestyle, with strong rural communities and local self-reliance, while enjoying the efficiencies of the modern world.[5] If that quite simple vision appealed to people then, how much more would an alternative that was already well underway appeal to people now?

In sum, the picture is not as bleak as some might imagine. I do not deny that, in the short and medium terms, this alternative would be fighting an uphill battle in the developed world. It would have to overcome generations of cultural damage and a well-oiled sales machine that persistently sings the praises of modernity. But I do think that, in the long run, the restoration of a timeless decency and a well-ordered society could happen anywhere. Belloc and Chesterton mused on reestablishing a peasantry in England, and nothing happened. Even in the best scenario, with the economy of values flourishing and the global political landscape changing, we shall not see a new peasantry of sorts in the developed world for at least a century. But if developed countries could lose a humane way of life in a century or less, surely they could rebuild it in the same span of time.

For the North and even for parts of the South, this alternative means rolling back much of what the modern world has wrought. It defies the tide of recent history with a clear conscience. For the poorest and most neglected parts of the world, however, it builds on what people already have. Here is the real hope it holds out: the hope of continuity in your way of life and the dignity of knowing that, whatever others might say, you have a place in the future. Supposedly doomed communities embody an economy of values that extends back across the centuries. We can rebuild that economy now from the grassroots. Surely this promise of continuity lends a depth and plausibility that would be absent in any alternative conjured out of thin air. I suggest, quite simply, that Pomatambans today should be able to look forward across the generations and recognize the spirit and strengths of their community. As they walk towards the sunrise, they should be able to keep walking on a path of their own.

→ → →

One August morning in 2069, Suhay walked into the hallway of his house. He kicked off his slippers by the door and leaned down to pull on his boots. He did not like to think of himself as aging, but he had to admit that his back was a bit stiffer in the morning nowadays than it used to be. His boots on, he straightened, slipped his poncho over his shoulders, and donned his hat.

Suhay swung open the door of his house and felt a wave of cold, crisp air flood in. It was certainly a change from the warmth of the hallway. He tugged his gloves out of his pocket as he stepped into the street and pulled the door closed behind him. The sky was mostly dark, with the last few twinkling stars visible in the west over the hills. A few street lamps cast a pale yellowish glow over the shiny glazed-adobe house fronts. He knew the lamps would go off automatically in a few minutes now that the first brightness of dawn was rising fast in the eastern sky.

A few small puddles were drying here and there on the street, Suhay noticed as he stepped down from the curb. It must have rained during the night. The weather forecast had been for a dry night and rain during the day, which was why he had struggled to put on his boots. Probably not necessary after all, he muttered. Even with the newest satellites and supercomputers, it seemed the forecasters could never quite get it right. The weather was about as predictable as human beings—never what the experts expected.

Feeling invigorated by the cold, he strode along the street and into Pomatambo's square. He had not imagined that he would see anyone else there at such an hour, but two people were already climbing aboard the shuttle bus parked in front of the village hall. Puriq and Illari, he concluded from their shapes as he got closer. "Morning," he greeted them as he stepped into the small bus and deftly swiped his card.

"You're going to drive, right?" Illari asked as she sat down in one of the back seats. It seemed more like an assumption than a question, so Suhay nodded as he slid behind the wheel. He liked driving anyway, at least short distances. He glanced around the square in case anyone else was coming. No one was, so they were ready to go. He pressed the start button and the dashboard lit up. These new electric engines were so quiet that you often couldn't hear them when a strong wind was blowing or a loud conversation was going on. The batteries lasted so much longer now, too. Only in the rainy season did they ever have to charge them from the village grid; usually the sun performed the task for days at a time. They had chosen the fleet of buses well, he thought with some satisfaction, since he had suggested them. Six villages together had bought twenty from the company after he had returned from visiting the factory near Lake Titicaca. Small wonder the company had grown so quickly by selling these high-altitude vehicles. During the day you would pass at least a couple on the road into town.

Suhay released the brake and swiftly turned into the square. He was going to be earlier than he had planned, he realized as the bus glided over the bridge and out of Pomatambo. It would take only about ten minutes to drive along the hills, past the lagoon, and into Vilcashuamán. Puriq and Illari were chattering away about something or other in the back, so he was left to his own thoughts.

They turned naturally to his destination: his granddaughter's school at Vilcashuamán. He was on his way to help set up for the school assembly. He was on the committee. Apparently the director had thought that Suhay, given his habits, would arrive early enough to get a head start. And his granddaughter was going to receive one of the prizes for her world geography project. He smiled as he remembered the many hours she had spent online working on it a couple of weeks earlier. It had not seemed like work to her, so transfixed was she with curiosity. He had had to go up to her room to retrieve her for dinner at least four nights in a row. Family conversation at those meals had revolved mainly around what she was hoping to do with her animated model of India.

His granddaughter had inherited her fondness for far-flung corners of the world. Her uncle, his younger son, was still in Mali and quite smitten with the place. He had gone there a few years ago, soon after graduation, in search of adventure. Now in his late twenties, he was immersed in one or another project there. It seemed he was putting his irrigation-technology training from the institute to good use. Suhay could tell how much he loved doing that kind of work. Global warming and desertification in the Sahel meant there was never any shortage of stuff to do. His eyes always seemed to light up when he told tales about the villages he visited and the people he met. Suhay had never had that wanderlust himself, but he appreciated hearing the stories whenever his son came back to Pomatambo. This year he had returned three times, for about a month each stay.

Twice that year, Suhay's son had brought his fiancée back with him. She had spoken Spanish to Suhay, with a strong Quebecois French accent. His son had met her while they were working together in Mali. The young couple had hit it off as they tried to perfect their French and Spanish on one another. At first they had talked mostly about their home villages and how different from the Malian near-desert the Andean pastures and the North American forests and snow were. They both liked the adventure of their work, though they had decided that later they would be a bit more settled. Each year, they would probably spend at least a couple of months in Pomatambo and at least a couple at her family farm near Montreal. There were projects that could be done at both of those places, after all.

Suhay's thoughts turned to his daughter. She did not live in Pomatambo year-round either, but she was nearby. She came out to visit at least every couple of weeks, usually on one of her trips to the countryside for consultations with the villages. She had become quite a force to be reckoned with at her law partnership in Ayacucho. The firm mostly handled community law cases, defending the interests of the villages in administrative disputes, sometimes even on constitutional questions. And they had a good track record. So good, in fact, that her friends often joked about how they felt torn between wanting to keep her there and urging her to stand for office during the next election.

Suhay was proud of how his daughter had put her education to use. UNSCH and then San Marcos had prepared her well, and she possessed a good share of the old Pomatamban spirit of fighting injustices. Maybe they were rarer and milder injustices now, but one had to be vigilant. Suhay was thankful that they could count on good advocates nowadays. He remembered his mother telling him how helpless her family had felt when the soldiers beat her uncle long ago.

They were humble people but they had come a long way, Suhay thought as he drove up the sloping road beyond the lagoon. Hard work made a difference. Take his elder son, for example. He had promised the night before to be at the school assembly for his daughter's prize. And he would come, though it would mean tearing himself away from his meetings in Vilcashuamán. He had been so much busier lately, now that Suhay had been taking on more and more of the duties in Pomatambo: president of the endowment board of trustees, infrastructure committee chair, and this year *varayoq*. Suhay had been eager to take on those jobs, and he was the right age to do more such things, but he knew that they meant his son had had to take up much of the slack.

Their cooperative seemed to be none the worse for it. His son had done much over the last ten years to expand it. He always seemed to be on the lookout for new opportunities, or even just new ways of making the work better for himself and the other members. It was only natural that they chose him as the new manager when his father stepped down. Suhay was proud of how well his son had taken to the business after coming back from college to take up experimental farming. He worked hard and expected a lot from the others. But he got along with them well. Just the night before, he had been out with them at the tavern on the square until after Suhay went to sleep. They always drank *chicha* and had a hearty drawn-out dinner right after the weekly planning meeting.

The biggest thing Suhay's son had done for the cooperative was to persuade it to complete the deal with their new partners in Addis Ababa. It all started when he met the Ethiopian fellow and his wife while getting a quick lunch at his usual café in Vilcashuamán. They had come out to the area for a couple of days during their drive down the spine of the Andes. They had got to talking, after trial and error with different languages, and struck up a rapport as fellow mountain folk, albeit from opposite sides of the world. Suhay's son had invited them out to dinner in Pomatambo the night before they left. With some jocularity, the chubby fellow had taken to the local cuisine, including roast guinea pig, more enthusiastically than some other guests had done in the past.

In their conversations, Suhay's son discovered that the Ethiopian helped run an exchange clearinghouse for hundreds of cooperatives in the eastern African highlands. When they talked about the Ethiopian staple grain, teff, they found out that it was not so different from quinoa, an Andean counterpart. On the basis of their friendship, they entered into an agreement for crop experimentation over the next few years. The new hybrids, suitable for different altitudes, were already starting to circulate between Pomatambo's experimental farming cooperative and the network headquartered in Addis Ababa. They joked that they had invented a new cuisine, *injera* bread made from modified quinoa. It took some getting used to, though the Ethiopian fellow liked it well enough. Then again, he was a bit of a glutton, Suhay thought as he smiled.

He was driving down the hill into the Vilcashuamán square, he realized with a bit of a start as he came out of his daydream. He steered the bus around the corner and into the entrance of the parking ramp. The attendant waved as he ambled up to the side, ready to park it underground. There were already three other buses at the line on the square, and they were not supposed to have too many out at a time.

The three Pomatambans disembarked. Suhay could see signs of morning bustle already beginning around the square. The sun was about to crack over the horizon. It was a clear day. He glanced at his companions, ready to bid them goodbye. Illari was looking up at the sky. She shook her head slightly as she turned to him with a gleam of mischief in her eye.

"You're going to say they got it wrong again, aren't you?" It had become something of a running joke lately that Suhay was always complaining about the weather forecasters.

He paused. It was too nice a morning to be a curmudgeon. "No," he answered. "I was going to say it turned out better than anyone expected."

Notes

I. Big Questions from a Backwater

1. International Monetary Fund, *World Economic Outlook Database* (April 2007). World Bank, *World Bank Development Indicators Database* (July 1, 2007).

2. Raúl González, "Ayacucho: Por los caminos de Sendero," *Quehacer* 19 (October 1992): 70.

3. Rodrigo Montoya, "Ayacucho: Una introducción necesaria," in *Perú: El problema agrario en debate,* eds. Fernando Eguren *et al.* (Ayacucho: Universidad Nacional San Cristóbal de Huamanga, 1988), 425.

4. A good overview of the period of Inka rule is Michael A. Malpass, *Daily Life in the Inca Empire* (Westport, CT: Greenwood Press, 1996).

5. On the difficulty of political mobilization amid this ethnic fragmentation, see David Scott Palmer, "'Revolution from Above': Military Government and Popular Participation in Perú, 1968–1972," Ph.D. diss., Cornell University, 1973, 196–99. On the emergence of a common "Indian" peasant identity under Spanish rule, see Irene Silverblatt, "Becoming Indian in the Central Andes of Seventeenth-Century Peru," in *After Colonialism: Imperial Histories and Post-colonial Displacements,* ed. Gyan Prakash (Princeton, NJ: Princeton University Press, 1995).

6. For this and other archeological information on the area, I am indebted to Di Hu, "Between the Sword and the Wall: Inca and Modern Peruvian State Strategies of Control in Pomat-ambo–Vilcashuamán," unpublished thesis, University of Pennsylvania (2007).

7. Tupac Katari, November 15, 1781. On nostalgia for the Inka empire, see Manuel Burga, *Nacimiento de una utopía: Muerte y resurrección de los incas* (Lima: Instituto de Apoyo Agrario, 1988); and Alberto Flores Galindo, *Buscando un inca: Identidad y utopía en los Andes* (Havana: Ediciones Casa de las Américas, 1986).

8. Virgilio Galdo Gutiérrez, *Ayacucho: Conflictos y pobreza: Historia regional (siglos XVI–XIX)* (Ayacucho: Universidad Nacional San Cristóbal de Huamanga, 1992), 67–82. Alfonso Or-rego Moreno, *Ayacucho: Capital de la revolución mundial?* (Lima: Ediciones Jurídicas Sociales, 1987), 52.

9. I first encountered the poem set to music in *Panorama ayacuchano,* a cassette (circa 1994) containing recordings of Senderista songs and distributed by the movement's sympathizers abroad.

10. The Lagos story and its implications are discussed sympathetically in Victoria Guerrero, "El cuerpo muerto y el fetiche en Sendero Luminoso: El caso de Edith Lagos," *Ciberayllu* (March 9, 2006).

11. Ladislao Landa Vásquez and Juan Alberto López Alarcón, *Proyecto Qhapaq Ñan Plan Piloto de Vilcashuamán: Informe etnográfico 2004* (Lima: Instituto Nacional de Cultura, 2005), 49–50, 198. Severo Baldeón Malpartida, Teófilo Allende Ccahuana, and Cirilo Vivanco Pomacanchari, *Proyecto Qhapac Ñan: Análisis territorial de Vilcashuamán* (Lima: Instituto Nacional de Cultura, 2005), vol 1, 26, 39–40, 144–45. Rosario Pérez Liu, "Violencia, migración y productividad: Cuatro estudios de caso en las comunidades ayacuchanas," in *Perú: El problema agrario en debate,* 523. Antonio Díaz Martínez, *Ayacucho: Hambre y esperanza* (Lima: Mosca Azul Editores, 1985 [1969]), 113–14. Carlos Iván Degregori, *Ayacucho: Raíces de una crisis* (Ayacucho: Instituto de Estudios Regionales José María Arguedas, 1986), 93.

12. Landa and López, 21, 23. Baldeón, Allende, and Vivanco, 163 (quoting INEI statistics of 2002).

13. Major overviews of the movement include Degregori, *Ayacucho 1969–1979: El surgimiento de Sendero* Luminoso (Lima: Instituto de Estudios Peruanos, 1990), and *The Shining Path of Peru,* ed. David Scott Palmer (New York: St. Martin's Press, 1992).

14. See my *Beyond the Global Culture War* (New York: Routledge, 2006).

15. Grupo ALLPA, "Número de comunidades nativas y comunidades campesinas por departamento," statistics compiled from Ministerio de Agricultura, *Directorio de Comunidades Campesinas* (2002), accessed at http://www.cepes.org.pe/allpa/estad-cc_y_cn_departamento.shtml (August 6, 2007). Office of the General Registrar (India), *Census of India* (2001). There is no straightforward way to estimate the number of peasants in the world today, given the different ways rural areas are defined and the mix of agricultural and nonagricultural livelihoods within them. Sources suggest that the world's urban population passed fifty percent for the first time in 2007 or 2008. See "Mayday 23: World Population Becomes More Urban than Rural," *Science Daily,* reprinted news release from North Carolina State University, May 25, 2007; and David E. Bloom and Tarun Khanna, "The Urban Revolution," *Finance and Development* 44:3 (September 2007), 9–14. As of 2000, approximately forty-four percent of the world's economically active population was in agricultural employment. See statistics on website of the Food and Agriculture Organization of the United Nations, at faostat.fao.org.

16. Included among the *Panorama ayacuchano* recordings; composer and date unknown.

II. Small Worlds, Small Fortunes

1. Waman Puma de Ayala, *Nueva corónica y buen gobierno,* drawing 147 (digital image of original).

2. Howard J. Wiarda, *The Soul of Latin America: The Cultural and Political Tradition* (New Haven, CT: Yale University Press, 2001).

3. Linda A. Newson, "The Demographic Impact of Colonization," in *The Cambridge Economic History of Latin America,* eds. Victor Bulmer-Thomas, John H. Coatsworth, and Roberto Cortés Conde (Cambridge: Cambridge University Press, 2006). Magnus Mörner, *The Andean Past: Land, Societies, and Conflicts* (New York: Columbia University Press, 1985). Claudio Esteva-Fa-

bregat, "El campesinado andino como terminal estructural," *Revista de Indias* 42:169, 384.

4. Galdo, 35–65. Steve J. Stern, *Peru's Indian Peoples and the Challenge of Spanish Conquest: Huamanga to 1640* (Madison: University of Wisconsin Press, 1982). Nathan Wachtel, *The Vision of the Vanquished: The Spanish Conquest of Peru Through Indian Eyes, 1530–1570* (New York: Harper & Row, 1977). Franklin Pease G. Y., "Continuidad y resistencia de lo andino," *Allpanchis* 17/18 (1981). Elinor G. K. Melville, "Land Use and the Transformation of the Environment," and John M. Monteiro, "Labor Systems," both in *The Cambridge Economic History of Latin America*. On later peasant experience of labor demands from the state, see Peter Gose, *Deathly Waters and Hungry Mountains: Agrarian Ritual and Class Formation in an Andean Town* (Toronto: University of Toronto Press, 1994), 224, 238–45; and Billie Jean Isbell, *To Defend Ourselves: Ecology and Ritual in an Andean Village* (Prospect Heights, IL: Waveland Press, 1978), 177.

5. David Slater, *Territory and State Power in Latin America: The Peruvian Case* (London: Macmillan Press, 1989), 59–70. The relative independence of many indigenous villages is also noted in John H. Coatsworth, "Political Economy and Economic Organization," in *The Cambridge Economic History of Latin America*.

6. Eric R. Wolf, "Types of Latin American Peasantry: A Preliminary Discussion," *American Anthropologist* 57 (1955): 456–58. Henry A. Landsberger, "The Role of Peasant Movements and Revolts in Development," in *Latin American Peasant Movements,* ed. Landsberger (Ithaca, NY: Cornell University Press, 1969), 2. The embeddedness of premodern economies in social relationships is stressed in Karl Polanyi, *The Great Transformation: The Political and Economic Origins of Our Time* (Boston: Beacon Press, 1957).

7. Robert Redfield, *The Little Community: Viewpoints for the Study of a Human Whole* (Chicago: University of Chicago Press, 1955), 52–65. Gary Urton, "Communalism and Differentiation in an Andean Community," *Andean Cosmologies Through Time: Persistence and Emergence,* eds. Robert V. H. Dover, Katharine E. Seibold, and John H. McDowell (Bloomington: Indiana University Press, 1992).

8. In addition to my own interviews, for such details I have drawn on an ethnographic study of Pomatambo by my research assistant, Óscar Fredy Castillo Vílchez, in 1995. The description of agricultural tasks, for example, comes from Óscar Fredy Castillo Vílchez, "Cambios económicos-sociales en la comunidad campesina de Pomatambo–Vilcashuamán, 1969–1990," unpublished thesis, Universidad Nacional San Cristóbal de Huamanga (1998), 51.

9. Galdo, 128. On one aspect of the later significance of the lack of large haciendas in much of rural Ayacucho, see Isbell, "The Emerging Patterns of Peasants' Responses to Sendero Luminoso," paper presented to NYU–Columbia University Conference (December 9, 1988), 3.

10. Adolfo Figueroa, *Capitalist Development and the Peasant Economy in Peru* (Cambridge: Cambridge University Press, 1984), 106. A sympathetic outsider's impressions of Andean subsistence agriculture appears in Wendell Berry, "An Agricultural Journey in Peru," reprinted in *The Gift of Good Land: Further Essays Cultural and Agricultural* (San Francisco: North Point Press, 1981 [1979]).

11. "Vertical complementarity" during the Inka period is discussed in John Victor Murra, *The Economic Organization of the Inka State* (Greenwich, CT: JAI Press, 1980); and Charles Stanish, *Ancient Andean Political Economy* (Austin: University of Texas Press, 1992). For a more contemporary discussion, see Stephen B. Brush, *Mountain, Field, and Family: The Economy and Human Ecology of an Andean Valley* (Philadelphia: University of Pennsylvania Press, 1977),

1–16. Present numbers for Vilcashuamán appear in Baldón, Allende, and Vivanco, 149. On Pomatambo, see Castillo, 16, 55–56.

12. Castillo, 28, 53.

13. Mörner, op. cit.

14. Among my interviewees in 1995, there was no statistical correlation between having one of the five surnames of rich peasant families and having a higher income level. They were slightly more likely to have a nonagricultural source of income, however.

15. César Fonseca Martel and William W. Stein, trans., "Peasant Differentiation in the Peruvian Andes," in *Peruvian Contexts of Change,* ed. William W. Stein (New Brunswick, NJ: Transaction Books, 1985), 159. Jorge C. Loayza Camargo, Elvira Cárdenas Laurente, and Rubén Jáuregui Benavides, "Condoray: Proceso productivo, espacio económico y diferenciación," in *Comunidades campesinas de Ayacucho: Economía, ideología y organización social,* ed. Instituto de Estudios Regionales José Maria Arguedas (Ayacucho: Comisión de Coordinación de Tecnología Andina, 1985), 25–29. Julián Laite, "Expansión capitalista, migración y diferenciación social entre los campesinos de Perú," *Revista Mexicana de Sociología* 43:1 (January 1981): 196–98, 217.

16. These figures come from Castillo, 51. Only about one percent of the land in rural Vilcashuamán is naturally irrigated; see Landa and López, 49.

17. Ibid., 36.

18. Ibid., 35, 38. District-wide (including the town of Vilcashuamán), fewer than seven percent of land parcels are fully titled and registered, according to Baldón, Allende, and Vivanco, 146–47.

19. The proportion holds across Vilcashuamán district; see the agricultural census data cited in Landa and López, 198.

20. Carlos Sempat Assadourian, and Amílcar Challú and John H. Coatsworth (trans.), "Agriculture and Land Tenure," in *The Cambridge Economic History of Latin America,* 285–86.

21. Landa and López, 55.

22. Law Number 24656 (1987), Article 11, reprinted in *Compendio de nuevas leyes de comunidades campesinas* (Lima: Editorial El Carmen, 2006).

23. On traditional patterns of land rotation, see David Guillet, *Agrarian Reform and Peasant Economy in Southern Peru* (Columbia, MO: University of Missouri Press, 1979), 78–79, 83; and Daniel Cotlear, *Desarrollo campesino en los Andes* (Lima: Instituto de Estudios Peruanos, 1989), 35.

24. Detailed discussions of *ayni* and *minka* appear in Gose, 12, 15; Guillet, 73; Figueroa, 64–65; Abilio Vergara Figueroa, Genaro Zaga Saufle, and Juan Arguedas Chávez, "Culluchaca: Algunos elementos sobre la ideología comunal," in *Comunidades campesinas de Ayacucho,* 131; Pérez Liu, 525–26; and Enrique José Mayer, "Reciprocity, Self-Sufficiency and Market Relations in a Contemporary Community in the Central Andes of Peru," Ph.D. diss., Cornell University (1974), 12.

25. Gose, 8–11, 228. Vergara, Zaga, and Chávez, 132. Isbell, *To Defend Ourselves,* 168. Fonseca, 131–33, 160.

26. Vergara, Zaga, and Chávez, 131. Mayer, 4, 135–37. Fonseca, 159. Laite, 215. Jane L. Collins, "The Household and Relations of Production in Southern Peru," *Comparative Studies in Society and History* 28:4 (October 1986): 653, 656. Gavin Smith, "Reflections on the Social Relations of Simple Commodity Production," *Journal of Peasant Studies* 13:1 (October

1985): 100–06; and *Livelihood and Resistance: Peasants and the Politics of Land in Peru* (Berkeley: University of California Press, 1989), 23, 158–66. Brush, 104–14. On similar calculations in southeast Asia, see Michael Moerman, *Agricultural Change and Peasant Choice in a Thai Village* (Berkeley: University of California Press, 1968), 127, 133–37; and James C. Scott, *The Moral Economy of the Peasant: Rebellion and Subsistence in Southeast Asia* (New Haven, CT: Yale University Press, 1976), 43.

27. Slater, 89–94, 114.

28. Orrego, 152–53. Degregori, *Ayacucho: Raíces de una crisis,* 44. Slater, 122 (citing A. Ponce). Sociedad Geográfica de Lima, *Anuario geográfico departamental, Opúsculo No. 24.05.a: Perfil antropogeográfico de Ayacucho* (Lima: Sociedad Geográfica de Lima, 1990), 98.

29. José María Caballero, "Agriculture and the Peasantry Under Industrialization Pressures: Lessons from the Peruvian Experience," *Latin American Research Review* 19:2 (1984): 27.

30. Andrew Pearse, "Agrarian Change Trends in Latin America," in *Agrarian Problems and Peasant Movements in Latin America,* ed. Rodolfo Stavenhagen (Garden City, NY: Doubleday and Company, 1970), 34–35. Howard Handelman, *Struggle in the Andes: Peasant Political Mobilization in Peru* (Austin: University of Texas Press, 1975), 58.

31. Mayer, 14, 256. Laite, 195. Isbell, *To Defend Ourselves,* 71. A broader upsurge of social mobility or "cholification" is discussed in Julio Cotler, "The Mechanics of Internal Domination and Social Change in Peru," in *Peruvian Nationalism: A Corporatist Revolution,* ed. David Chaplin (New Brunswick, NJ: Transaction Books, 1976). For a comparison to rural Mexico, see Charles J. Erasmus, "Culture Change in Northwest Mexico," in *Contemporary Change in Traditional Communities of Mexico and Peru,* ed. Julian H. Steward (Urbana: University of Illinois Press, 1967), 124.

32. Degregori, "'Sendero Luminoso': Los hondos y mortales desencuentros," in *Movimientos sociales y crisis: El caso peruano* ed. Eduardo Ballón (Lima: Centro de Estudios y Promoción del Desarrollo, 1986), 251–52; and *Qué difícil es ser Dios: Ideología y violencia política en Sendero Luminoso* (Lima: El Zorro de Abajo Ediciones, 1989), 17.

33. *Anuario geográfico,* vii. Degregori, *Ayacucho: Raíces de una crisis,* 51.

34. Erwin H. Epstein, "Peasant Consciousness Under Peruvian Military Rule," *Harvard Educational Review* 52:3 (August 1982): 291.

35. Jaime Urrutia Ceruti, Adriano Araujo, and Haydeé Joyo, "Las comunidades en la región de Huamanga, 1824–1968," in *Perú: El problema agrario en debate,* 456–58.

36. Cynthia McClintock, *Peasant Cooperatives and Political Change in Peru* (Princeton, NJ: Princeton University Press, 1981), 76. Wolf, "Types of Latin American Peasantry," 456. John Strasma, "Agrarian Reform," in *Peruvian Nationalism,* 292–300.

37. Gérard Chaliand, *Revolution in the Third World: Myths and Prospects* (Hassocks: Harvester Press, 1977), 117–28. Alfred Stepan, *The State and Society: Peru in Comparative Perspective* (Princeton, NJ: Princeton University Press, 1978). Slater, 144–58. E. V. K. FitzGerald, *The Political Economy of Peru, 1956–1978* (Cambridge: Cambridge University Press, 1979).

38. General Jorge Fernández Maldonado, cited indirectly in Linda J. Seligmann, "The Burden of Visions Amidst Reform: Peasant Relations to Law in the Peruvian Andes," *American Ethnologist* 20:1 (February 1993): 25–51. On ideological tendencies among the officer corps, see Liisa L. North, "Ideological Orientations of Peru's Military Rulers," in *The Peruvian Experiment Reconsidered,* eds. Cynthia McClintock and Abraham F. Lowenthal (Princeton, NJ: Princeton University Press, 1983).

39. Juan Velasco Alvarado, speech to the nation on June 24, 1969, reprinted in *Velasco: La voz de la revolución: Discursos del Presidente de la República General de División Juan Velasco Alvarado* (Lima: Ediciones Participación, 1972), vol. 1, 43–55. Chaliand, op. cit. Norman Long and David Winder, "From Peasant Community to Production Cooperative: An Analysis of Recent Government Policy in Peru," *Journal of Development Studies* 12:1 (October 1975): 77–78. Some of the goals and legal provisions are listed in Supreme Decree Number 37-70-AG, "Estatuto Especial de Comunidades Campesinas" (1970), Articles 1–9 and 101–105, reprinted in *Compendio de nuevas leyes de comunidades campesinas*. The 1960s ideal of rural prosperity following from a moderate agrarian reform is discussed in Luis Llambi, "Emergence of Capitalized Family Farms in Latin America," *Comparative Studies in Society and History* 31:4 (October 1989): 745–74.

40. Seligmann, op. cit.

41. Castillo, 53.

42. David Scott Palmer, "'Revolution from Above,'" 195, 225. Montoya, 424. Carmen Diana Deere, "Changing Social Relations of Production and Peruvian Peasant Women's Work," *Latin American Perspectives* 4:1 (Winter 1977): 64. Julio Cotler, "Democracy and National Integration in Peru," and Daniel M. Schydlowsky and Juan J. Wicht, "The Anatomy of an Economic Failure," both in *The Peruvian Experiment Reconsidered*. For a more optimistic assessment in the early years, see Strasma, 300–23.

43. Seligmann, op. cit.

44. Ibid. Epstein, 282–83. Florencia E. Mallon, "Indian Communities, Political Cultures, and the State in Latin America, 1780–1990," *Journal of Latin American Studies* 24 (1992): 47–49.

45. Cotler, "Democracy and National Integration in Peru." Peter S. Cleaves and Henry Pease García, "State Autonomy and Military Policymaking," in *The Peruvian Experiment Reconsidered*.

46. Chaliand, 117–28. Guillet, 162, 170, 175. Isbell, "Emerging Patterns," 7–8. Cotler, "Democracy and National Integration in Peru." Stepan, op. cit. David Nugent, "Building the State, Making the Nation: The Bases and Limits of State Centralization in 'Modern' Peru," *American Anthropologist* 96:2 (June 1994).

47. A typical list of duties appears in Supreme Decree Number 37-70-AG, "Estatuto Especial de Comunidades Campesinas" (1970), reprinted in *Compendio de nuevas leyes de comunidades campesinas*. On the limited role of the formal legal system in earlier decades, see Fernando de Trazegnies Granda, *Law and Modernization in Nineteenth Century Peru* (Madison: Institute for Legal Studies, 1987).

48. On the role of brokers, especially in navigating the legal system, see Handelman, 32; Isbell, *To Defend Ourselves*, 20, 217; and Seligmann, op. cit. For a psychological account of broker self-confidence, see Erasmus, 111–13, 124.

49. On the role of the *varayoq*, see Isbell, *To Defend Ourselves*, 176.

50. Wolf, "Types of Latin American Peasantry," 458. Mayer, 210. Vergara, Zaga, and Chávez, 139. Joel S. Migdal, *Peasants, Politics, and Revolution: Pressures Toward Political and Social Change in the Third World* (Princeton, NJ: Princeton University Press, 1974), 67–69. Daisy Irene Núñez del Prado Béjar, "El rol de la mujer campesina quechua," *América Indígena* 35:2 (April–June 1975): 398.

51. Mayer, 240. Isbell, *To Defend Ourselves*, 85, 94–95.

52. For example, a generational divide between candidates for office in some villages, in Mayer, 251. On the role of young, literate peasants in political mobilization during the agrarian reform, as foreshadowing of responses during the Sendero years, see Mallon, "Chronicle of a Path Foretold? Velasco's Revolution, Vanguardia Revolucionaria, and 'Shining Omens' in the Indigenous Communities of Andahuaylas," in *Shining and Other Paths: War and Society in Peru, 1980–1995* ed., Steve J. Stern (Durham, NC: Duke University Press, 1998).

53. Landsberger, 39; and William Foote Whyte and Giorgio Alberti, *Power, Politics and Progress: Social Change in Rural Peru* (New York: Elsevier, 1976), 244.

54. Pearse, *The Latin American Peasant* (London: Frank Cass and Company, 1975), 255. Moerman, 80. Pérez Liu, op. cit. Susan C. Bourque and Kay Barbara Warren, *Women of the Andes: Patriarchy and Social Change in Two Peruvian Towns* (Ann Arbor, MI: University of Michigan Press, 1981), 153–54.

55. Slater, 120 (citing V. Roel), 137 (citing ministerial data).

56. Gose, 46, 51, 56. Migdal, 138, 142. Bourque and Warren, 158. Isbell, *To Defend Ourselves*, 67. Handelman, 199. Mayer, 252–54. Wolf, "Types of Latin American Peasantry," 458. Scott, *The Moral Economy of the Peasant*, 61.

57. Law Number 24656 (1987), Article 14, reprinted in *Compendio de nuevas leyes de comunidades campesinas*.

58. Orrego, 154–55, 284.

59. Castillo, 4, 33.

60. Caballero, 21. Vergara, Zaga, and Chávez, 125. Efraín Gonzales de Olarte, *Inflación y campesinado: Comunidades y microrregiones frente a la crisis* (Lima: Instituto de Estudios Peruanos, 1987), 98–99. Loayza, Cárdenas, and Jáuregui, 44–46. Bourque and Warren, 206.

61. Vergara, Zaga, and Chávez, 140. Isbell, *To Defend Ourselves*, 11, 19, 220.

62. McClintock, "Why Peasants Rebel: The Case of Peru's Sendero Luminoso," *World Politics* 37:1 (October 1984): 49, 71, 80, 83. Slater, 167, 172.

III. Socialism and Scorched Earth

1. Castillo, 93.

2. David Scott Palmer, presentation at Harvard University, October 1993. For overviews of the rise of Sendero, see Palmer, "Rebellion in Rural Peru: The Origins and Evolution of Sendero Luminoso," *Comparative Politics* 18:2 (1986): 127–46; and *The Shining Path of Peru*, ed. Palmer. On Sendero's relationship with the rest of the left, see Iván Hinojosa, "On Poor Relations and the Nouveau Riche: Shining Path and the Radical Peruvian Left," in *Shining and Other Paths*.

3. Partido Comunista del Perú (SL), *Sétima conferencia nacional: Sobre el carácter de la sociedad y los problemas de la revolución peruana* (n.p., 1972); and *Entrevista al Presidente Gonzalo* (Lima: Ediciones Bandera Roja, 1989) [reprint from *El Diario* interview of July 1988].

4. Degregori, "Sendero Luminoso," 260; and *Ayacucho 1969–79*, 205. González, 43.

5. Ricardo Melgar Bao, "Una guerra etnocampesina en el Perú: Sendero Luminoso," *Anales de Antropología* 23 (1986): 173. Orin Starn, "Antropología andina, 'andinismo' y Sendero Luminoso," *Allpanchis* 23:39 (January–June 1992): 30. Degregori, "Harvesting Storms: Peasant

Rondas and the Defeat of Sendero Luminoso in Ayacucho," in *Shining and Other Paths.*

6. McClintock, "Why Peasants Rebel," 71. Degregori, "Sendero Luminoso," 228–29.

7. McClintock, "Why Peasants Rebel," 59, 68. Figueroa, 109. Gonzales de Olarte, 43, 102, 108, 114, 157–58. Isbell, "Emerging Patterns," 9. For a more nuanced discussion of shifting terms of trade, see Waldo E. Mendoza Bellido, "La crisis agraria en el departamento de Ayacucho, 1980–1985," in *Perú: El problema agrario en debate,* 486.

8. Fonseca, 148–49. Handelman, 191–202. Vergara, Zaga, and Arguedas, 153. Scott, *The Moral Economy of the Peasant,* 193–94, 201–03. Migdal, 87–88, 154, 229–32, 252–53. James C. Davies, "Toward a Theory of Revolution," *American Sociological Review* 27:1 (February 1962): 5–19. Gerrit Huizer, *The Revolutionary Potential of Peasants in Latin America* (Lexington MA: Lexington Books, 1972), 53, 144, 182. Wolf, *Peasant Wars of the Twentieth Century* (New York: Harper and Row, 1969), 279.

9. Jo-Marie Burt, "Shining Path and the 'Decisive' Battle in Lima's *Barriadas:* The Case of Villa El Salvador," and Ponciano del Pino Huamán, "Family, Culture, and 'Revolution': Everyday Life with Sendero Luminoso," both in *Shining and Other Paths.*

10. Vergara, Zaga, and Arguedas, 126.

11. Ibid., 141. González, 44–45. Melgar, 168. Whyte and Alberti, 235, 265.

12. Henri Favre, "Sendero Luminoso y horizontes ocultos," *Cuadernos Americanos* 1:4 (1987): 54. Ronald H. Berg, "Sendero Luminoso and the Peasantry of Andahuaylas," *Journal of Interamerican Studies and World Affairs* 28:4 (1986/1987): 190.

13. Melgar, 191. Favre, 43. Gustavo Benavides, "Poder político y religión en el Perú," *Márgenes* 4 (December 1988): 52. Alain Hertoghe and Alain Labrousse, *Le Sentier lumineux du Pérou: Un nouvel intégrisme dans le tiers monde* (Paris: Éditions la Découverte, 1989), 91, 206.

14. Castillo, 95.

15. Isbell, "Emerging Patterns," 6, 11. Starn, "Antropología andina," 41. Burt, op. cit. González, op. cit. Yolanda Rodríguez, "Los actores sociales y la violencia política en Puno," *Allpanchis* 23:39 (January–June 1992): 136–37. José E. Gonzales, "Guerrillas and Coca in the Upper Huallaga Valley," in *The Shining Path of Peru,* 110. Colin Harding, "Notes on Sendero Luminoso," *Communist Affairs* 3 (1984): 48. Félix Valencia Quintanilla, *Ayacucho: Sangre y miseria* (Lima: Tierra y Liberación, 1986), 28. Sendero's harsh justice also garnered praise from others on the left. See Federación Departamental de Rondas Campesinas de Cajamarca, *Primer Congreso Departamental Rondas Campesinas Cajamarca: Documentos* (Chota: Federación de Rondas Campesinas de Cajamarca, 1985), 19–21, 29–32; and Hugo Blanco, *Comunidad campesina: SL, PUM, Patria Roja* (Lima: n.p., 1988), 9.

16. Castillo, 96.

17. On the push for autarky, see Isbell, "Emerging Patterns," 10; Favre, 51; Degregori, "Sendero Luminoso," 255; Harding, "Antonio Díaz Martínez and the Ideology of Sendero Luminoso," *Bulletin of Latin American Research* 7:1 (1988): 72; and Simon Strong, *Shining Path: The World's Deadliest Revolutionary Force* (London: HarperCollins, 1992), 98–100.

18. Isbell, "Emerging Patterns," 12.

19. Díaz Martínez, 116–17, 199–200. Harding, "Antonio Díaz Martínez," 68–69, 72–73.

20. Hertoghe and Labrousse, 212–13. González, 72–73. Melgar, 181. An early critique of Allpachaka is in Díaz Martínez, 37–41.

21. Migdal, 211–12, 255.

22. McClintock, "Why Peasants Rebel," 81.

23. On gaps in the safety net, see Isbell, *To Defend Ourselves,* 72.

24. Díaz Martínez, 206–07.

25. Isbell, "Emerging Patterns,"11.

26. Guillet, 12, 172–74. See also Brush, 134–40.

27. Karl Marx, *The Eighteenth Brumaire of Louis Bonaparte* (New York: International Publishers, 1963 [1852]), 124. On tensions between peasant values and state-run agriculture, see also Jane Jacobs, *Systems of Survival: A Dialogue on the Moral Foundations of Commerce and Politics* (New York: Random House, 1992), 117–19.

28. Scott, *The Moral Economy of the Peasant,* 9–10, 18, 28, 38, 45. Mayer, 12, 45–46. Wolf, "Types of Latin American Peasantry," 464. Pearse, *The Latin American Peasant,* 256. Cotlear, 187–89.

29. Murra, 130–34. Terence N. D'Altroy and Timothy K. Earle, "Staple Finance, Wealth Finance, and Storage in the Inka Political Economy," in *Inka Storage Systems,* ed. Terry Y. LeVine (Norman, OK: University of Oklahoma Press, 1992).

30. Núñez, "El rol de la mujer campesina quechua." Ruth Dixon-Mueller, *Women's Work in Third World Agriculture* (Geneva: International Labor Organization, 1985), 20. Florence E. Babb, "Women and Men in Vicos, Peru: A Case of Unequal Development," in *Peruvian Contexts of Change,* 170. Juan Lázaro, "Women and Political Violence in Contemporary Peru," *Dialectical Anthropology* 15 (1990): 234. On women in Pomatambo specifically, see Castillo, 44–45.

31. Núñez, "El rol de la mujer campesina quechua," 394–95. Cotlear, 23. Laite, 194. Gose, 11. Jacqueline A. Ashby, "Women and Agricultural Technology in Latin America and the Caribbean," in *Women, Agriculture, and Rural Development in Latin America,* eds. Jacqueline A. Ashby and Stella Gómez (Cali: Centro Internacional de Agricultura Tropical, 1985): 14, 16. For arguments that this complementarity is not always respected, see Bourque and Warren, 119–21; and Deere and and Magdalena León de Leal, *Women in Andean Agriculture: Peasant Production and Rural Wage Employment in Colombia and Peru* (Geneva: International Labor Office, 1982), 6, 48, 51.

32. Babb, 198. Isbell, "Emerging Patterns," 4–5. Collins, 665–66. Laite, 205. Deere, 62. Sarah A. Radcliffe, "Between Hearth and Labor Market: The Recruitment of Peasant Women in the Andes," *International Migration Review* 24:2 (Summer 1990): 235–36. On Pomatambo, see Castillo, 48.

33. Mayer, 319. Bourque and Warren, 131, 172, 200–01. Babb, 171, 187. Lázaro, 235, 240. Catherine V. Scott, *Gender and Development: Rethinking Modernization and Dependency Theory* (Boulder, CO: Lynne Rienner Publishers, 1995), 71. Mary Bouquet, "The Differential Integration of the Rural Family," *Sociologia Ruralis* 24:1 (1984): 72.

34. Starn, "New Literature on Peru's Sendero Luminoso," *Latin American Research Review* 27:2 (1992): 217. Carol Andreas, "Women at War," *NACLA Report on the Americas* 24:4 (December/January 1990/1991): 20–27. For an argument that Sendero was more patriarchal than it pretended, see Isabel Coral Cordero, "Women in War: Impact and Responses," in *Shining and Other Paths.*

35. Blanco, 11. Gose, 252. Hobart A. Spalding, "Peru Today: Still on the Brink," *Monthly Review* 44:10 (March 1993): 36.

36. The numbers come from the truth commission, cited in Landa and López, 92.

37. Degregori, "Harvesting Storms." Harding, "Notes on Sendero Luminoso," 48. César Franco, *Cajatambo: Experiencia de un desarrollo posible* (Lima: Centro de Estudios para el Desarrollo y la Participación, 1990), 72–73. Spalding, 36. On the anti-Sendero patrols organized by some communities and supported by the military as part of its counterinsurgency strategy, see Starn, "Villagers at Arms: War and Counterrevolution in the Central-South Andes," in *Shining and Other Paths;* and Mario Antonio Fumerton, *From Victims to Heroes: Peasant Counter-Rebellion and Civil War in Ayacucho, Peru, 1980–2000* (Amsterdam: Rozenberg Publishers, 2002). On killings in Pomatambo, see Castillo, 89–90.

38. Mendoza, 491.

39. Baldón, Allende, and Vivanco, 125 (citing 1993 census).

40. Castillo, 93.

41. Degregori, "Sendero Luminoso," 255–57. On communities in northern Ayacucho that remained strong enough to organize against Sendero, see del Pino, op. cit.

42. Many of my interviewees mentioned this incident. For the full details in sequence, I am indebted to the witness accounts compiled in Castillo, 103–05.

43. On economic policy during the García years, see Manuel Pastor and Carol Wise, "Peruvian Economic Policy in the 1980s: From Orthodoxy to Heterodoxy and Back," *Latin American Research Review* 27:2 (1992): 83–117.

44. Favre, 50.

IV. Homeward and Hopeful

1. *Anuario geográfico,* 102. Isbell, "Emerging Patterns," 9. Loayza, "El repliegue de la economía comunera en Ayacucho," in *Perú: El problema agrario en debate,* 503.

2. *Atlas Departamental del Perú: Imagen geográfica, estadística, histórica y cultural, N° 8, Ayacucho/Ica* (Lima: Ediciones PEISA, 2003), 26.

3. On similar patterns in Ecuador, see Anthony Bebbington, "Reencountering Development: Livelihood Transitions and Place Transformations in the Andes," *Annals of the Association of American Geographers* 90:3 (September 2000): 495–520. That migrants still form part of Pomatambo's economy is a recurring theme in Castillo, op. cit., though he sees their role entirely through a Marxist lens of class differentiation.

4. Landa and López, 50–51.

5. Cotlear, 55, 60–61. McClintock, "Why Peasants Rebel," 63. Garrett Hardin, "The Tragedy of the Commons," *Science* 162 (1968): 1243–48. George M. Foster, "Peasant Society and the Image of Limited Good," *American Anthropologist* (1965): 301. Some conflict over land involving returned migrants in the 1990s is noted in Castillo, 17. On the land rights of returning migrants and the figure on land out of use, see Landa and López, 44–45.

6. Moerman, 144. Esteva-Fabregat, 380. Epstein, 285. Marga Stahr and Marisol Vega, "El conflicto tradición–modernidad en mujeres de sectores populares," *Márgenes* 2:3 (1988): 60–62.

7. Castillo, 49–50.

8. A brief overview of the revival of the *varayoq* system appears in Landa and López, 42–43.

9. I refer mainly to theories of the "new class." See, *inter alia,* Alvin W. Gouldner, *The Future of Intellectuals and the Rise of the New Class* (New York: Seabury Press, 1979); and Peter L. Berger,

"The Worldview of the New Class: Secularity and Its Discontents," in *The New Class?* ed. B. Bruce-Briggs (New York: McGraw-Hill Book Company, 1979).

10. Landa and López, 37–38.

11. Programa Nacional de Manejo de Cuencas Hidrográficas y Conservación de Suelos (PRONAMACHS), "Impacto Social MIMA–Pomatambo" (electronic copy of report provided in August 2006).

12. Supreme Decree Number 008-91-TR (1987), Articles 60–68, reprinted in *Compendio de nuevas leyes de comunidades campesinas*.

13. Oficina Nacional de Procesos Electorales (ONEP), "Elecciones municipales 2002, Vilcashuamán," election data at www.onpe.gob.pe. November 2006 municipal election results for Ayacucho provinces accessed at Transparencia website, www.transparencia.org.pe. Much of the electoral victory in 2002 was apparently due to kinship networks; see Landa and López, 42.

14. Bruce H. Kay, "Fujipopulism and the Liberal State in Peru, 1990–1995," *Journal of Interamerican Studies and World Affairs* 38:4 (Winter 1996): 55–98. Moisés Arce, *Market Reform in Society: Post-Crisis Politics and Economic Change in Authoritarian Peru* (University Park PA: Pennsylvania State University Press, 2005), 14, 24–25, 107–20. Pedro Francke, "Institutional Change and Social Programs," and Carlos Monge Salgado, "Decentralization: An Opportunity for Democratic Governance," both in *Making Institutions Work in Peru: Democracy, Development, and Inequality Since 1980*, ed. John Crabtree (London: Institute for the Study of the Americas, 2006).

15. PRONAMACHS, "Impacto Social MIMA–Pomatambo."

16. Kay, op. cit. On support for Fujimori by an electorate disillusioned with democratic institutions, see Fernando Rospigliosi, "Democracy's Bleak Prospects," and Francisco Sagasti and Max Hernández, "The Crisis of Governance," both in *Peru in Crisis: Dictatorship or Democracy*, eds. Joseph S. Tulchin and Gary Bland (Boulder, CO: Lynne Rienner, 1994).

17. On delegative democracy, see Guillermo O'Donnell, "Delegative Democracy," *Journal of Democracy* 5:1 (1994): 55–69. One well-known study of the technopol approach in Mexico is Miguel Ángel Centeno, *Democracy Within Reason: Technocratic Revolution in Mexico* (University Park, PA: Pennsylvania State University Press, 1997). On the political psychology behind popular support for painful economic reforms, see Kurt Weyland, *The Politics of Market Reform in Fragile Democracies: Argentina, Brazil, Peru, and Venezuela* (Princeton, NJ: Princeton University Press, 2002).

18. Arce, 17, 41–53. Francisco Durand, "The Problem of Strengthening Business Institutions," in *Making Institutions Work in Peru*. Patricia Oliart, "Alberto Fujimori: 'The Man Peru Needed?'" in *Shining and Other Paths*. The market-reform agenda had broad support across the Peruvian elite, including among those who opposed Fujimori for political reasons, e.g. Álvaro Vargas Llosa, *The Madness of Things Peruvian* (New Brunswick, NJ: Transaction Publishers, 1994).

19. ONPE, "Segunda elección presidencial 2001."

20. Rosa Pizarro, Laura Trelles, and Eduardo Toche, "La protesta social durante el toledismo," in *Perú hoy: Los mil días de Toledo* (Lima: Centro de Estudios y Promoción del Desarrollo, 2004).

21. Francke, op. cit. The program's goals and scope are detailed on its website, www.juntos. gob.pe.

22. ONPE, "Segunda elección presidencial 2006."

V. Peasantry of the Future

1. Law Number 24656 (1987), Articles 1–2, reprinted in *Compendio de nuevas leyes de comunidades campesinas.*

2. A vivid description of the Pomatamban work ethic appears in Castillo, 46.

3. Kurt Weyland, "'Growth with Equity' in Chile's New Democracy?" *Latin American Research Review* 32:1 (1997). Jorge Nef, "The Chilean Model: Fact and Fiction," *Latin American Perspectives* 30:5 (September 2003): 16–40. Xavier Rambla, "Globalization, Educational Targeting, and Stable Inequalities: A Comparative Analysis of Argentina, Brazil, and Chile," *International Review of Education* 52:3/4 (May–July 2006): 353–70.

4. PRONAMACHS, "Impacto Social MIMA–Pomatambo."

5. Samuel L. Popkin, *The Rational Peasant: The Political Economy of Rural Society in Vietnam* (Berkeley: University of California Press, 1979); Gary S. Becker, *The Economic Approach to Human Behavior* (Chicago: University of Chicago Press, 1976); and Thomas L. Friedman, *The Lexus and the Olive Tree* (New York: Farrar Straus Giroux, 2000), 348. For a critical perspective on this discourse, see Tariq Banuri, "Modernization and Its Discontents: A Cultural Perspective on Theories of Development," in *Dominating Knowledge: Development, Culture, and Resistance,* eds. Frédérique Apffel Margin and Stephen A. Marglin (Oxford: Oxford University Press, 1990); and Thomas Frank, *One Market Under God: Extreme Capitalism, Market Populism, and the End of Economic Democracy* (New York: Doubleday, 2000).

6. Hernando de Soto, *The Other Path: The Economic Answer to Terrorism* (New York: Basic Books, 1989 [1987]); and *The Mystery of Capital: Why Capitalism Triumphs in the West and Fails Everywhere Else* (New York: Basic Books, 2000). For a critique of de Soto's vision as too simplistic a solution to poverty, see Heather Bourbeau, "Property Wrongs: How Weak Ideas Gain Strong Appeal in the World of Development Economics," *Foreign Policy* 127 (November 2001): 78–79.

7. Law Number 24657 (1987), reprinted in *Compendio de nuevas leyes de comunidades campesinas.*

8. Supreme Decree Number 011-97-AG (1997); Law Number 26845 (1997); and Supreme Decree Number 064-2000-AG (2000), "Proyecto Especial Titulación de Tierras y Catastro Rural," all reprinted in *Compendio de nuevas leyes de comunidades campesinas.*

9. Fumerton, 301–2.

10. Cotlear, 65, 69, 76–77, 84, 264–66. Vergara, Zaga, and Arguedas, 153.

11. Fernando Eguren, "Agrarian Policy, Institutional Change, and New Actors in Peruvian Agriculture," in *Making Institutions Work in Peru.* See also John Crabtree, "The Impact of Neoliberal Economics on Peruvian Peasant Agriculture in the 1990s," *Journal of Peasant Studies* 29:3/4 (April–July 2002): 131–61. The difficulty smallholders in Vilcashuamán have in getting agricultural development loans is mentioned in Landa and López, 54. On the complexities of smallholder-focused development across Latin America, see Llambi, op. cit.

12. On out-migration and stagnation, see Esteva-Fabregat, 381; and Everett M. Rogers, "Motivations, Values, and Attitudes of Subsistence Farmers: Toward a Subculture of Peasantry," in *Subsistence Agriculture and Economic Development,* ed. Clifton R. Wharton (Chicago: Aldine Publishing Company, 1969): 120.

13. On the contrast between traditional and modern ways of dealing with displaced children

in Ayacucho, see Jessaca B. Leinaweaver, "On Moving Children: The Social Implications of Andean Child Circulation," *American Ethnologist* 34:1 (February 2007): 163–80.

14. Arturo Éscobar, "Culture, Economics, and Politics in Latin American Social Movements Theory and Research," in *The Making of Social Movements in Latin America: Identity, Strategy, and Democracy,* eds. Arturo Éscobar and Sonia E. Álvarez (Boulder, CO: Westview Press, 1992), 62–85; and "Place, Economy, and Culture in a Post-Development Era," in *Places and Politics in an Age of Globalization* eds. Arif Dirlik and Roxann Prazniak (New York: Rowman and Littlefield, 2001). In a similar vein, see many of the essays in *The Spirit of Regeneration: Andean Culture Confronting Western Notions of Development,* ed. Frédérique Appfel-Marglin (New York: Zed Books, 1998).

15. Pithy statements of the agrarian vision are Berry, "The Agrarian Standard," Maurice Telleen, "The Mind-Set of Agrarianism . . . New and Old," and Norman Wirzba, "Placing the Soul: An Agrarian Philosophical Principle," all in *The Essential Agrarian Reader,* ed. Norman Wirzba (Washington: Shoemaker and Hoard, 2003).

16. Marcus Tullius Cicero, *On Duties,* eds. M. T. Griffin and E. M. Atkins (New York: Cambridge University Press, 1991), Book I, §151. Mencius, *The Works of Mencius,* trans. James Legge (New York: Dover Publications, 1970 [1895]), VII:2:xiv.

17. *Distributist Perspectives: Essays on the Economics of Justice and Charity,* eds. John Sharpe *et al.* (Norfolk, VA: IHS Press, 2004). G. K. Chesterton, *What's Wrong with the World* (Fort Collins, CO: Ignatius Press, 1994 [1910]); and *The Outline of Sanity* (London: Methuen and Company, 1926). Arthur J. Penty, *The Gauntlet: A Challenge to the Myth of Progress* ed. Peter Chojnowski (Norfolk, VA: IHS Press, 2003). For a more recent articulation of distributism, see John C. Médaille, *The Vocation of Business: Social Justice in the Marketplace* (New York: Continuum, 2007), especially 294–316.

18. This and other texts appear in *Catholic Social Teaching: The Documentary Heritage,* eds. David J. O'Brien and Thomas A. Shannon (Maryknoll, NY: Orbis Books, 1992).

19. Hilaire Belloc, *The Servile State* (Indianapolis: Liberty Fund, 1977 [1913]); and *An Essay on the Restoration of Property* (Norfolk, VA: IHS Press, 2002 [1936]).

20. Margaret Canovan, *G. K. Chesterton: Radical Populist* (New York: Harcourt Brace Jovanovich, 1977), 8–9.

21. On guild socialism, see S. T. Glass, *The Responsible Society: The Ideas of the English Guild Socialists* (London: Longmans, Green and Company, 1966).

22. Liang Shuming, *Zhongguo ren: shehui yu rensheng* (Beijing: Zhongguo Wenlian Chuban Gongsi, 1996 [1921–70]). Guy S. Alitto, *The Last Confucian: Liang Shuming and the Chinese Dilemma of Modernity* (Berkeley: University of California Press, 1979). Alfred H. Y. Lin, "Confucianism in Action: A Study of Liang Shuming's Theory and Practice of Rural Reconstruction in the 1930s," in *Journal of Oriental Studies* 28:1 (1990).

23. Mohandas K. Gandhi, *Hind Swaraj: Indian Home Rule* (Madras: G. A. Nateson and Company, 1921 [1908]); and *The Essential Gandhi: An Anthology of His Writings on His Life, Work, and Ideas,* ed. Louis Fischer (New York: Vintage Books, 2002 [1962]).

24. E. F. Schumacher, *Small Is Beautiful: Economics as if People Mattered* (New York: Harper and Row, 1973).

25. Wolf, *Peasant Wars of the Twentieth Century,* 295. Scott, *The Moral Economy of the Peasant,* 5, 40. The classic work arguing otherwise is Popkin, op. cit.

26. Scott, *The Moral Economy of the Peasant;* and *Seeing Like a State: How Certain Schemes to Improve the Human Condition Have Failed* (New Haven, CT: Yale University Press, 1998).

27. Tom Brass, "Populism, Peasants, and Intellectuals, or What's Left of the Future," *Journal of Peasant Studies* 21:3/4 (April–July 1994): 246–86.

28. Scott, *Seeing Like a State.*

29. W. E. Tate, *The English Village Community and the Enclosure Movements* (London: Victor Gollancz, 1967). Michael Turner, *Enclosures in Britain, 1750–1830* (London: Macmillan Press, 1984). Robert C. Allen, "The Efficiency and Distributional Consequences of Eighteenth Century Enclosure," *Economic Journal* 92:368 (December 1982): 937–53. For a competing view, see Gregory Clark, "Commons Sense: Common Property Rights, Efficiency, and Institutional Change," *Journal of Economic History* 58:1 (March 1998): 73–102. On the increased "legibility" of enclosed land for states, see Scott, *Seeing Like a State,* 37–44.

30. On the uneasy relationship between American conservatives and Karl Polanyi, for example, see Allan Carlson, "The Problem of Karl Polanyi," *Intercollegiate Review* 41:1 (Spring 2006): 32–39.

31. Bruce M. S. Campbell and Ricardo Godoy, "Commonfield Agriculture: The Andes and Medieval England Compared," in *Making the Commons Work: Theory, Practice, and Policy,* ed. Daniel W. Bromley (San Francisco: ICS Press, 1992); Glenn G. Stevenson, *Common Property Economics: A General Theory and Land Use Applications* (Cambridge: Cambridge University Press, 1991); and Timothy Earle, "Archeology, Property, and Prehistory," *Annual Review of Anthropology* 29 (2000): 39–60.

32. Belloc, *The Servile State,* 82–83, 98–101; and *Essay on the Restoration of Property,* 19, 41–42, 77.

33. Burga, op. cit. Flores, op. cit. José Carlos Mariátegui, *Seven Interpretive Essays on Peruvian Reality,* trans. Marjory Urquidi (Austin, TX: University of Texas Press, 1971 [1928]), especially 74–76, note 15. For a typical myth, see Peter G. Roe, "The Josho Nahuanbo Are All Wet and Undercooked: Shipibo Views of the Whiteman and the Incas in Myth, Legend, and History," in *Rethinking History and Myth,* ed. Jonathan D. Hill (Chicago: University of Illinois Press, 1988), 106–35.

34. Scott, *The Moral Economy of the Peasant,* 192. Landsberger, 52. Wolf, *Peasants* (Englewood Cliffs NJ: Prentice-Hall, 1966), 106–08.

VI. Building an Economy of Values

1. Hannah Arendt, *The Human Condition* (Chicago: University of Chicago Press, 1958); Sheldon Wolin, *Politics and Vision. Continuity and Innovation in Western Political Thought* (Princeton, NJ: Princeton University Press, 2004 [1960]); and Michael Sandel, *Democracy's Discontent: America in Search of a Public Philosophy* (Cambridge MA: Harvard University Press, 1996).

2. Belloc, *Essay on the Restoration of Property,* 55.

3. J. K. Gibson-Graham, *A Postcapitalist Politics* (Minneapolis: University of Minnesota Press, 2006), 167. Bebbington, "Reencountering Development."

4. PRONAMACHS, "Impacto Social MIMA–Pomatambo." Cotlear, 116, 197–98. Bebbington, "Modernization from Below: An Alternative Indigenous Development," *Economic Geography* 69:3 (July 1993).

5. Various accounts of PRATEC's efforts appear in *The Spirit of Regeneration,* ed. Appfel-Marglin. For a complementary defense of the efficiency of traditional agricultural patterns, see Vandana Shiva, "Globalization and the War Against Farmers and the Land," in *The Essential Agrarian Reader.*

6. Landa and López, 51. Baldeón, Allende, and Vivanco, 125.

7. Ibid., 47.

8. Ibid., 46–47, 181–82.

9. The decline of crafts in Pomatambo specifically is discussed in Castillo, 56, 69. The undercutting of rural artisans by commercial goods goes back decades; see Slater, 112.

10. Foster, 296–98. Scott, *The Moral Economy of the Peasant,* 41. On the diversion of investment from agriculture, see Pearse, "Agrarian Change Trends in Latin America," 38; and Palmer, *The Impact of Male Out-Migration on Women in Farming* (West Hartford, CT: Kumarian Press, 1985), 4.

11. The vision of microlending was described by its most famous founder, Muhammad Yunus, in his Nobel lecture at Oslo (December 10, 2006). Because of its focus on small businesses, microlending has received some guarded support from distributists, e.g. Médaille, 258–66. A more orthodox market-oriented appropriation of microlending appears in Phil Smith and Eric Thurman, *A Billion Bootstraps: Microcredit, Barefoot Banking, and the Business Solution for Ending Poverty* (New York: McGraw-Hill, 2007); and Mario La Torre and Gianfranco A. Vento, *Microfinance* (New York: Palgrave Macmillan, 2006). On the uneasy relationship between early microlending nonprofits and the for-profit sector, see Mark Sappenfield and Mark Trumbull, "Big Banks Find Little Loans a Nobel Winner, Too," *Christian Science Monitor* (October 16, 2006); and Andrew Curry, "Poor Vision: Why Nobel Laureate Muhammad Yunus Will Doom Microfinance," *The New Republic Online* (December 7, 2006).

12. Esteva-Fabregat, 388.

13. Probably the best overview of Mondragón's history is in William Foote Whyte, *Making Mondragón: The Growth and Dynamics of the Worker Cooperative Complex* (Ithaca, NY: ILR Press, 1988). See also the website of Mondragón Corporación Cooperativa, at www.mcc.es. For praise of Mondragón from the perspective of Catholic social thought, see Médaille, 267–79.

14. Ana Gutiérrez Johnson and Whyte, "The Mondragón System of Worker Production Cooperatives," *Industrial and Labor Relations Review* 31:1 (October 1977): 18–30.

15. George Cheney, *Values at Work: Employee Participation Meets Market Pressure at Mondragón* (Ithaca, NY: ILR Press, 1999). Peter Leigh Taylor, "The Rhetorical Construction of Efficiency: Restructuring and Industrial Democracy in Mondragón, Spain," *Sociological Forum* 9:3 (September 1994): 459–89. Sharryn Kasmir, *The Myth of Mondragón: Cooperatives, Politics, and Working-Class Life in a Basque Town* (Albany: SUNY Press, 1996).

16. Andrew Hindmoor, "Free Riding Off Capitalism: Entrepreneurship and the Mondragón Experiment," *British Journal of Political Science* 29:1 (January 1999): 217–24. On the problems alleged to be inherent in a cooperative economy and how Mondragón overcame many of them, see Alasdair Clayre, "The Political Economy of a 'Third Sector,'" and Robert Oakeshott, "A Cooperative Sector in a Mixed Economy," both in *The Political Economy of Co-operation and Participation,* ed. Alasdair Clayre (Oxford: Oxford University Press, 1980).

17. Landa and López, 54, 198.

18. Stevenson, 40, 43.

231

19. Murra, 16–20, 34–35. Cirilo Vivanco Pomacanchari, "Tecnología andina," in *Proyecto Qhapac Ñan: Análisis territorial de Vilcashuamán,* vol 2.

20. Law Number 24656 (1987), Articles 2, 4, 7, 25–27; and Supreme Decree Number 045-93-AG (1993); both reprinted in *Compendio de nuevas leyes de comunidades campesinas.*

21. Castillo, 31.

22. PRONAMACHS, "Impacto Social MIMA–Pomatambo."

23. Émile Durkheim, *The Division of Labor in Society,* trans. Lewis A. Coser (New York: Free Press, 1997).

24. Peter Barnes, *Capitalism 3.0: A Guide to Reclaiming the Commons* (San Francisco: Berrett-Koehler Publishers, 2006).

25. Richard Douthwaite, *Short Circuit: Strengthening Local Economies for Security in an Unstable World* (Totnes: Green Books, 1996); Michael H. Shuman, *Going Local: Creating Self-Reliant Communities in a Global Age* (New York: The Free Press, 1998); and Bill McKibben, *Deep Economy: The Wealth of Communities and the Durable Future* (New York: Times Books, 2007). In a different vein but a somewhat similar spirit are visions of a "participatory economy," more or less a bottom-up socialism of nested councils. One example is Michael Albert, *Parecon: Life After Capitalism* (New York: Verso, 2003).

26. Liang, op. cit. Lin, op. cit. Alitto, op. cit. Lyman P. van Slyke, "Liang Shuming and the Rural Reconstruction Movement," *The Journal of Asian Studies* 18:4 (August 1959).

27. Deborah J. Yashar, *Contesting Citizenship in Latin America: The Rise of Indigenous Movements and the Postliberal Challenge* (Cambridge: Cambridge University Press, 2005), 224–78.

28. Monge, op. cit. John Crabtree, "Political Parties and Intermediation in Peru," and Paulo Drinot, "Nation-Building, Racism, and Inequality: Institutional Development in Peru in Historical Perspective," both in *Making Institutions Work in Peru.*

29. On Toledo's failed decentralizing efforts, see Javier Azpur, "La descentralización: Una reforma democratizadora que avanza sin norte ni conducción estratégica," in *Perú hoy.* The Decentralist Coalition's website is http://www.concertaciondescentralista.com.

30. Azpur, 124–25, 129.

31. Scott, *The Moral Economy of the Peasant,* 43–44. Handelman, 197.

32. Migdal, 222–23. Christopher Lasch, *The Revolt of the Elites and the Betrayal of Democracy* (New York: W. W. Norton, 1995). Richard J. Herrnstein and Charles Murray, *The Bell Curve: Intelligence and Class Structure in American Life* (New York: Free Press, 1994), 29–43. For a satirical account of how this works, see Michael Young, *The Rise of the Meritocracy, 1870–2033: An Essay on Education and Equality* (Baltimore: Penguin Books, 1961 [1958]), 48–49, 150.

VII. Dawn over the Andes

1. Antonio Gramsci, *Selections from the Prison Notebooks* (New York: International Publishers, 1971). George H. Nash, *The Conservative Intellectual Movement in America Since 1945* (Wilmington, DE: Intercollegiate Studies Institute, 1996). Sara Diamond, *Not by Politics Alone: The Enduring Influence of the Christian Right* (New York: Guilford Press, 1998).

2. Bloom and Khanna, 12. For a narrower discussion of the issues involved in crossing the divide between a rural-centered agrarian vision and urban life, see Benjamin E. Northrup

and Benjamin J. Bruxvoort Lipscomb, "Country and City: The Common Vision of Agrarians and New Urbanists," in *The Essential Agrarian Reader.*

3. Rod Dreher, *Crunchy Cons* (New York: Crown Forum, 2006). Arthur J. Versluis, "The Revolutionary Conservatism of Jefferson's Small Republics," *Modern Age* 48:1 (Winter 2006): 6–12. Catherine McNicol Stock, *Rural Radicals: Righteous Rage in the American Grain* (Ithaca, NY: Cornell University Press, 1996). Gibson-Graham, op. cit. Russell Nieli, "Social Conservatives of the Left," *Political Science Reviewer* 22:1 (1993).

4. Neil Howe and William Strauss, *Millennials Rising: The Next Great Generation* (New York: Vintage Books, 2000).

5. Luke Lea, "The Soft Path: Notes for a New Way of Life in America," electronic pamphlet (2007).

Bibliography

Albert, Michael. *Parecon: Life After Capitalism*. New York: Verso, 2003.

Alberts, Tom. "Agrarian Reform and Rural Poverty: A Case Study of Peru." Ph.D. diss., *University of Lund*, 1981.

Alitto, Guy S. *The Last Confucian: Liang Shu-ming and the Chinese Dilemma of Modernity.* Berkeley, CA: University of California Press, 1979.

Allen, Robert C. "The Efficiency and Distributional Consequences of Eighteenth Century Enclosure." *Economic Journal* 92:368 (December 1982): 937–53.

Andreas, Carol. "Women at War." *NACLA Report on the Americas* 24:4 (December/January 1990/1991): 20–27.

Ansión, Juan. "Sendero Luminoso: La política como religión." *Cristianismo y Sociedad* 106 (1990): 115–29.

Appfel-Marglin, Frédérique, ed. *The Spirit of Regeneration: Andean Culture Confronting Western Notions of Development*. New York: Zed Books, 1998.

Arce, Moisés. *Market Reform in Society: Post-Crisis Politics and Economic Change in Authoritarian Peru*. University Park PA: Pennsylvania State University Press, 2005.

Arendt, Hannah. *The Human Condition*. Chicago: University of Chicago Press, 1958.

Ashby, Jacqueline A. "Women and Agricultural Technology in Latin America and the Caribbean." In Jacqueline A. Ashby and Stella Gómez, eds., *Women, Agriculture, and Rural Development in Latin America*. Cali: Centro Internacional de Agricultura Tropical, 1985.

Atlas Departamental del Perú: Imagen geográfica, estadística, histórica y cultural, N° 8, Ayacucho/Ica. Lima: Ediciones PEISA, 2003.

Azpur, Javier. "La descentralización: Una reforma democratizadora que avanza sin norte ni conducción estratégica." *Perú hoy: Los mil días de Toledo*. Lima: Centro de Estudios y Promoción del Desarrollo, 2004.

Babb, Florence E. "Women and Men in Vicos, Peru: A Case of Unequal Development." William W. Stein, ed., 163–210. *Peruvian Contexts of Change*. New Brunswick, NJ: Transaction Books, 1985.

Baldeón Malpartida, Severo, Teófilo Allende Ccahuana, and Cirilo Vivanco Pomacanchari. *Proyecto Qhapac Ñan: Análisis territorial de Vilcashuamán*. 2 vols. Lima: Instituto Nacional de Cultura, 2005.

Banuri, Tariq. "Modernization and Its Discontents: A Cultural Perspective on Theories of Development." In Frédérique Apffel Margin and Stephen A. Marglin, eds., *Dominat-*

ing Knowledge: Development, Culture, and Resistance. Oxford: Oxford University Press, 1990.

Barnes, Peter. Capitalism 3.0: A Guide to Reclaiming the Commons. San Francisco: Berrett-Koehler Publishers, 2006.

Bebbington, Anthony. "Modernization from Below: An Alternative Indigenous Development." Economic Geography 69:3 (July 1993): 274–92.

——— "Reencountering Development: Livelihood Transitions and Place Transformations in the Andes." Annals of the Association of American Geographers 90:3 (September 2000): 495–520.

Becker, Gary S. The Economic Approach to Human Behavior. Chicago: University of Chicago Press, 1976.

Belloc, Hilaire. An Essay on the Restoration of Property. Norfolk VA: IHS Press, 2002 [1936].

——— The Servile State. Indianapolis: Liberty Fund, 1977 [1913].

Benavides, Gustavo. "Poder político y religión en el Perú." Márgenes 4 (December 1988): 21–54.

Berg, Ronald H. "Sendero Luminoso and the Peasantry of Andahuaylas." Journal of Interamerican Studies and World Affairs 28:4 (1986/1987): 165–96.

Berger, Peter L. "The Worldview of the New Class: Secularity and Its Discontents." B. Bruce-Briggs, ed. The New Class? New York: McGraw-Hill Book Company, 1979.

Berry, Wendell. "The Agrarian Standard." In Norman Wirzba, ed., The Essential Agrarian Reader. Washington: Shoemaker and Hoard, 2003.

———. "An Agricultural Journey in Peru." The Gift of Good Land: Further Essays Cultural and Agricultural. San Francisco: North Point Press, 1981 [1979].

Blanco, Hugo. Comunidad campesina: SL, PUM, Patria Roja. Lima: n.p., 1988.

Bloom, David E. and Tarun Khanna. "The Urban Revolution." Finance and Development, 44:3 (September 2007): 9–14.

Bouquet, Mary. "The Differential Integration of the Rural Family." Sociologia Ruralis 24:1 (1984): 65–77.

Bourbeau, Heather. "Property Wrongs: How Weak Ideas Gain Strong Appeal in the World of Development Economics." Foreign Policy 127 (November 2001): 78–79.

Bourque, Susan C. "Cholification and the Campesino: A Study of Three Peruvian Peasant Organizations in the Process of Societal Change." Ph.D. diss., Cornell University, 1971.

——— and Kay Barbara Warren. Women of the Andes: Patriarchy and Social Change in Two Peruvian Towns. Ann Arbor, MI: University of Michigan Press, 1981.

Brass, Tom. "Populism, Peasants, and Intellectuals, or What's Left of the Future." Journal of Peasant Studies 21:3/4 (April–July 1994): 246–86.

Brush, Stephen B. Mountain, Field, and Family: The Economy and Human Ecology of an Andean Valley. Philadelphia: University of Pennsylvania Press, 1977.

Burga, Manuel. Nacimiento de una utopía: Muerte y resurrección de los incas. Lima: Instituto de Apoyo Agrario, 1988.

Burt, Jo-Marie. "Shining Path and the 'Decisive' Battle in Lima's Barriadas: The Case of Villa El Salvador." In Steve J. Stern, ed., Shining and Other Paths: War and Society in Peru, 1980–1995. Durham, NC: Duke University Press, 1998.

Caballero, José María. "Agriculture and the Peasantry Under Industrialization Pressures:

Lessons from the Peruvian Experience." *Latin American Research Review,* 19:2 (1984): 3–41.

Campbell, Bruce M. S. and Ricardo Godoy. "Commonfield Agriculture: The Andes and Medieval England Compared." In Daniel W. Bromley, ed., *Making the Commons Work: Theory, Practice, and Policy.* San Francisco: ICS Press, 1992.

Canovan, Margaret. *G. K. Chesterton: Radical Populist.* New York: Harcourt Brace Jovanovich, 1977.

Carlson, Allan. "The Problem of Karl Polanyi." *Intercollegiate Review* 41:1 (Spring 2006): 32–39.

Castillo Vílchez, Óscar Fredy. "Cambios económicos-sociales en la comunidad campesina de Pomatambo–Vilcashuamán, 1969–1990." Unpublished thesis, Universidad Nacional San Cristóbal de Huamanga, 1998.

Centeno, Miguel Ángel. *Democracy Within Reason: Technocratic Revolution in Mexico.* University Park, PA: Pennsylvania State University Press, 1997.

Chaliand, Gérard. *Revolution in the Third World: Myths and Prospects.* Hassocks: Harvester Press, 1977.

Cheney, George. *Values at Work: Employee Participation Meets Market Pressure at Mondragón.* Ithaca, NY: ILR Press, 1999.

Chesterton, G. K. *The Outline of Sanity.* London: Methuen and Company, 1926.

——— *What's Wrong with the World.* Fort Collins, CO: Ignatius Press, 1994 [1910].

Cicero, Marcus Tullius. *On Duties.* M. T. Griffin and E. M. Atkins, eds. New York: Cambridge University Press, 1991.

Clark, Gregory. "Commons Sense: Common Property Rights, Efficiency, and Institutional Change." *Journal of Economic History* 58:1 (March 1998): 73–102.

Clayre, Alasdair. "The Political Economy of a 'Third Sector.'" In Alasdair Clayre, ed., *The Political Economy of Co-operation and Participation.* Oxford: Oxford University Press, 1980.

Cleaves, Peter S. and Henry Pease García. "State Autonomy and Military Policymaking." In Cynthia McClintock and Abraham F. Lowenthal, eds., *The Peruvian Experiment Reconsidered.* Princeton, NJ: Princeton University Press, 1983.

Coatsworth, John H. "Political Economy and Economic Organization." In Victor Bulmer-Thomas, John H. Coatsworth, and Roberto Cortés Conde, eds., *The Cambridge Economic History of Latin America.* Cambridge: Cambridge University Press, 2006.

Collins, Jane L. "The Household and Relations of Production in Southern Peru." *Comparative Studies in Society and History* 28:4 (October 1986): 651–71.

Compendio de nuevas leyes de comunidades campesinas. Lima: Editorial El Carmen, 2006.

Confederación Campesina del Perú. *Sétimo consejo nacional: Alto a la militarización y a la violencia.* Lima: Prensa de la Confederación Campesina del Perú, 1986.

Coral Cordero, Isabel. "Women in War: Impact and Responses." In Steve J. Stern, ed., *Shining and Other Paths.*

Coser, Lewis A. *Continuities in the Study of Social Conflict.* New York: The Free Press, 1967.

Cotlear, Daniel. *Desarrollo campesino en los Andes.* Lima: Instituto de Estudios Peruanos, 1989.

Cotler, Julio. "Democracy and National Integration in Peru." In Cynthia McClintock and Abraham F. Lowenthal, eds., *The Peruvian Experiment Reconsidered.*

A Path of Our Own

————— "The Mechanics of Internal Domination and Social Change in Peru." *Peruvian Nationalism: A Corporatist Revolution.* New Brunswick, NJ: Transaction Books, 1976.

Crabtree, John. "The Impact of Neoliberal Economics on Peruvian Peasant Agriculture in the 1990s." *Journal of Peasant Studies* 29:3/4 (April–July 2002): 131–61.

————— "Political Parties and Intermediation in Peru." *Making Institutions Work in Peru: Democracy, Development, and Inequality Since 1980.* London: Institute for the Study of the Americas, 2006.

Cueva Sánchez, Luis. *Sierra central: Comunidad campesina, problemas y alternativas.* Lima: Fundación Friedrich Ebert, 1987.

Curry, Andrew. "Poor Vision: Why Nobel Laureate Muhammad Yunus Will Doom Microfinance." *The New Republic Online,* December 7, 2006.

D'Altroy, Terence N. and Timothy K. Earle. "Staple Finance, Wealth Finance, and Storage in the Inka Political Economy." In Terry Y. LeVine, ed., *Inka Storage Systems.* Norman, OK: University of Oklahoma Press, 1992.

Davies, James C. "Toward a Theory of Revolution." *American Sociological Review* 27:1 (February 1962): 5–19.

Deere, Carmen Diana. "Changing Social Relations of Production and Peruvian Peasant Women's Work." *Latin American Perspectives* 4:1 (Winter 1977): 48–68.

————— and León de Leal, Magdalena. *Women in Andean Agriculture: Peasant Production and Rural Wage Employment in Colombia and Peru.* Geneva: International Labor Office, 1982.

Degregori, Carlos Iván. "A Dwarf Star." *NACLA Report on the Americas* 24:4 (December/January 1990/1991): 10–16.

————— *Ayacucho 1969–1979: El surgimiento de Sendero Luminoso.* Lima: Instituto de Estudios Peruanos, 1990.

————— *Ayacucho: Raíces de una crisis.* Ayacucho: Instituto de Estudios Regionales José María Arguedas, 1986.

————— "Harvesting Storms: Peasant *Rondas* and the Defeat of Sendero Luminoso in Ayacucho." In Steve J. Stern, ed., *Shining and Other Paths.*

————— *Qué difícil es ser Dios: Ideología y violencia política en Sendero Luminoso.* Lima: El Zorro de Abajo Ediciones, 1989.

————— "'Sendero Luminoso': Los hondos y mortales desencuentros." In Eduardo Ballón, ed., 225–67, *Movimientos sociales y crisis: El caso peruano.* Lima: Centro de Estudios y Promoción del Desarrollo, 1986.

del Pino Huamán, Ponciano. "Family, Culture, and 'Revolution': Everyday Life with Sendero Luminoso." In Steve J. Stern, ed. *Shining and Other Paths.*

de Soto, Hernando. *The Mystery of Capital: Why Capitalism Triumphs in the West and Fails Everywhere Else.* New York: Basic Books, 2000.

————— *The Other Path: The Economic Answer to Terrorism.* New York: Basic Books, 1989 [1987].

de Trazegnies Granda, Fernando. *Law and Modernization in Nineteenth Century Peru.* Madison, WI: Institute for Legal Studies, 1987.

Diamond, Sara. *Not by Politics Alone: The Enduring Influence of the Christian Right.* New York: Guilford Press, 1998.

Díaz Martínez, Antonio. *Ayacucho: Hambre y esperanza.* Lima: Mosca Azul Editores, 1985 [1969].

Dixon-Mueller, Ruth. *Women's Work in Third World Agriculture*. Geneva: International Labor Organization, 1985.

Douthwaite, Richard. *Short Circuit: Strengthening Local Economies for Security in an Unstable World*. Totnes: Green Books, 1996.

Dreher, Rod. *Crunchy Cons*. New York: Crown Forum, 2006.

Drinot, Paulo. "Nation-Building, Racism, and Inequality: Institutional Development in Peru in Historical Perspective." In John Crabtree, ed., *Making Institutions Work in Peru*.

Durand, Francisco. "The Problem of Strengthening Business Institutions." In John Crabtree, ed., *Making Institutions Work in Peru*.

Durkheim, Émile. *The Division of Labor in Society*. Lewis A. Coser, trans. New York: Free Press, 1997.

Earle, Timothy. "Archeology, Property, and Prehistory." *Annual Review of Anthropology* 29 (2000): 39–60.

Eguren, Fernando. "Agrarian Policy, Institutional Change, and New Actors in Peruvian Agriculture." In John Crabtree, ed., *Making Institutions Work in Peru*.

Epstein, Erwin H. "Peasant Consciousness Under Peruvian Military Rule." *Harvard Educational Review* 52:3 (August 1982): 280–300.

Erasmus, Charles J. "Culture Change in Northwest Mexico." In Julian H. Steward, ed., 1–131, *Contemporary Change in Traditional Communities of Mexico and Peru*. Urbana, IL: University of Illinois Press, 1967.

Éscobar, Arturo. "Culture, Economics, and Politics in Latin American Social Movements Theory and Research." In Arturo Éscobar and Sonia E. Álvarez, eds., 62–85, *The Making of Social Movements in Latin America: Identity, Strategy, and Democracy*. Boulder, CO: Westview Press, 1992.

———. "Place, Economy, and Culture in a Post-Development Era." In Arif Dirlik and Roxann Prazniak, eds., *Places and Politics in an Age of Globalization*. New York: Rowman and Littlefield, 2001.

Esteva-Fabregat, Claudio. "El campesinado andino como terminal estructural." *Revista de Indias* 42:169 (1982): 371–92.

Favre, Henri. "Sendero Luminoso y horizontes ocultos." *Cuadernos Americanos* 1:4 (1987): 29–58.

Federación Agraria Departamental de Ayacucho. *Ayacucho: Primer encuentro de comunidades campesinas*. Ayacucho: FADA, 1986.

Federación Departamental de Rondas Campesinas de Cajamarca. *Primer Congreso Departamental Rondas Campesinas Cajamarca: Documentos*. Chota: Federación de Rondas Campesinas de Cajamarca, 1985.

Figueroa, Adolfo. *Capitalist Development and the Peasant Economy in Peru*. Cambridge: Cambridge University Press, 1984.

FitzGerald, E. V. K. *The Political Economy of Peru, 1956–1978*. Cambridge: Cambridge University Press, 1979.

Flores Galindo, Alberto. *Buscando un inca: Identidad y utopía en los Andes*. Havana: Ediciones Casa de las Américas, 1986.

Fonseca Martel, César. "Peasant Differentiation in the Peruvian Andes." William W. Stein, trans. In William W. Stein, ed., 124–62, *Peruvian Contexts of Change*.

A Path of Our Own

Food and Agriculture Organization of the United Nations. Statistical database at faostat.fao.org.

Foster, George M. "Peasant Society and the Image of Limited Good." *American Anthropologist* (1965): 293–312.

Francke, Pedro. "Institutional Change and Social Programs." In John Crabtree, ed., *Making Institutions Work in Peru*.

Franco, César. *Cajatambo: Experiencia de un desarrollo posible*. Lima: Centro de Estudios para el Desarrollo y la Participación, 1990.

Frank, Thomas. *One Market Under God: Extreme Capitalism, Market Populism, and the End of Economic Democracy*. New York: Doubleday, 2000.

Freyfogle, Eric T. "Private Property Rights in Land." In Norman Wirzba, ed., *The Essential Agrarian Reader*.

Friedman, Thomas L. *The Lexus and the Olive Tree*. New York: Farrar Straus Giroux, 2000.

Fumerton, Mario Antonio. *From Victims to Heroes: Peasant Counter-Rebellion and Civil War in Ayacucho, Peru, 1980–2000*. Amsterdam: Rozenberg Publishers, 2002.

Galdo Gutiérrez, Virgilio. *Ayacucho: Conflictos y pobreza: Historia regional (siglos XVI–XIX)*. Ayacucho: Universidad Nacional San Cristóbal de Huamanga, 1992.

Gandhi, Mohandas K. *The Essential Gandhi: An Anthology of His Writings on His Life, Work, and Ideas*. Louis Fischer, ed. New York: Vintage Books, 2002 [1962].

——— *Hind Swaraj: Indian Home Rule*. Madras: G. A. Nateson and Company, 1921 [1908].

Georgescu-Roegen, Nicholas. "The Institutional Aspects of Peasant Communities." In Clifton R. Wharton, ed., 61–93, *Subsistence Agriculture and Economic Development*. Chicago: Aldine Publishing Company, 1969.

Gibson-Graham, J. K. *A Postcapitalist Politics*. Minneapolis: University of Minnesota Press, 2006.

Glass, S. T. *The Responsible Society: The Ideas of the English Guild Socialists*. London: Longmans, Green and Company, 1966.

Gonzales, José E. "Guerrillas and Coca in the Upper Huallaga Valley." In David Scott Palmer, ed., 105–25, *The Shining Path of Peru*. New York: St. Martin's Press, 1992.

Gonzales de Olarte, Efraín. *Inflación y campesinado: Comunidades y microrregiones frente a la crisis*. Lima: Instituto de Estudios Peruanos, 1987.

González, Raúl. "Ayacucho: Por los caminos de Sendero." *Quehacer* 19 (October 1992): 36–77.

Gorriti Ellenbogen, Gustavo. *Sendero: Historia de la guerra milenaria en el Perú*. Lima: Editorial Apoyo, 1990.

Gose, Peter. *Deathly Waters and Hungry Mountains: Agrarian Ritual and Class Formation in an Andean Town*. Toronto: University of Toronto Press, 1994.

Gouldner, Alvin W. *The Future of Intellectuals and the Rise of the New Class*. New York: Seabury Press, 1979.

Gramsci, Antonio. *Selections from the Prison Notebooks*. New York: International Publishers, 1971.

Grupo ALLPA. "Número de comunidades nativas y comunidades campesinas por departamento." Statistics compiled from Ministerio de Agricultura, *Directorio de Comunidades Campesinas*, 2002. Accessed at http://www.cepes.org.pe/allpa/estad-cc_y_cn_departamento.shtml, August 6, 2007.

Bibliography

Guerrero, Victoria. "El cuerpo muerto y el fetiche en Sendero Luminoso: El caso de Edith Lagos." *Ciberayllu,* March 9, 2006.

Guillet, David. *Agrarian Reform and Peasant Economy in Southern Peru.* Columbia, MO: University of Missouri Press, 1979.

Handelman, Howard. *Struggle in the Andes: Peasant Political Mobilization in Peru.* Austin: University of Texas Press, 1975.

Hardin, Garrett. "The Tragedy of the Commons." *Science* 162 (1968): 1243–48.

Harding, Colin. "Antonio Díaz Martínez and the Ideology of Sendero Luminoso." *Bulletin of Latin American Research* 7:1 (1988): 65–73.

———. "Notes on Sendero Luminoso." *Communist Affairs* 3 (1984): 45–49.

Herrnstein, Richard J. and Charles Murray. *The Bell Curve: Intelligence and Class Structure in American Life.* New York: Free Press, 1994.

Hertoghe, Alain and Alain Labrousse. *Le Sentier lumineux du Pérou: Un nouvel intégrisme dans le tiers monde.* Paris: Éditions la Découverte, 1989.

Hindmoor, Andrew. "Free Riding Off Capitalism: Entrepreneurship and the Mondragón Experiment." *British Journal of Political Science* 29:1 (January 1999): 217–24.

Hinojosa, Iván. "On Poor Relations and the Nouveau Riche: Shining Path and the Radical Peruvian Left." In Steve J. Stern, ed., *Shining and Other Paths.*

Howe, Neil and William Strauss. *Millennials Rising: The Next Great Generation.* New York: Vintage Books, 2000.

Hu Di. "Between the Sword and the Wall: Inca and Modern Peruvian State Strategies of Control in Pomatambo–Vilcashuamán." Unpublished thesis, University of Pennsylvania, 2007.

Huamantinco Cisneros, Francisco. *Los refugiados internos en el Perú: Un estudio de aproximación en dos asentamientos humanos de Lima.* Lima: Ediciones y Publicidad de Comercio Exterior, n.d.

Huizer, Gerrit. *The Revolutionary Potential of Peasants in Latin America.* Lexington, MA: Lexington Books, 1972.

International Monetary Fund. *World Economic Outlook Database,* April 2007.

Isbell, Billie Jean. "The Emerging Patterns of Peasants' Responses to Sendero Luminoso." Paper presented to NYU–Columbia University Conference, December 9, 1988.

———. "Shining Path and Peasant Responses in Rural Ayacucho." In David Scott Palmer, ed., 59–81, *The Shining Path of Peru.*

——— *To Defend Ourselves: Ecology and Ritual in an Andean Village.* Prospect Heights, IL: Waveland Press, 1978.

Jacobs, Jane. *Systems of Survival: A Dialogue on the Moral Foundations of Commerce and Politics.* New York: Random House, 1992.

Johnson, Ana Gutiérrez and William Foote Whyte. "The Mondragón System of Worker Production Cooperatives." *Industrial and Labor Relations Review* 31:1 (October 1977): 18–30.

Juntos—Programa Nacional de Apoyo Directo a los Más Pobres. Website at www.juntos. gob.pe.

Kasmir, Sharryn. *The Myth of Mondragón: Cooperatives, Politics, and Working-Class Life in a Basque Town.* Albany: SUNY Press, 1996.

Kay, Bruce H. "Fujipopulism and the Liberal State in Peru, 1990–1995." *Journal of Interamerican Studies and World Affairs* 38:4 (Winter 1996): 55–98.

Kervyn, Bruno. *La economía campesina en el Perú: Teorías y políticas*. Cusco: Centro de Estudios Rurales Andinos "Bartolomé de las Casas." 1988.

Laite, Julián. "Expansión capitalista, migración y diferenciación social entre los campesinos de Perú." *Revista Mexicana de Sociología* 43:1 (January 1981): 193–219.

Landa Vásquez, Ladislao and Juan Alberto López Alarcón. *Proyecto Qhapaq Ñan Plan Piloto de Vilcashuamán: Informe etnográfico 2004*. Lima: Instituto Nacional de Cultura, 2005.

Landsberger, Henry A. "The Role of Peasant Movements and Revolts in Development." In Henry A. Landsberger, ed., 1–61, *Latin American Peasant Movements*. Ithaca, NY: Cornell University Press, 1969.

Lara, Jesús. *El Tawantinsuyu: Origen. Organización política, económica y social*. Cochabamba: Editorial Los Amigos del Pueblo, 1974.

Lasch, Christopher. *The Revolt of the Élites and the Betrayal of Democracy*. New York: W. W. Norton, 1995.

La Torre, Mario and Gianfranco A. Vento. *Microfinance*. New York: Palgrave Macmillan, 2006.

Lázaro, Juan. "Women and Political Violence in Contemporary Peru." *Dialectical Anthropology* 15 (1990): 233–47.

Lea, Luke. "The Soft Path: Notes for a New Way of Life in America." Electronic pamphlet, 2007.

Leinaweaver, Jessaca B. "On Moving Children: The Social Implications of Andean Child Circulation." *American Ethnologist* 34:1 (February 2007): 163–80.

Liang Shuming. *Zhongguo ren: Shehui yu rensheng*. Beijing: Zhongguo Wenlian Chuban Gongsi, 1996 [1921–70].

Lin, Alfred H. Y. "Confucianism in Action: A Study of Liang Shuming's Theory and Practice of Rural Reconstruction in the 1930s." *Journal of Oriental Studies* 28:1 (1990): 21–40.

Llambi, Luis. "Emergence of Capitalised Family Farms in Latin America." *Comparative Studies in Society and History* 31:4 (October 1989): 745–74.

Loayza Camargo, Jorge C. "El repliegue de la economía comunera en Ayacucho." In Fernando Eguren et al., eds., 495–514, *Perú: El problema agrario en debate*. Ayacucho: Universidad Nacional San Cristóbal de Huamanga, 1988.

———, Elvira Cárdenas Laurente, and Rubén Jáuregui Benavides. "Condoray: Proceso productivo, espacio económico y diferenciación." Instituto de Estudios Regionales José Maria Arguedas, 13–51. *Comunidades campesinas de Ayacucho: Economía, ideología y organización social*. Ayacucho: Comisión de Coordinación de Tecnologia Andina, 1985.

Long, Norman and Winder, David. "From Peasant Community to Production Cooperative: An Analysis of Recent Government Policy in Peru." *Journal of Development Studies* 12:1 (October 1975): 75–94.

Mallon, Florencia E. "Chronicle of a Path Foretold? Velasco's Revolution, Vanguardia Revolucionaria, and 'Shining Omens' in the Indigenous Communities of Andahuaylas." In Steve J. Stern, ed., *Shining and Other Paths*.

——— *The Defense of Community in Peru's Central Highlands: Peasant Struggle and Capitalist Transition, 1860–1940*. Princeton, NJ: Princeton University Press, 1983.

———— "Indian Communities, Political Cultures, and the State in Latin America, 1780–1990." *Journal of Latin American Studies* 24 (1992): 35–53.

Malpass, Michael A. *Daily Life in the Inca Empire.* Westport, CT: Greenwood Press, 1996.

Manrique, Nelson. "Time of Fear." *NACLA Report on the Americas* 24:4 (December/January 1990/1991): 28–38.

Mariátegui, José Carlos. *Seven Interpretive Essays on Peruvian Reality.* Marjory Urquidi, trans. Austin, TX: University of Texas Press, 1971 [1928].

Marx, Karl. *The Eighteenth Brumaire of Louis Bonaparte.* New York: International Publishers, 1963 [1852].

"Mayday 23: World Population Becomes More Urban than Rural." *Science Daily,* May 25, 2007 [reprinted news release from North Carolina State University].

Mayer, Enrique José. "Reciprocity, Self-Sufficiency and Market Relations in a Contemporary Community in the Central Andes of Peru." Ph.D. diss., Cornell University, 1974.

McClintock, Cynthia. *Peasant Cooperatives and Political Change in Peru.* Princeton, NJ: Princeton University Press, 1981.

———— "Why Peasants Rebel: The Case of Peru's Sendero Luminoso." *World Politics* 37:1 (October 1984): 48–84.

McKibben, Bill. *Deep Economy: The Wealth of Communities and the Durable Future.* New York: Times Books, 2007.

Médaille, John C. *The Vocation of Business: Social Justice in the Marketplace.* New York: Continuum, 2007.

Melgar Bao, Ricardo. "Una guerra etnocampesina en el Perú: Sendero Luminoso." *Anales de Antropología* 23 (1986): 163–94.

Melville, Elinor G. K. "Land Use and the Transformation of the Environment." In Victor Bulmer-Thomas, John H. Coatsworth, and Roberto Cortés Conde, eds., *The Cambridge Economic History of Latin America.*

Mencius. *The Works of Mencius.* James Legge, trans. New York: Dover Publications, 1970 [1895].

Mendoza Bellido, Waldo E. "La crisis agraria en el departamento de Ayacucho, 1980–1985." Fernando Eguren et al., eds., 469–93, *Perú: El problema agrario en debate.*

Migdal, Joel S. *Peasants, Politics, and Revolution: Pressures Toward Political and Social Change in the Third World.* Princeton, NJ: Princeton University Press, 1974.

Moerman, Michael. *Agricultural Change and Peasant Choice in a Thai Village.* Berkeley, CA: University of California Press, 1968.

Mondragón Corporación Cooperativa website, at www.mcc.es.

Monge Salgado, Carlos. "Decentralization: An Opportunity for Democratic Governance." In John Crabtree, ed., *Making Institutions Work in Peru.*

Monteiro, John M. "Labor Systems." In Victor Bulmer-Thomas, John H. Coatsworth, and Roberto Cortés Conde, eds., *The Cambridge Economic History of Latin America.*

Montoya, Rodrigo. "Ayacucho: Una introducción necesaria." In Fernando Eguren et al., eds., 421–28, *Perú: El problema agrario en debate.*

Mörner, Magnus. *The Andean Past: Land, Societies, and Conflicts.* New York: Columbia University Press, 1985.

Murra, John Victor. *The Economic Organization of the Inka State.* Greenwich, CT: JAI Press, 1980.

Nash, George H. *The Conservative Intellectual Movement in America Since 1945.* Wilmington, DE: Intercollegiate Studies Institute, 1996.

Nef, Jorge. "The Chilean Model: Fact and Fiction." *Latin American Perspectives* 30:5 (September 2003): 16–40.

Newson, Linda A. "The Demographic Impact of Colonization." In Victor Bulmer-Thomas, John H. Coatsworth, and Roberto Cortés Conde, eds., *The Cambridge Economic History of Latin America.*

Nieli, Russell. "Social Conservatives of the Left." *Political Science Reviewer* 22:1 (1993): 198–292.

North, Liisa L. "Ideological Orientations of Peru's Military Rulers." In Cynthia McClintock and Abraham F. Lowenthal, eds., *The Peruvian Experiment Reconsidered.*

Northrup, Benjamin E. and Benjamin J. Bruxvoort Lipscomb. "Country and City: The Common Vision of Agrarians and New Urbanists." In Norman Wirzba, ed., *The Essential Agrarian Reader.*

Nugent, David. "Building the State, Making the Nation: The Bases and Limits of State Centralization in 'Modern' Peru." *American Anthropologist* 96:2 (June 1994): 333–69.

Núñez del Prado Béjar, Daisy Irene. "El poder de decisión de la mujer quechua andina." *América Indígena* 35:2 (July–September 1975): 623–30.

———. "El rol de la mujer campesina quechua." *América Indígena* 35:2 (April–June 1975): 391–401.

Oakeshott, Robert. "A Cooperative Sector in a Mixed Economy." In Alasdair Clayre, ed., *The Political Economy of Co-operation and Participation.*

O'Brien, David J. and Thomas A. Shannon, eds. *Catholic Social Teaching: The Documentary Heritage.* Maryknoll, NY: Orbis Books, 1992.

O'Donnell, Guillermo. "Delegative Democracy." *Journal of Democracy* 5:1 (1994): 55–69.

Office of the General Registrar (India). *Census of India, 2001.*

Oficina Nacional de Procesos Electorales. Election results accessed at www.onpe.gob.pe.

Oliart, Patricia. "Alberto Fujimori: 'The Man Peru Needed?'" In Steve J. Stern, ed., *Shining and Other Paths.*

Orlove, Benjamin. "Inequality Among Peasants: The Forms and Uses of Reciprocal Exchange in Andean Peru." In Rhoda Halperin and James Dow, eds., 201–14, *Peasant Livelihood: Studies in Economic Anthropology and Cultural Ecology.* New York: St. Martin's Press, 1977.

Orrego Moreno, Alfonso. *Ayacucho: Capital de la revolución mundial?* Lima: Ediciones Jurídicas Sociales, 1987.

Painter, Michael. "The Value of Peasant Labor Power in a Prolonged Transition to Capitalism." *Journal of Peasant Studies* 13:4 (July 1986): 221–39.

Palmer, David Scott. "Rebellion in Rural Peru: The Origins and Evolution of Sendero Luminoso." *Comparative Politics* 18:2 (1986): 127–46.

——— "'Revolution from Above': Military Government and Popular Participation in Perú, 1968–1972." Ph.D. diss., Cornell University, 1973.

Palmer, Ingrid. *The Impact of Male Out-Migration on Women in Farming.* West Hartford, CT: Kumarian Press, 1985.

Panorama ayacuchano. Audio cassette distributed by Committee to Defend the Life of Abimael Guzmán (circa 1994).

Bibliography

Parkin, David J. *Palms, Wine and Witnesses: Public Spirit and Private Gain in an African Farming Community.* Prospect Heights, IL: Waveland Press, 1972.

Partido Comunista del Perú (SL). *Entrevista al Presidente Gonzalo.* Lima: Ediciones Bandera Roja, 1989. (Reprint from *El Diario* interview of July 1988.)

——— *Sétima conferencia nacional: Sobre el carácter de la sociedad y los problemas de la revolución peruana.* n.p., 1972.

Pastor, Manuel and Carol Wise. "Peruvian Economic Policy in the 1980s: From Orthodoxy to Heterodoxy and Back." *Latin American Research Review* 27:2 (1992): 83–117.

Pearse, Andrew. "Agrarian Change Trends in Latin America." In Rodolfo Stavenhagen, ed., 11–40, *Agrarian Problems and Peasant Movements in Latin America.* Garden City, NY: Doubleday and Company, 1970.

——— *The Latin American Peasant.* London: Frank Cass and Company, 1975.

Pease G. Y., Franklin. "Continuidad y resistencia de lo andino." *Allpanchis* 17/18 (1981): 104–18.

Penty, Arthur J. and Peter Chojnowski, eds. *The Gauntlet: A Challenge to the Myth of Progress.* Norfolk, VA: IHS Press, 2003.

Pérez Liu, Rosario. "Violencia, migración y productividad: Cuatro estudios de caso en las comunidades ayacuchanas." In Fernando Eguren et al., eds., 515–36, *Perú: El problema agrario en debate.*

Pizarro, Rosa, Laura Trelles, and Eduardo Toche. "La protesta social durante el toledismo." *Perú hoy.*

Polanyi, Karl. *The Great Transformation: The Political and Economic Origins of Our Time.* Boston: Beacon Press, 1957.

Poole, Deborah and Gerardo Rénique. *Peru: Time of Fear.* London: Latin America Bureau, 1992.

Popkin, Samuel L. *The Rational Peasant: The Political Economy of Rural Society in Vietnam.* Berkeley, CA: University of California Press, 1979.

Portugal Vizcarra, José A. *La reforma agraria en las microrregiones de Ayacucho, Apurímac y Huancavelica.* Lima: SINAMOS, 1987.

Programa Nacional de Manejo de Cuencas Hidrográficas y Conservación de Suelos (PRONAMACHS). "Impacto Social MIMA–Pomatambo." Electronic copy of report provided in August 2006.

Proyecto Andino de Tecnologías Campesinas. *Manchay tiempo: Proyectos de desarrollo en tiempos de temor en Ayacucho.* Lima: PRATEC, 1989.

Radcliffe, Sarah A. "Between Hearth and Labor Market: The Recruitment of Peasant Women in the Andes." *International Migration Review* 24:2 (Summer 1990): 229–49.

Rambla, Xavier. "Globalization, Educational Targeting, and Stable Inequalities: A Comparative Analysis of Argentina, Brazil, and Chile." *International Review of Education* 52:3/4 (May–July 2006): 353–70.

Ramírez A., Antonio. *A propósito de la autodefensa de masas: Rondas campesinas.* Chota: Federación de Rondas Campesinas de Cajamarca, 1986.

Redfield, Robert. *The Little Community: Viewpoints for the Study of a Human Whole.* Chicago: University of Chicago Press, 1955.

Rénique, José L. "Apogeo y crisis de la 'tercera vía': Campesinismo, 'guerra popular' y contrainsurgencia en Puno." Paper presented to University of Wisconsin/Madison International Symposium, April 26–30, 1995.

Revolutionary Communist Party USA. "En Perú el pueblo se está liberando a si mismo," in *Obrero Revolucionario* 16:4 (May 22, 1994): 8–10.

Rodríguez, Yolanda. "Los actores sociales y la violencia política en Puno." *Allpanchis* 23:39 (January–June 1992): 131–54.

Roe, Peter G. "The Josho Nahuanbo Are All Wet and Undercooked: Shipibo Views of the Whiteman and the Incas in Myth, Legend, and History." In Jonathan D. Hill, ed., 106–35, *Rethinking History and Myth*. Chicago: University of Illinois Press, 1988.

Rogers, Everett M. "Motivations, Values, and Attitudes of Subsistence Farmers: Toward a Subculture of Peasantry." In Clifton R. Wharton, ed., 111–35, *Subsistence Agriculture and Economic Development*.

Rospigliosi, Fernando. "Democracy's Bleak Prospects." In Joseph S. Tulchin and Gary Bland, eds., *Peru in Crisis: Dictatorship or Democracy*. Boulder, CO: Lynne Rienner, 1994.

Sagasti, Francisco and Max Hernández. "The Crisis of Governance." In Joseph S. Tulchin and Gary Bland, eds., *Peru in Crisis*.

Sandel, Michael. *Democracy's Discontent: America in Search of a Public Philosophy*. Cambridge, MA: Harvard University Press, 1996.

Sappenfield, Mark, and Mark Trumbull. "Big Banks Find Little Loans a Nobel Winner, Too." *Christian Science Monitor,* October 16, 2006.

Schumacher, E. F. *Small Is Beautiful: Economics as if People Mattered*. New York: Harper and Row, 1973.

Schydlowsky, Daniel M. and Juan J. Wicht. "The Anatomy of an Economic Failure." In Cynthia McClintock and Abraham F. Lowenthal, eds., *The Peruvian Experiment Reconsidered*.

Scott, Catherine V. *Gender and Development: Rethinking Modernization and Dependency Theory*. Boulder, CO: Lynne Rienner, 1995.

Scott, James C. *The Moral Economy of the Peasant: Rebellion and Subsistence in Southeast Asia*. New Haven, CT: Yale University Press, 1976.

Scott, James C. *Seeing Like a State: How Certain Schemes to Improve the Human Condition Have Failed*. New Haven, CT: Yale University Press, 1998.

Seligmann, Linda J. "The Burden of Visions Amidst Reform: Peasant Relations to Law in the Peruvian Andes." *American Ethnologist* 20:1 (February 1993): 25–51.

Sempat Assadourian, Carlos. "Agriculture and Land Tenure." Amílcar Challú and John H. Coatsworth, trans. In Victor Bulmer-Thomas, John H. Coatsworth, and Roberto Cortés Conde, eds., *The Cambridge Economic History of Latin America*.

Sharpe, John et al., eds. *Distributist Perspectives: Essays on the Economics of Justice and Charity*. Norfolk, VA: IHS Press, 2004.

Shiva, Vandana. "Globalization and the War Against Farmers and the Land." In Norman Wirzba, ed., *The Essential Agrarian Reader*.

Shuman, Michael H. *Going Local: Creating Self-Reliant Communities in a Global Age*. New York: The Free Press, 1998.

Silverblatt, Irene. "Becoming Indian in the Central Andes of Seventeenth-Century Peru." In Gyan Prakash, ed., *After Colonialism: Imperial Histories and Postcolonial Displacements*. Princeton, NJ: Princeton University Press, 1995.

Slater, David. *Territory and State Power in Latin America: The Peruvian Case.* London: Macmillan Press, 1989.

Smith, Gavin. *Livelihood and Resistance: Peasants and the Politics of Land in Peru.* Berkeley, CA: University of California Press, 1989.

———. "Reflections on the Social Relations of Simple Commodity Production." *Journal of Peasant Studies* 13:1 (October 1985): 99–239.

Smith, Phil and Eric Thurman. *A Billion Bootstraps: Microcredit, Barefoot Banking, and the Business Solution for Ending Poverty.* New York: McGraw-Hill, 2007.

Sociedad Geográfica de Lima. *Anuario geográfico departamental, Opúsculo No. 24.05.a: Perfil antropogeográfico de Ayacucho.* Lima: Sociedad Geográfica de Lima, 1990.

Spalding, Hobart A. "Peru Today: Still on the Brink." *Monthly Review* 44:10 (March 1993): 31–37.

Stahr, Marga and Marisol Vega, "El conflicto tradición–modernidad en mujeres de sectores populares." *Márgenes* 2:3 (1988): 47–62.

Stanish, Charles. *Ancient Andean Political Economy.* Austin: University of Texas Press, 1992.

Starn, Orin. "Antropología andina, 'andinismo' y Sendero Luminoso." *Allpanchis* 23:39 (January–June 1992): 15–62.

———. "'I Dreamed of Foxes and Hawks': Reflections on Peasant Protest, New Social Movements, and the Rondas Campesinas of Northern Peru." In Arturo Éscobar and Sonia E. Álvarez, eds., 89–111, *The Making of Social Movements in Latin America.*

———. "New Literature on Peru's Sendero Luminoso." *Latin American Research Review* 27:2 (1992): 212–26.

———. "Villagers at Arms: War and Counterrevolution in the Central-South Andes." In Steve J. Stern, ed., *Shining and Other Paths.*

Stepan, Alfred. *The State and Society: Peru in Comparative Perspective.* Princeton, NJ: Princeton University Press, 1978.

Stern, Steve J. *Peru's Indian Peoples and the Challenge of Spanish Conquest: Huamanga to 1640.* Madison, WI: University of Wisconsin Press, 1982.

Stevenson, Glenn G. *Common Property Economics: A General Theory and Land Use Applications.* Cambridge: Cambridge University Press, 1991.

Stock, Catherine McNicol. *Rural Radicals: Righteous Rage in the American Grain.* Ithaca, NY: Cornell University Press, 1996.

Strasma, John. "Agrarian Reform." In David Chaplin, ed., *Peruvian Nationalism.*

Strong, Simon. *Shining Path: The World's Deadliest Revolutionary Force.* London: HarperCollins, 1992.

Tagore, Rabindranath. *Towards Universal Man.* [Reprinted articles, 1892–1941.] New York: Asia Publishing House, 1961.

Tate, W. E. *The English Village Community and the Enclosure Movements.* London: Victor Gollancz, 1967.

Taylor, Peter Leigh. "The Rhetorical Construction of Efficiency: Restructuring and Industrial Democracy in Mondragón, Spain." *Sociological Forum* 9:3 (September 1994): 459–89.

Telleen, Maurice. "The Mind-Set of Agrarianism . . . New and Old." In Norman Wirzba, ed., *The Essential Agrarian Reader.*

Tovar, Teresa. *Las luchas populares en el siglo XIX (1780–1920).* Lima: Centro de Estudios y Promoción del Desarrollo, 1983.

Transparencia—Observatorio Electoral. Website at www.transparencia.org.pe

Turner, Michael. *Enclosures in Britain, 1750–1830.* London: Macmillan Press, 1984.

Urrutia Ceruti, Jaime, Adriano Araujo, and Haydeé Joyo. "Las comunidades en la región de Huamanga, 1824–1968." In Fernando Eguren et al., eds., 429–67, *Perú: El problema agrario en debate.*

Urton, Gary. "Communalism and Differentiation in an Andean Community." In Robert V. H. Dover, Katharine E. Seibold, and John H. McDowell, eds., *Andean Cosmologies Through Time: Persistence and Emergence.* Bloomington: Indiana University Press, 1992.

Valencia Quintanilla, Félix. *Ayacucho: Sangre y miseria.* Lima: Tierra y Liberación, 1986.

——— *Luchas campesinas en el contexto semifeudal del oriente de Lucanas, Ayacucho.* Lima: Centro Popular de Estudios Agrarios, 1984.

van Slyke, Lyman P. "Liang Shuming and the Rural Reconstruction Movement." *The Journal of Asian Studies* 18:4 (August 1959): 457–74.

Vargas Llosa, Álvaro. *The Madness of Things Peruvian.* New Brunswick, NJ: Transaction Publishers, 1994.

Velasco Alvarado, Juan. *Velasco: La voz de la revolución: Discursos del Presidente de la República General de División Juan Velasco Alvarado.* 2 vols. Lima: Ediciones Participación, 1972.

Vergara Figueroa, Abilio, Genaro Zaga Saufle, and Juan Arguedas Chavez. "Culluchaca: Algunos elementos sobre la ideología comunal." Instituto de Estudios Regionales José María Arguedas, 107–56. *Comunidades campesinas de Ayacucho: Economía, ideología y organización social.* Ayacucho: Comisión de Coordinación de Tecnología Andina, 1985.

Versluis, Arthur J. "The Revolutionary Conservatism of Jefferson's Small Republics." *Modern Age* 48:1 (Winter 2006): 6–12.

Villacrez R., Eloy. *Nuestra guerra civil: Ayacucho 80.* Lima: Graphos 100 Editores, 1985.

Villalobos de Urrutia, Gabriela. *Diagnóstico de la situación social y económica de la mujer peruana.* Lima: Centro de Estudios de Población y Desarrollo, 1975.

Wachtel, Nathan. *The Vision of the Vanquished: The Spanish Conquest of Peru Through Indian Eyes, 1530–1570.* New York: Harper & Row, 1977.

Waman Puma de Ayala. *Nueva corónica y buen gobierno.* Digital image of original.

Weyland, Kurt. "'Growth with Equity' in Chile's New Democracy?" *Latin American Research Review* 32:1 (1997): 37–67.

——— *The Politics of Market Reform in Fragile Democracies: Argentina, Brazil, Peru, and Venezuela.* Princeton, NJ: Princeton University Press, 2002.

Whyte, William Foote. *Making Mondragón: The Growth and Dynamics of the Worker Cooperative Complex.* Ithaca, NY: ILR Press, 1988.

——— and Giorgio Alberti. *Power, Politics and Progress: Social Change in Rural Peru.* New York: Elsevier, 1976.

Wiarda, Howard J. *The Soul of Latin America: The Cultural and Political Tradition.* New Haven, CT: Yale University Press, 2001.

Wirzba, Norman. "Placing the Soul: An Agrarian Philosophical Principle." In Norman Wirzba, ed., *The Essential Agrarian Reader.*

Wolf, Eric R. *Peasants.* Englewood Cliffs, NJ: Prentice-Hall, 1966.

——— *Peasant Wars of the Twentieth Century.* New York: Harper and Row, 1969.

———. "Types of Latin American Peasantry: A Preliminary Discussion." *American Anthropologist* 57 (1955): 452–71.

Wolin, Sheldon. *Politics and Vision. Continuity and Innovation in Western Political Thought.* Princeton, NJ: Princeton University Press, 2004 [1960].

World Bank. *World Bank Development Indicators Database,* July 1, 2007.

Yashar, Deborah J. *Contesting Citizenship in Latin America: The Rise of Indigenous Movements and the Postliberal Challenge.* Cambridge: Cambridge University Press, 2005.

Young, Michael. *The Rise of the Meritocracy, 1870–2033: An Essay on Education and Equality.* Baltimore: Penguin Books, 1961 [1958].

Yunus, Muhammad. Nobel Lecture, Oslo, December 10, 2006.

Acknowledgments

This book had a long and somewhat irregular path to fruition, spanning fourteen years from start to finish. Along the way, I have incurred a debt of gratitude to a wide range of people on two continents and in several walks of life.

None of the research on Pomatambo would have been possible without the extensive and generous help from my Peruvian friends, both in the village and elsewhere. I am especially grateful to the Castillo family. In particular, Óscar Fredy Castillo Vílchez first introduced me to his home village in 1995, and Sergio Sekov Canchari Castillo helped me during my follow-up research in 2006. Both worked long and hard winning the confidence of villagers, doing interview translations between Quechua and Spanish, and trudging around the mountains with me. I have also enjoyed many a lively conversation with them on their experiences and on the social problems and prospects of the highlands. During my first visit to Ayacucho, my research was also facilitated by Ponciano del Pino and other faculty at the Universidad Nacional San Cristóbal de Huamanga.

In doing thesis research on this community in 1995, I was fortunate to have as an advisor David Scott Palmer. His long familiarity with and contacts in Ayacucho helped greatly in launching me into the area, and I have much appreciated his friendship and advice in the years since. As an undergraduate working on this topic, I also benefited from helpful suggestions from Harvard faculty at the time, including Deborah Yashar, John Coatsworth, Martin Kilson, and David Maybury-Lewis.

While teaching at Harvard more recently, I was fortunate to have a supportive and intellectually engaging group of colleagues in the Social

Studies program. Particularly valuable responses to this project and the preoccupations behind it came from Darra Mulderry, Thomas Ponniah, Amelie Rorty, Patti Lenard, David Meskill, Bo-Mi Choi, and Paul Lachelier. My students in several years of the "Global Culture Clash" seminar also inspired me with their lively discussions on the nature of modernity and tradition.

In 2007 and 2008, I was kindly invited to participate in the annual "Rethinking Development" conferences in New Hampshire. At crucial points in writing and revising the manuscript, I benefited from thoughtful critiques and encouragement from members of this circle, including Stephen Marglin, Frédérique Appfel-Marglin, and Smitu Kothari.

More broadly, insightful comments on the project came from David Yang, Li Yuyu, Joshua Neff, John Médaille, and Luke Lea.

Funding for the research was generously provided in 1995 by the Center for International Affairs and the Harvard College Research Program, and in 2006 by Social Studies.

As the book made its way through the publication process, the editors and staff at ISI Books showed an impressive attentiveness to the project and its potential. I especially wish to thank Jeremy Beer, Richard Brake, Bill Kauffman, and Jennifer Connolly. My agent, Sorche Fairbank, was helpful with the practical details of the book.

Finally, I wish to thank Di Hu for her moral support while writing, her advice on the region's complex pre-Conquest history, and above all for her companionship in many rural Andean adventures.

Index

Bebbington, Anthony, 163
Belaúnde, Fernando, 36–37, 40, 55
Belloc, Hilaire, 146, 147, 150, 156,
    163, 211
Berry, Wendell, 142
Beyond the Global Culture War (Webb),
    11, 203
Bolivia, 195
Brazil, 127
Buddhism, 150

C

Calvinism, 191
capitalism, 108, 147, 148, 151, 153, 170,
    172, 187, 189–90, 191; de Soto,
    Hernando, and, 152
Capitalism 3.0 (Barnes), 183
Carrasco, Elena, 22
Castro Mendoza, Otto, 125
Castroites, 53
Catholicism, 6, 147, 150
junta and, 38
cattle rustlers, 60
Chanka confederation, 4
Chesterton, G. K., 146, 147, 150, 156,
    211
chicha, see corn beer
Chile, 127
China, 11, 29, 64, 109–10, 127, 146,
    149, 154, 190
Cultural Revolution of, 8, 53, 57, 64;
    "Great Leap Forward" of, 73; "ru-
    ral reconstruction" movement in,
    194; Senderista uniforms and, 71
Chirapaq (NGO), 167–68
Christianity; junta and, 38; leftism
    and, 38
Chuschi, Peru, 8, 52, 63
Cicero, 146
CNN (cable network), 12
collectivism, 190

Colpapampa, Peru, 17, 28, 81
communal land, 24
Communist Party of Peru
see Sendero Luminoso
communists, 151
"Comrade Feliciano"
see Durand, Óscar Ramírez
Confucianism, 149
conquistadores, 18
corn beer, 82, 86, 89, 97
Cotswolds, 167
Cuban revolution, 37
Cuzco, Peru, 4, 5, 167

D

de Soto, Hernando, 130, 131–32, 137,
    153, 154, 201; capitalism and, 152;
    Institute for Liberty and Democ-
    racy and, 132
Decentralist Coalition, 196
"decentralization," 128
"delegative democracy," 117
Deng Xiaoping, 64
distributism, 148, 156, 163, 172
Distributists, 146, 147, 189–90, 191
Durand, Óscar Ramírez (aka "Com-
    rade Feliciano"), 51
Durkheim, Émile, 180

E

Economist, 12
"economy of values," 183, 185, 188,
    203
Ecuador, 136, 195
education, 32, 105, 108, 119; Andean
    peasantry and, 34–35; village
    school as agent of change, 33–35
El otro sendero (de Soto); see *Other Path,
    The*
"enclosure movement," 154
England, 154, 191, 211

About the Author

A dam K. Webb grew up in England, Spain, and the United States. After attending Harvard as an undergraduate, he received a Ph.D. in politics from Princeton in 2002. He has taught at Princeton, Harvard, and the Johns Hopkins–Nanjing Center and has been a Visiting Scholar at the American Academy of Arts and Sciences. Webb is the author of *Beyond the Global Culture War*. His interests span the impact of globalization, social and political thought, and critiques of the modern world.